MICHAEL DOUGLAS

MICHAEL DOUGLAS

Acting on Instinct

John Parker

HEADLINE

First published in 1994
by HEADLINE BOOK PUBLISHING

10 9 8 7 6 5 4 3 2 1

British Library Cataloguing in Publication Data

Parker, John
Michael Douglas
I. Title
791.43028092

ISBN 0-7472-1035-7

Typeset by
Avon Dataset Ltd., Bidford-on-Avon, B50 4JH

Printed and bound in Great Britain by
Mackays of Chatham PLC, Chatham, Kent

HEADLINE BOOK PUBLISHING
A division of Hodder Headline PLC
338 Euston Road
London NW1 3BH

Contents

Prologue

Michael Douglas is an irritatingly nice guy. His working relationships are, by and large, happy, and his fellow actors will talk gushingly of his generosity and coolness. Few emerge from making a picture with him feeling daunted by the experience; no prima donna attitudes, no tongue lashings except when deserved and no sulks.

He has his private demons, of course, which have shown up mainly in the turbulence of his marriage and other habits that stemmed from his free-loving, liberal adventures of the 1960s. For some, he provided a living reminder that the era of activism was not dead, just a good deal more affluent. Along the way, he did acquire a ruthless professional streak born out of rejection, an inner core that is as hard as steel and sometimes stubbornly and selfishly impenetrable.

He isn't boastful by nature, but he's not modest about his successes either. He is a man driven, throughout his adult life, towards some kind of secret goal that appears not to be entirely motivated by money, although that subject invariably crops up in conversation with him because money is the talk of Hollywood: development money', budgets, percentages, grosses, a piece of this and a piece of that; it's been his life.

For a man who was kicked out of college after his first semester and who had the most minimal of training for an actor, he pulled off some remarkable coups when people around him, people in power, laughed in his face, tauntingly suggesting he was mad to try and that he would end up face-down in a manure heap.

He battled tenaciously to prove them wrong, and within six

1

years of entering the profession of his father had become a multimillionaire and had an Oscar on the mantelpiece. Michael Douglas would not have been surprised if that's where it stopped: a one-hit wonder who rode off anonymously into the sunset to enjoy a quiet life.

It wasn't, and he didn't.

He merely kept repeating the procedure, never sure if or when it would end, until he became one of the most successful Hollywood actor-producers of this last half-century, and the people who said he'd never make it were laughing on the other side of their faces. Revenge, he said, would be sweet but there is no real evidence, either, that when he made it to the top he was in any way vengeful of people who had kicked him when he was down. He secured his revenge by the well-publicised balance sheets of the movies he made, for which, as producer, he banked well over $1 billion – and that was before he became a major movie star.

His fortune was secured at a remarkably early age by producing a couple of the most politically influential movies of the 1970s, and then swinging right across the entertainment spectrum by producing one of the biggest romantic-comedy hits of all time. Yet the recognition he sought remained elusive.

If money was a constant as he travelled on towards a greater fame, so were references to his father, Kirk Douglas.

For more than two decades he fought valiantly, often in vain, to shake off the overpowering image of his father, the actor who created so many huge roles. 'My father and I are very different people,' he pleaded repeatedly, imploring the world to take note. And yet, when he finally overcame the hurdle of being his father's son, he himself would then constantly refer to him not as a mentor but as a figure in his life whose actions, beginning from the time Kirk was divorced from Michael's mother when Michael was five, always appear to have some relevance in the way he shaped his career.

For years he struggled in that shadow of The Great Kirk Douglas, a problem made more difficult as he got older by striking granite-chinned and oral similarities. Michael, too, possessed pulsating temples when roused, intense sincerity and, occasionally, the nostrils flared. More often, though, he was seen in the early days as a bland, unflappable young man lacking in the fire of his old man.

Michael Douglas recognised from an early age that his father was going to be a big act to follow. 'In my childhood,' he said, 'I saw him as making love to Lana Turner, as a gladiator, nailed to a cross, as an artist who has his ear cut off – doing these superhuman things that made me cry and think, "How can I possibly be the man this man was?" That image remained for a long, long time.'

And, of course, the media kept it up well into his mid-life, and the headline clichés charted their own story from a very early stage in his life: Michael Douglas was the son of a *Champion* who *Cast a Giant Shadow*. He was a boy raised in that other *Glass Menagerie* known as Hollywood, which is also a *Town without Pity*. He was son of *Spartacus*, that marvellous, larger-than-life character of whom there could be only one in any family. He saw his father revelling among *The Bad and the Beautiful* and, yes indeed, for a time father and son were *Strangers When We Meet*, leaving Michael perpetually confronted by the reputation of a man who had a *Lust for Life* and for whom *Once Is Not Enough*. Even at seventy, dad was still among the *Tough Guys*, although by then his star – but not his persona – was waning and Mike himself was able finally to slip under the wire and discover his own *Paths of Glory*.

In a way, it was true. With a modicum of imagination, Kirk's long list of film titles – of which those above are a small sample – provided a curiously fitting and accurate signposting of both his own extraordinary career and the way it reflected upon his family, and Michael in particular.

It was only when declining film roles and retirement began to force their unwelcome way on to Kirk's horizon that his son broke out. By then, Michael was just as rich, if not richer, and more successful in all respects other than as an actor – where he was nowhere near the status of 'superstar'. He was a worrying fortysomething before he managed to reverse the roles and Kirk Douglas was transposed, almost overnight, into The Father of

Michael Douglas. Michael became a suddenly famous film star whose fans saw him only as a modern star and not in the image of his father.

This was important. Being his father's son had never given him a professional boost, no leg up in his chosen career. More often than not it had worked against him . . . i.e. with accusations of being born with the silver spoon and that he expected everyone to fall in front of him, or, from casting directors: 'Yes, but he's no Kirk Douglas, is he?' And he wasn't, and deliberately shied away from trying to be – but everyone attempted to make the comparison.

As he said, Michael knew he couldn't follow his father. Douglas senior was one of that Golden Age school of actors of whom there could be only one of each of a kind they don't make any more – Bogart, Cagney, Gable, Grant, Stewart, Tracy, Cooper, Lancaster, Fonda.

Kirk would be a barrier in many ways, so much so that Michael relied upon his father only twice in his life, once to help get himself a job with Kirk's oldest friend in the business, Karl Malden, in the long-running television series *The Streets of San Francisco*, and secondly to obtain the film rights to his production of the stirring 1970s movie starring Jack Nicholson, *One Flew Over the Cuckoo's Nest*, which Kirk had owned for ten years.

Both events, however, became milestones in Michael's life. The latter also became a milestone in Kirk's life, because it made him $15 million – more money from his smallish percentage of the profits from *Cuckoo's Nest* than he made from any of the seventy movies he has appeared in during a career spanning almost half a century.

Michael won his first Oscar as producer of the film long before he became a box office star and so was credited with a far greater business-savvy quotient than is normally expected of a Hollywood actor. So perhaps, after all, he had a knowledge that might in part have been picked up through his upbringing – which brings us back to his father. Kirk was one of the first among major Hollywood actors to produce his own movies through his own independent company.

4

In normal circumstances it ought to be enough to record a father's influence on the subject of a biography and move quickly on to other matters. These are not, however, normal circumstances. Kirk Douglas cannot easily be dismissed from anything, and certainly not in a few paragraphs at the appropriate points in his son's early life.

He remains ever visible, the founding-father of the clan Douglas and who crops up intermittently, often looms large and, even when he is not even involved in the action, still manages to cast that giant shadow over the whole proceedings.

In the end, although the writer may understand the subject's concern to establish that father and son are two very different people, it is never really possible to ignore Kirk's presence in telling Michael's story. Perhaps that is the way it should be, for a number of reasons. But Michael was fired by a determination – which eventually became an obsession – to make his mark in life without trading on his old man's past glories.

Kirk himself was not unaware of the problems of a family born of a famous father. Once, while playing a round of golf with Joseph Kennedy, he raised the question of sons. 'Give them a guiding hand, sure,' said Joe, 'and keep a gentle hand on the tiller yourself. But make your boys independent. Let them find their own course in life – that way, they will always come back to you. For advice and as a family.'

From all accounts, Kirk followed the recommendation with rather more wit and style than old Joe Kennedy himself, who had his sons running for office as soon as they could walk and then determined to run their lives. Kirk did not do that, though not always because he wanted to stay out of his son's life. He was a vain, self-obsessed man when the boys were growing up, always looking at himself and acting out the role of a big star. But at least he kept his family functioning, to use a modern term, and although some diversions were tried and tested, particularly by Michael's free-loving, dope-infested days of the 1960s, the Douglas clan was steered by its womenfolk away from the pit that has devoured other offspring of the Hollywood famous, and most notably described (in Stephen Farber's and Marc Green's book

5

Dynasties) by Jesse Lasky, son of the founder of Paramount studios:

'I have known the others: the drug victims, the perverts, the well-meaning, misdirected, badly aimed projectiles of their fathers' ruthless power drives. I've seen neurotic wrecks, overdriven like engines unable to attain the high-speed ascendencies they thought their fathers demanded of them – because the fault was not always the father's. It was as often due to the son's inability to accept his own mediocrity.'

Kirk was always willing – much later in life – to admit to his own failings as a father and as a husband. Michael, on the other hand, would not accept he was of mediocre talent which, in spite of early spectacular success as a producer, was a description that could well have been applied to his acting well into his career.

Then, as Kirk Douglas ruefully acknowledged, 'Every kid has to kick his father in the balls'. That time came when Michael Douglas decided he was going to get out from under . . .

1
Tense Beginnings

Michael Douglas grew up with a firm hatred and contempt for the world of entertainment which surrounded his father. From as far back as he can remember, he and his brothers were subordinate to the inflated egos of Hollywood which were apparent in all who came into his father's house, starting when Kirk was a young star struggling to survive in the heady glamour days of the postwar era, the dying years of the Golden Age.

Michael was the first of Kirk's four sons, two from each of two wives. They were bound to Kirk by the power of his personality – and bound to each other by his temper and disapproval. A rare first-generation dynasty emerged, despite the fact that his two sets of sons were deposited on opposite coasts of America. Each pair was brought up under the stable reign of its own mother, but goaded and admonished by letters from their father, anchored as he so often was in some far-off hotel room.

The dynastic elements of the family seemed to take on some importance and recognition much later in the century than was ever imagined when the first born in the new Douglas household arrived on 25 September 1944, in New Brunswick, New Jersey.

At the time, Kirk himself was struggling for recognition and, as he describes in his enthralling autobiography, *The Ragman's Son*, spent his early life in abject poverty, the son of illiterate Russian-Jewish immigrants in Amsterdam, New York.

His was the epitome of the American dream: the nobody who rose to fame and fortune through his own grit and determination. It was also a story that became a classic, and very public, Hollywood rags-to-riches saga. There were plenty of them around,

7

and they are being retold to this day with a greater degree of frankness than was once allowed by the image-conscious studio publicists. Sean Connery's similarly self-inspired rise from the slums of Edinburgh springs to mind, though some were less inclined to dwell upon the past as either Connery or Douglas have done so candidly.

When he became famous, Kirk never concealed his background. He revelled in it. His present wife Anne says he dined out on his childhood for years; he would tell all who would listen that he was the poorest, most miserable child that ever lived. He would chip in with some self-mocking, ego-piercing remark when the company talked of the finer things in life, such as owning horses. 'Oh, yeah,' said Kirk at one swank affair. 'My dad owned a horse – it used to pull his junk cart.' If Connery had been sitting next to him, he might well have rejoined; 'Yeah, and mine towed a milk float.'

Kirk would have snorted and blustered. He did not enjoy having someone in his midst who could outdo his stories of childhood deprivations, who was poorer than he had been, or who had suffered more because of their ethnic background. He made much of the 'No Jews' rule of the time, complaining that he could not even get a job as a newspaper delivery boy because of it, and admitted that he, too, like most Jews in the harsh world of redneck and WASP communities, went through a phase of hating being Jewish.

In reality, of course, the background of the Douglas clan was no different to that of a million and one other impoverished immigrant families who arrived in America at the turn of the century, and were among the worst hit when the Depression came.

In every city throughout the land there were streets full of such people, and from those streets came some very successful men and women of modern America. There was the difference – that he, Kirk Douglas, was one of those who eventually became rich and famous through the most self-promoting of all media but never attempted to mask his past with snobbery. Today, it might even be classed as inverted snobbery.

And so the driving theatrical passions and self-improvement motivations of Kirk, and eventually Michael to a lesser degree, were rooted in ancestry, and Douglas senior never let anyone forget it. Nor should he, because it is an integral and vital ingredient of their tale.

His upbringing, his thoughts, his style, which a father often unconsciously passes on to his offspring, were moulded in the heartland of the New World in which the European immigrants arrived and settled. This itself would provide the thesis for many books, plays and films on families who came to the great melting-pot across the ocean, and spread out across the land from that formidable sorting-house of human flotsam called Ellis Island, through which 16 million immigrants passed between 1892 and 1924.

Michael Douglas's grandparents, Herschel and Bryna Danielovitch, arrived there towards the end of 1908 on a ship jammed with escapees from poverty, anti-Semitism and the impending chaos of Russian and European wars. Kirk, born on 9 December 1916 and named Issur Danielovitch, was the middle of seven children. The rest were all girls, which posed some difficult problems in his adolescent years.

A house awash with women to the point of domination probably contributed to those striking facial expressions he became noted for as an actor, expressions that verged upon a kind of earnest, contorted, angry frustration. Michael picked up some of them himself, subconsciously copied no doubt, as he saw his father in action, either on the domestic front or on screen.

Herschel turned out to be a poor provider. Even by the educational standards of non-English-speaking immigrants, he was of a fairly low order. He found he was unable to get a decent job, not even at any of the three huge mills of Amsterdam which produced carpets and silk but which made no bones about their dislike of employing Jewish workers. He supplemented occasional employment by becoming a ragman, touting for scrap iron and cast-off clothing.

Home was also in the nether regions, beside a familiar landscape in stories of poverty: the slaughterhouse, the railroad track and the polluted, putrid river. 'Yes ... I know, it sounds like the plot for a 1930s B-movie,' Kirk admitted. 'But that's the way it was.'

Kirk dragged himself by his clog-straps, followed his mother's advice and concentrated on his education – as opposed to his father's wish that he should get out and start earning a living as soon as he was able. Kirk proved himself an enthusiastic scholar. Just as his parents had sought escape from Russia, he longed to flee the grimness of Amsterdam and reject the local one-track alternative of factory employment. The route out seemed beyond the family's meagre means. A university education cost money, and they had none.

Even his mother and sisters had had enough. They were planning to leave their depressing surroundings and escape to Schenectady, fifteen miles away, abandoning Herschel to his self-created ragman's squalor. One way or another, Kirk managed to scrape together some funds by working all hours, hitch-hiked to Canton, New York, and there explained his plight direct to the powers that be at St Lawrence University.

Impressed by both his honesty and his intensity, the dean arranged loans, and Douglas took out-of-school work to help pay his way, including that of janitor. This also for a time solved the accommodation problem, as a room came with the job. After a difficult beginning, in which his impoverished background and Jewish origins were ammunition for cruel first-year taunts, he began to flourish through a mixture of self-determination and popularity among fellow students and tutors alike.

The latter manifested itself in his university activities. He was elected to office of several student groups, including president of the German club, president of the drama society and, most surprising of all, president of the university student body. At the time Jews were barred from a number of university groups, including fraternities, and it was the first time in the university's history that a non-fraternity member had been elected to the presidency, a move which caused displeasure in some circles. The Alumni Association angrily commented: 'What's this university coming to – electing a Jewish boy as students' president?'

Issur Demsky, as Kirk was known by then, left St Lawrence in 1939 after his four-year stint a good deal wiser, armed with a BA and possessed by a dream that was his next major goal in life – to reach the hub of New York's theatrical scene and study at the American Academy of Dramatic Arts. He aimed high, to the very pinnacle of prestigious learning.

Without money or a scholarship, he set about overcoming the seemingly insurmountable obstacles with the same determination he had displayed so far in his life.

He badgered, pleaded and begged his way to an AADA audition in which he gave an impressive, hard-selling performance, having established a talent which caught the imagination of the selection body. Though there were no scholarships available, they made an exception – and Kirk made a triumphant entrance to one of the most acclaimed drama establishments in the world during that autumn of 1939. Practical experience was gained in the summer, first as a stagehand and then in walk-on roles at the Tamarack Playhouse at Lake Pleasant, New York.

He would doubtless have met one Mladen Sekulovich from Gary, Indiana, at some future date, but, like so many who ended up in Hollywood, paths often crossed early in their careers in the summer stock playhouses around New York. That early encounter would be recalled later when Sekulovich, having changed his name to Karl Malden, also became famous and was instrumental in giving Michael Douglas a much-needed hand. It was also at Tamarack during one of several debates about what he would call himself – Issy Demsky did not sound suitable for star billing – that he chose the name Kirk Douglas.

There were other fateful meetings as he began his student days at the academy. Betty (later Lauren) Bacall was barely sixteen and in her junior year at the academy when they first met in 1940. Today, she has fond memories of the days when they were struggling to make ends meet, Kirk more so than herself.

He was, she recalls, very poor, 'absolutely no money at all', and out of school he became the best busboy and then the best waiter at Schrafft's on Broadway, close to Bacall's little apartment. She was infatuated by his presence – 'he was my hero when I saw him on stage at the academy' – and loved to watch him work. She took him home that winter and persuaded her uncle Charlie to give him one of his overcoats. In her own words, Lauren was a nice Jewish girl and 'nice Jewish girls stayed virgins until they were married'.

Even so, she apparently had hopes of a relationship. They dated and did some intensive necking in his tiny little flat, which he rented for $2 a week. She admits ruefully, however, that he did not pursue her, and she would write poetry about her unrequited love.

He was more interested in one of the seniors at the academy, a girl named Diana Dill. She was, coincidentally, a good friend of Lauren's and had warned Lauren off 'getting involved with actors' one day when Kirk's name cropped up in conversation. Lauren did not mention that secretly she daydreamed of a future with Kirk, both romantically and acting together on Broadway. Not long afterwards, Lauren discovered that Kirk and Diana were dating and her hopes of a romance were dashed. But Bacall had yet an important role in Kirk's life – helping him get his first big break in Hollywood.

At the time, Diana Dill was no more than a casual date. They were both more interested in finishing their studies. There remained, in him at least, a certain longer-lasting attraction which would not materialise until later, long after they had left the academy. Kirk described it as an attraction of opposites. Diana came from a socially élite, though not especially wealthy, family of British origin in Bermuda. Her father was Thomas Neville Dill, Crown solicitor in the British colonial administration on the island.

When they both graduated from AADA in 1941, neither had a particular hankering to see each other again. He hung around New York, trying for work on Broadway, while Diana had ambitions of making it to Hollywood. She went west, and the next time Kirk saw her was on the cover of *Life* magazine for some movieland feature. By this time he had been drafted for military service, in the navy, as a communication officer in anti-

12

submarine warfare, having spent 120 days furthering his education at the Notre Dame Midshipman's School.

Legend has it that when he saw Diana on the front of the magazine, he boasted to his shipmates: 'I know her . . . and furthermore I'm going to marry her.'

No one took him very seriously, but Kirk wrote to Diana care of *Life* magazine, who eventually forwarded the 'Remember me?' missive to her agent. By then, she was back in New York; the Hollywood vision of discovery had faded and she had resorted to modelling. Eventually, during a two-week leave, they got together in New York and spent a good deal of time together. They met as often as they were able and wrote to each other daily. The romance blossomed during the uncertainties of war, with snatched meetings between leave, and overshadowed always by the fear that, one day, Kirk might not return.

In the autumn of 1943, when an altogether more serious involvement in the hostilities beckoned, Kirk proposed. On 2 November he and Diana Dill were married. They managed less than a month together before his ship was sent off to the Pacific for the duration, chasing Japanese submarines, for which he won some medals.

Though his own education had smoothed off some of Kirk's rougher edges, his marriage to Diana – like so many wartime affairs – went against the convention of like with like, a convention more prevalent among the society in which Diana had been reared than in America's so-called classless one. Diana's childhood education had been spent in England, and the whole aura of her family's life in Bermuda was slotted in the privileged upper class.

The only similarity in her background to Kirk's was that she came from a large family. She was the youngest of six. She had three brothers, all heading for the legal profession, one of whom would receive a knighthood, and two sisters, Ruth and Fanny.

In spite of the stiffness of the background, supervised by a father whose views on life were typically conservative, Diana was an easy-going young woman with a sharp sense of humour. Her parents had long since given up trying to push her towards the social élite which she had shunned in favour of her chosen career on the fringes of the theatre and modelling. But parents and brothers all remained observant and protective towards the youngest and most headstrong of the Dill offspring.

Similarly, Kirk's own family, poor though they were, had about them the rigid traditions of orthodox Jewry and were probably more shocked than Diana's relatives that he had married a shiksa, a non-Jew.

The differences in their social circumstances, ethnic or otherwise, were never a problem for either at the time. Kirk, however, was quite evidently taken aback by the opulent lifestyle of the family he had married into. He became exposed to this when his service days ended after he sustained a severe injury in a South Pacific encounter with the Japanese, and he returned to civilian life in 1944.

Diana's sister Ruth was married to Seward Johnson, of the Johnson and Johnson family, and had kindly offered to accommodate Diana and her new husband until they found their feet. Kirk was totally unprepared for what confronted him on arrival at his new quarters – a massive English-style castle set in an estate of vast acreage by the Raritan River outside New Brunswick, New Jersey. The house reeked of richness, and the multimillions with which Seward was blessed. It was filled with priceless antiques and works of arts and heavily attended by servants and flunkeys.

Mr Johnson himself was not present, since he was at the time in the middle of divorce proceedings from Ruth, who had herself moved into one of the smaller houses in the grounds. Kirk and Diana had the run of the west wing of the castle, which became their temporary home while they both began the task of re-establishing their theatrical careers.

Broadway was surprisingly active, given that the war was reaching its climax in Europe, the Far East and the Pacific. As in London, where the theatre was giving birth to a new Golden Age, New York was staging the work of some of its finest dramatists and actors. As Kirk began the round of casting calls and auditions, he admitted to surprise at landing a major role so quickly. The producers of a frothy comedy, *Kiss and Tell*, which had been running on Broadway for more than a year, were looking for a replacement for Richard Widmark, who was going into another play. The role as a romantic young serviceman rather fitted his immediate past, and Kirk was off and running.

Diana, however, had been unable to pursue her own ambitions, having given Kirk the news that they were expecting their first child. He was still appearing in *Kiss and Tell,* and moonlighting with some radio work in the mornings, when he returned to the Johnson castle, where they still lived, late one night to find Diana ready to go into hospital.

Michael Douglas was born the following day, 25 September 1944. Though he could by no means be classed as a silver spoon baby, Michael's surroundings during his first few weeks on this earth were certainly opulent. Forty-three years later, a matter of particular interest to Michael was the battle of Seward Johnson's children for possession of their late father's fortune, the billion-dollar estate having been left to his most recent bride, a young Polish girl who had been employed as his chambermaid.

Michael's presence at the New Brunswick castle was brief. With Ruth's divorce from Seward reaching its completion, coupled with Kirk's increasing workload in New York, the time had come for the family Douglas to move into its own home. Kirk and Diana chose an apartment on West 11th Street in Greenwich Village, then a very fashionable haven in the heart of New York populated by artists and theatrical people. Kirk, especially, was in his element among the heady atmosphere of the neighbourhood as the war ended.

New opportunities abounded, but there were also tensions and pressures upon their marriage. Kirk admitted that because they had married in a rush during the war, he and Diana hardly knew each other, not in a deep, real sense of knowing what makes a person tick, the foibles, the character traits, and so on. Curiously enough, the same problem would arise for Michael years later, when he married in similar haste. The similarity was uncanny.

Kirk, as he sought to make his way, suffered from the insecurities faced by many actors and artists, fears that centred on whether he would get the next role, and then, if he got it, whether he would be successful in it. All of these things, and the opening up of a world of which, for the time being, Diana was not a part, caused problems in their first couple of years of married life.

Just before Michael's first birthday, Diana sought relief from it and took Michael to Bermuda for a lengthy stay. Kirk himself was supposed to be going on tour in a new play, which in fact never opened, and there was no other work on the immediate horizon.

Unbeknown to either of them, another diversion in their destiny was taking shape, for Kirk and ultimately his young son.

2
Parental Discord

The early days of his father's career are important to Michael Douglas. He heard his dad reminiscing so often that he knew some of the stories off by heart. He absorbed the colourful descriptions of the movie stars and the moguls, the studio life and the politics of moviemaking; indeed, he was bounced on the knees of many a famous name. Later, as he got older and could understand all the nuances and intrigues, he would begin to form opinions and make mental notes that would, without doubt, be drawn upon in the future, even if subconsciously. And so Kirk's story is part of Michael's, providing the formative influences of the future.

There was also another aspect, less discussed, which would show why Michael Douglas needed to distance himself from Kirk in later life, quite apart from the 'shadow of my father' syndrome. This aspect also provides an additional explanation as to why Michael took so long to get started and get on in Hollywood, where nepotism – and just about every other kind of 'ism' – has flourished one way or another since the place was invented. Almost from the moment he arrived there, Kirk Douglas began acquiring enemies, quite a few of them in high places.

Even his associates and friends sometimes wondered at his suitability for the Hollywood 'system' of being told what to do – and what not to do – what to wear, who to go out with, who to be seen with at premières and who to avoid; in short, bowing and scraping to the moguls who controlled the studios. As Clark Gable so prophetically remarked soon after returning to Louis B. Mayer's MGM after war service: 'They're absolute bastards. They encourage you to be larger than life, they give actors anything they want, take any crap provided they interest the public, but the moment they slip, oh, brother! Look at the young talent on the Metro lot today – Garland, Taylor, Gardner, Rooney – they'll probably ruin them all.'

Kirk would not submit easily to that system, as was evident quite early on when he had to fight to retain what became his most notable facial feature, his dimpled chin. The studio bosses wanted him to have his chin smoothed out by plastic surgery, little realising that it would be his mark of valour, a signature almost, in the progression of his career.

Therapists might have – and eventually *did* have – a field day with the complexities of Kirk's personality. An almighty chip on his shoulder manifested itself in verbal belligerence and an aggressive physical presence. The therapists would conclude that Kirk's bluster was a combination of several factors, some connected with genetics which Michael would inherit.

Kirk's built-in attitude problem came partly from his Russian heritage – his 'crazed Russian temper', which his sons would speak of – and partly from his attempt to compensate for his poverty-stricken background. He was also possessed by a driving ambition – and seldom has there been a man more driven than he – in spite of quite deep insecurities, which hardly seemed possible for a man of such bold stature.

When these attitudes were all piled into the Kirk Douglas personality melting-pot, the result was a man filled with charm, wit and even great sensitivity who, when attacked, would give way to an explosion of temperament. It was so bad that *Photoplay* magazine, one of those great fanzines of the era, would later vote him the Most Hated Man in Hollywood; and, since memories are long in Hollywood, it was a title that Michael Douglas would find had not been forgotten when he came looking.

So those early Hollywood days of Douglas senior provide ample clues to the foundation of Michael Douglas's own personality and attitudes. Lauren Bacall is convinced of the similarities. She remembers the starting-point for Kirk, and watched the arrival of baby Michael in his mother's arms. Since she was more or less responsible for Kirk getting a screen test, she took more than a mere passing interest in developments.

By the time Kirk arrived, Lauren already knew her way around Hollywood, and half a century later admits to helping to change her old flame's life, and, in consequence, observing the collapse of his marriage to her former best friend, Diana. Bacall said she has no doubt at all that he would have made it to the West Coast anyway, regardless of her helping hand, but her intervention at the very least speeded up the process.

Bacall herself had been discovered by talent scouts in New York very soon after leaving the academy and taking modelling work.

She spent the first year after moving to the West Coast being shown around before even being given a try-out for a film. Hotshot director of the moment, Howard Hawks, had sent his partner Charlie Feldman, an actors' agent and one of Hollywood's sharpest and most renowned dealmakers, to New York to 'view' her. He liked what he saw, brought her to Los Angeles for a screen test and then put her on ice until the right part came along. One day, towards the end of 1943, she was called for her first audition, to read a scene from *To Have and Have Not* – the 'whistle' scene, as it turned out, and her most famous to this day. She also met and later married her co-star, Humphrey Bogart, and was an overnight sensation.

By then, Kirk was trying to make headway in the New York theatre, and Diana and baby Michael were in Bermuda, when producer Hal B. Wallis of Paramount came looking for him. The reason for this interest by a major Hollywood producer was one of those life-changing coincidences.

Wallis had mentioned to Bacall in conversation one day that he was looking for fresh male talent, and wanted a young lead to star opposite Barbara Stanwyck. It was a general problem among the major studios. The *Los Angeles Times* had recently run an article on the plight of postwar Hollywood, and how the studio moguls had watched their prewar idols returning from war, tired and often unsure of themselves, their temples tinged with grey.

The New York scene, which in the late 1940s and early 1950s

19

became a hothouse of burgeoning talent, was only just beginning to produce bright new actors at the end of the war. Many would eventually make their way to Hollywood, those of the next generation of actors of the silver screen – names like Charlton Heston, Montgomery Clift, Marlon Brando, Paul Newman, Steve McQueen and James Dean – but at the time most of them were some way off the starting-gate.

Bacall told Wallis she knew of a young man who might suit his requirements, and gave the big build-up to her old flame, stating that he was academy-trained and well versed in acting everything from Shakespeare and the classics to modern American drama. Wallis scribbled a note of the name; back at his office, he instructed an aide: 'Find me a guy named Kirk Douglas. He's in New York.'

Surprisingly, Kirk ignored the call. He still dreamed of success in the theatre and had high hopes for a new play, *The Wind Is Ninety*. But the job lasted only two months and Kirk left to join a new David Merrick production called *Raincheck for Joe;* that play was cancelled through lack of backing. Hal Wallis's approach suddenly looked inviting.

Wallis was still looking, though not for the original role he had thought of offering Kirk (that had already gone to Van Heflin). Instead, Kirk was offered a screen test to play Stanwyck's drunken husband in *The Strange Love of Martha Ivers*. Kirk discovered on arrival at the Paramount studios that it was no foregone conclusion, either. He was up against several other new actors fresh from New York, including Monty Clift, Richard Widmark and Wendell Corey. But Kirk won the part and he was on his way.

Kirk had been taken on by Charlie Feldman's agency and then became angry because he hung around for days trying to get an interview with Feldman himself, without success. He was instructed to join the party circuit and to get his face and name known; this he did with some gusto. He started smoking for the first time in his life. The women of Hollywood became an attraction to him, and vice versa.

Diana arrived from Bermuda with Michael and her mother at

a time when Kirk was so busy with his social and work commitments that he had not been able to find an apartment – which were in short supply in those days in Los Angeles. He was also virtually unable to leave the studio at the time because Hollywood was in the middle of a union dispute; once out of the compound, it was difficult to get back in. Diana arrived at the rail terminal to find no one to meet her. She telephoned the Feldman agency which, because Kirk's personal handler was away, said they had never heard of him. Mrs K. Douglas began to get the jitters, having visions of her and her baby son sleeping the night on the station.

Eventually, Kirk's agent Milt Grossman was located. He took them back to his house, where they stayed until Kirk was able to rent a small apartment. There, they seemed set to resume a more settled life in California. Diana soon revived aspirations of resuming her own acting career, but Kirk was dismissive of such notions, preferring to have a wife at home, keeping house and looking after their son. Consequently, the marriage was soon in trouble again, especially during that no man's land between finishing work on one picture and finding a new project, a period of pressure and insecurity.

Charlie Feldman's agency, Famous Artistes, failed to come up with a new offer to make Kirk famous. Kirk spent his time bobbing and weaving around Hollywood, looking for work, going to parties, getting known.

Finally, he returned to New York – leaving Diana and Michael at their new home in Laurel Canyon – to join a Broadway production of a satirical play, *Woman Bites Dog*. But the play was slated by the critics and closed after two nights. He returned, crestfallen, to Hollywood and went back to work for Hal Wallis, who had offered him a long-term personal contract starting at $500 a week.

Wallis had signed a number of actors, including Burt Lancaster and Lisabeth Scott, with whom he was having an affair. Another, arriving a couple of years later, was Charlton Heston, who told me: 'Wallis was a very shrewd man. He could see that the Hollywood studio system was dying on its feet, and he was signing

21

young actors under personal contract and loaning them out to studios like RKO for one-off picture deals.'

Wallis wanted Kirk to sign a deal for one picture every year for five years, then changed his mind and offered him a seven-year contract. Douglas rebelled and complained that to him it sounded like slavery. 'The contracts had their merits,' said Heston, 'inasmuch that you had the security of a long-term arrangement. But they could also be very restrictive, and you were virtually bound to take whatever work was offered.'

Kirk did not like that, and especially did not like the thought of being loaned out to RKO, where Robert Mitchum was their star of the moment and had the pick of the best parts. Wallis and Douglas argued a lot. Kirk would come home gnashing his teeth.

Diana provided understanding and compassion – and another diversion. Still only twenty-three, she fell pregnant again. On 23 January 1947 she presented Kirk with their second son, Joel. There was an obvious joy in that event which temporarily helped to paper over the deep cracks in their marriage. The heady, horrible atmosphere of Hollywood bore down on a union made in haste, of two people from different sides of the track and whose personal ambitions collided because they were so similar.

Michael Douglas the toddler would stroll into their rows and wonder, as best a child could, why his parents were scowling and shouting at each other. Later he was to describe his father unflatteringly as a 'screaming lunatic'.

The arrival of Michael's brother merely put a stay of execution on the inevitable separation. Kirk, meanwhile, was being offered roles he did not like and was the epitome of Hollywood's own angry young man, long before the phrase was even thought of. Equally inevitable was his split from Hal Wallis, a man whose eyes were fixed on money, the big deal, and little else. The artistic aspirations of Wallis's actors were seldom a matter of great concern.

Kirk went his own way. Wisely – and astoundingly to his colleagues – he turned down $50,000 to co-star in a major MGM picture with Gregory Peck and Ava Gardner, *The Great Sinner,* in favour of a lowly $15,000 plus a profit share from a small independent company headed by Stanley Kramer to star in *Champion* with Marilyn Maxwell. The film made him. Douglas's early caution was blown away in an instant. The Kirk Douglas that Kirk Douglas became famous for was created on that picture – the charismatic anti-hero in which he excelled.

Champion was a box office hit, and Kirk Douglas received an Academy nomination for best actor (although the Oscar that year went to Broderick Crawford for *All the King's Men*). Douglas had arrived. The major studios fell over themselves to sign him; scripts and contracts came fluttering through his door.

In one go, he graduated from the Hal Wallis school of journeyman stardom into the superleague, combining his acting talents with a clinically calculated style which was marked particularly in its contrast to all Hollywood's other leading men of the time. Whereas the likes of Brando would be heralded as great naturalistic actors, Douglas's characterisations were astutely self-engendered.

He virtually ignored interventionist directors. He prepared himself privately for each role he played, so that when the cameras were ready to roll he was suitably, and some would say egotistically and even selfishly, inspired to steal every scene in a manner comparable in modern times to Jack Nicholson's *modus operandi*.

The great presence he created for himself on screen was rapidly compounded in future roles, and the side-effects were obvious to all close to the Douglases.

As one of the most discussed new men-about-town, he held court in some famous watering-holes. He was less than discreet about his dalliances and affairs with actresses and starlets, including Marilyn Maxwell. Even before the release of *Champion* in 1949, his marriage was in name only.

Diana, a talented actress and with a similar pedigree to Kirk's, had been looking for work and was engaged for a short run in a play in Santa Barbara. Then, in the autumn of 1948, she took Michael and Joel to New York, to find some space of her own as the marriage became a continual shouting match. Hedda Hopper and Louella Parsons and the rest of the Hollywood sob-sisters

23

got wind of it and put them under the microscope.

Kirk angrily tried to ward off the publicity that followed the rumours that all was not well in the Douglas household. To purveyors of showbiz gossip, it was just another Hollywood story of a broken marriage, made all the more poignant by the fact that they were such recent arrivals in Tinsel Town. Kirk Douglas was 'hot' – so this was a 'hot' story.

For the first time in their lives, he and Diana found themselves gossip fodder. All his pleadings that his marriage was at stake, and that these columnists should consider the effects they might have on his two sons, were to no avail. The sob-sisters had heard it all before and never reacted to lines like 'Give us a break . . .'.

Neither was there any success in an attempt at reconciliation, when Diana returned to Laurel Canyon for Thanksgiving. Soon afterwards Kirk moved out of their home, into a small apartment nearby. Early in 1949 Diana began divorce proceedings in what was seen by many as the friendliest of partings. Only the lawyers tried to stoke up the fire of disharmony.

Diana was surprisingly understanding, especially with regard to the pressures of his career. She would tell their friends that the 'poor boy' had worked so hard to make it and was on the verge of a breakthrough and that she did not want to do anything to damage him.

While some might have attributed their troubles to Kirk's impenetrable ego and womanising, she rather handsomely accepted some of the blame. 'I wanted to act, and assert my own independence, and in a way that may have been a reaction to his success. Doug [as she called Kirk] spent his childhood dominated by women and simply could not come to terms with the fact that his role as the breadwinner might be challenged by my own ambitions. He wanted me to be the wife at home. He was also a complete perfectionist in everything, from the way I kept house to the way we dressed. But it was not a Hollywood break-up in the accepted sense. Our marriage was disintegrating long before we finally agreed to call it a day.'

Kirk, on his part, seemed ready to admit to his own failings even if he could not agree that he might be a model for male chauvinism. For some time afterwards, when he was more ready to discuss his marital troubles with inquiring newsmen, he could be relied upon for a quote that would make the blood of emerging feminists boil – not to mention Diana herself.

In an assessment that seemed more akin to his own situation, Douglas reckoned that, instead of trying to compete with men, women should 'train themselves to complement us. I am appalled by how little women know about how to run a home.' He would always add, as chauvinists always do, that he loved women. Two decades later, remarkably similar attitudes were emerging in his sons.

It was with the benefit of these marital reflections made in hindsight that a fair picture could be drawn of what had troubled him most in his relationship with Diana. More worrying to him at the time, however, was the fear that his relationship with his young sons might be torn asunder.

There is no doubt that in spite of his infidelities and his views on male–female cohabitation, the thought that he had failed his children weighed heavily. He went to see a psychiatrist. Early in 1949 he attended his first session on that other most widely used couch in Hollywood – after the one in the casting director's office – where he spilled out his innermost thoughts, and continued to do so weekly for the next five years with the same kind of intensity which he displayed on screen.

The search was not merely to establish a cause for or the effects of the breakdown of his marriage, or to obtain guidance on his handling on being separated from his sons. He wanted to 'look inside myself, find some kind of philosophy and discover how to cope with my success, so that it did not destroy me completely, as it has destroyed others'.

The psychiatrist very quickly pin-pointed some underlying troubles which, in his view, stemmed from Kirk's childhood and were specifically linked to a life dominated by women and to his relationship with his own father. Kirk recalled instances from his past, of the way his own father had been cold and distant, had never attempted a father–son relationship and could never show any kind of expression of pride in his son's achievements.

Kirk related what seemed to be a particularly harrowing story, of how his father had once asked to borrow some money from him. Kirk refused. 'What have you ever done for me?' he told his dad. And then he cried and said he never wanted that to happen to him.

There was a good deal of weeping as he lay on the psychiatrist's couch recalling his youth. And with Michael and Joel now removed from day-to-day contact, he ended each session of therapy with a determination to make sure that he would not become an absentee father, a distant and cold figure in his sons' lives. It may well have been his intent, but circumstances would dictate otherwise, largely because of the pressures of his life and the demands of his work.

Unknown to himself at the earliest stage of the separation procedure, Diana was already planning to get out of Hollywood. She pretty much hated the place anyhow, with all its phoniness, the hidden agendas and patronising double-talk, where people said one thing and meant another. At least in New York, you got it straight. She went east to take a part in a television drama; once back in New York she decided to stay.

Kirk accepted the fact that the boys would stay with their mother, even though she was planning to set up home on the other side of the country. In comparison with the often messy divorce scenarios of showbusiness and Hollywood couples where every last buck and Matisse are fought over, theirs was a remarkably calm and friendly untying of the bonds. Before they knew where they were, they were kissing goodbye. Kirk cried again. He remembered when his mother and sisters left his father and moved to Schenectady. Michael grabbed him around the neck and wouldn't let go.

So Kirk was out of it for the time being. He had much to do, anyway. Big pictures, brilliant directors, major studios were calling, even though Hollywood was in a mess financially and torn apart by the machinations of Senator Joe McCarthy and his Senate subcommittee, then conducting its witchhunts against suspected communists.

Kirk Douglas found himself a single man again at exactly the right time of his career and his life; if it was freedom he sought, he'd got it. And the brilliance of the man shone through in movies like *Ace in the Hole* and *The Bad and the Beautiful* which followed rapidly in a fast-moving career in which he built on his reputation as an SOB, both on and off the screen.

Diana Dill, meanwhile, established herself as a single parent in a modest apartment on West 84th Street within sight of Central Park, where she would take the boys riding on Sunday mornings. Though she had not bitten Kirk for every last cent in alimony, as she had been pressed to do by her lawyers, he was making plenty of money and – unlike his own father – ensured that he was a decent provider for his boys.

Michael and Joel were enrolled at a private school on 78th Street, not far from the academy where their parents had first met. They had to conform to strict rules, wearing uniforms and even a cap.

Michael was five when they moved to New York. As often happens when the father goes walkabout, the two brothers formed a strong bond. Kirk was a regular visitor, calling in to see them whenever he was passing through and having them over to Los Angeles for the holidays. But best-laid plans began to drift as work commitments increased and prevented his being a regular figure in their lives.

He tried to compensate by taking an extra interest in everything they did, even to the point of getting angry if their school work showed signs of slipping. But if one can be accused of patronising one's children, then that is perhaps a good description of Kirk's attitude towards his sons.

Michael was confused, and Joel would join him in the confusion when he was old enough to understand what confusion meant. He could not understand why his parents shouted at each other when they were together but fondly embraced now that they lived apart. Michael especially found the gulf between father and son widening; there was a void in their relationship which he could not understand.

Later, when he was much older, Michael analysed his own

feelings when a boy. He decided that it was not that he especially disliked his father; it was simply that 'I didn't want anyone rattling my cage'.

Kirk noticed the difference in Michael almost from the moment they moved to New York. The boy was old enough to be affected by what happened, father admitted, and he became quiet and uncooperative. Kirk would say that telephone conversations with young kids are always difficult. Face-to-face conversations also became less comfortable. It would be years before Kirk felt any warmth from Michael. And, on Kirk's own admission, months might pass between his seeing his sons, through pressure of work.

Michael, being the elder, was the first to suffer the effects of the public side of his father's life, too. The cruel innocence of the schoolboys often sent him home bitter and resentful after being teased about Kirk's very public lovelife after the divorce from Diana. Hollywood's newest heart-throb attracted much publicity, and he obliged by dating a string of the most famous of female faces: Evelyn Keyes, who was just divorcing John Huston, Ava Gardner, while she was still heavily involved with Frank Sinatra, Gene Tierney, Rita Hayworth . . . He also had a long-running affair with the nineteen-year-old Italian actress Pier Angeli, to whom he became secretly engaged in 1953 – secret, because her mother, a strict Roman Catholic, wanted her daughter to marry an Italian, not a divorced, high-profile star nudging forty. The affair, which started when they worked together on *The Story of Three Loves*, was to continue for almost two years.

For the time being, Kirk carried the Hollywood mantle of the village Lothario, more strident than anyone around but never lovable because he had acquired a reputation for being difficult to work with, hard to handle and easy to enrage. He could never understand it or explain it. 'I don't know why I got tagged with this reputation,' he moaned. 'True, I'd prepare myself beforehand, do my work as I felt fit, and of course I'd fight and argue if I didn't like what they were doing to me or my part. But if you'd asked Wyler, Wilder, Minnelli or Hawks – you would not find them complaining.'

His life had all the ingredients necessary for a tabloid saga that was set to run and run, and it did. His most recent screen success merely added to the maelstrom. As he began working on *The Story of Three Loves,* MGM rushed out *The Bad and the Beautiful* for release in early 1953; it was a major hit, positively bristling with good performances, especially from Lana Turner in probably her career best.

It was at this time that Michael found other confusions difficult to apprehend. He had come to terms with seeing his father on set, but he happened to visit him in Los Angeles at the time *The Bad and the Beautiful* was being filmed. Kirk had taken him to the set, and Michael walked in at a moment when his father was engaged in a heavy love scene with Lana. Kirk spotted him, and sent him away until they had finished the scene. Kirk then had to face the young boy's questions: 'Why were you kissing her, daddy . . . ?'

These echoes from the past came flooding back later when Michael experienced exactly the same situations with his own son, only worse because by then sexual explicitness allowed on screen had moved on apace, to the bare bottom stage.

The Bad and the Beautiful attracted six Oscar nominations. Ironically, the only one not to convert into an award was Kirk's own for Best Actor (it went that year to Gary Cooper for *High Noon*).

There was some discussion that the role he played in *The Bad and the Beautiful*, that of a detestable character who used anyone and everyone, was not far off Douglas's real-life image – a trifle undeserved. The columnist Sheilah Graham, with whom Kirk had several run-ins, described him as a boastful man who was so egotistical that he resented any kind of criticism, 'if anyone dare give it'.

There was, as one of his supporters suggested, evidence of a conspiracy against Douglas at this time. Not least among his detractors was the foul-mouthed boss of Columbia, Harry Cohn, who was heard distributing some colourful invective. If it was a conspiracy, perhaps it had some effect, for Kirk's career hit a bad patch during the mid-1950s before he changed tack and recovered.

Whatever he did, Kirk was at the eye of a hurricane. The media descended upon him as the focus for everything that was happening in Hollywood at the time. He was the heel, the adulterer, the son of a bitch who slugged his wheelchair-bound brother (in *Champion*) . . . He was the explosive personality, the rampant lover, the Hollywood stud with a cruel, sadistic edge. Fact and fiction, art and life became blurred.

Who was the real Kirk Douglas? For three or four years no one really knew.

The sons in New York, out of sight, were not oblivious of these developments. In summer Michael and Joel were put on planes to journey across America to their father's house, arriving nervously and with wonderment, the elder boy holding his brother's hand and dragging him along. Sometimes they would join Kirk on location in other parts of America or elsewhere in the world. They were never shielded from Kirk's temperament or from his background, which they were told they should never forget.

Whatever confusion rested in their minds over their parents' relationship, it was merely expanded by watching dad at work, or meeting his current girlfriend: would one of them end up as their stepmother?

Michael did not like the word, because he had heard about 'stepmothers and stepsisters' in *Cinderella*, and he wanted none of them. So Diana's disquiet over the headlines was not so much a matter of her own feelings. Her ex-husband could frequently be seen splashed across acres of newsprint with this star or that merry widow. Indeed, his name was at one time linked with a diamond-encrusted widow, Estelle Auguste, whose engagement to boxer Jack Dempsey foundered through an alleged liaison with Douglas.

Diana wasn't worried for herself; she was more troubled by the effects of the publicity on Kirk himself and on Michael, who was coming up to his ninth birthday. She feared that his growing introspection might become a problem. Though his father was often on the other side of the world, his very presence was never far away for one reason or another.

Kirk's meeting and subsequent relationship with Anne

Buydens, therefore, brought some measure of relief and hope –
that at last Kirk might settle down after three wild years on the
loose and give some order and direction to his sons' visits.

The 'taming of Kirk Douglas', as the tabloids called it, began
while he was in Paris filming *Act of Love* for Anatole Litvak but
was by no means an instant achievement. At the time Kirk was
looking for a public relations executive; local film people suggested
he should get in touch with Mrs Anne Buydens, who had earlier
worked with John Huston. She was, he was told, a strong-willed
and unflappable lady who knew the business.

Contact was made and Mrs Buydens invited Kirk to a meeting.
He was impressed. She was elegant, attractive and greeted him
in a formal and professional manner in her executive attire of
dark suit and white blouse.

She did not like Kirk Douglas, however; not immediately,
anyway. She turned down his offer of work and his invitation for
dinner. Later she explained that she was fed up with film people
and had just spent a harrowing time on the John Huston movie,
trying to keep a clamouring press and a jealous husband away
from the affair Huston was having with one of his leading ladies.
'Thanks, Mr Douglas, for the offer, but no thanks,' she said.

Kirk persisted. A couple of weeks later he persuaded Mrs
Buydens to come to work for him on a part-time basis. By then,
he wasn't too interested in the work she might do for him; he
was more intrigued by her personally. Over dinner one night he
discovered that she was trapped in an unhappy marriage to a
man whom she did not love, a man she had married to escape
from the Germans during the war, and who was well aware that
she was deeply involved in an affair with a married man.

Kirk sat listening to her story open-mouthed. Within a week
they had themselves become lovers, in spite of Anne's declared
resolution never to get involved with Hollywood again.

He had rented a house near the Bois de Boulogne. Anne began
to spend a good deal of time there, as filming *Act of Love* continued.
At Easter in 1953 Kirk telephoned Diana in New York to arrange
for the boys to fly out to join him for the holidays. Initially, she
was going to send them with a nurse, but Kirk invited her too;

they could all stay with him at the house.

Diana, Michael and Joel met Anne when they arrived. At that stage there was nothing to suggest the relationship between Kirk and Anne might become more permanent. Indeed, while Kirk and Diana were strolling in the park one afternoon with their sons, Michael caught hold of his parents' hands and remarked: 'Now we are a family again.'

3
Letters from Father

Seeing his parents on brief occasions of family togetherness disrupted Michael Douglas. He seemed reluctant to show affection, and according to his mother developed a deep sense of reserve. Although he has always dismissed the notion that his parents' divorce affected him in any way, there is little doubt that he was shattered by his parents' split and would cry and plead with them to get back together. It remained with him for the rest of his life, as was evident in virtually every major publicity interview he gave to media writers when he had become famous himself. The phrase, 'My parents were divorced when I was five—' was trotted out repeatedly.

Diana Dill knew she had to handle her elder son with kid gloves, and often had him around her. She had returned to her old love of stage-acting and starred in a couple of off-Broadway productions. When she was working, she used to take Michael to the theatre for rehearsals, parking him in the lighting booth with the electricians while she was working.

She found she had to keep a fairly strong grip on the boys, especially after they'd had time with their father.

They'd come back home having forgotten some of her own disciplines, like hanging up their clothes. 'Yes, but dad has a butler to do that!' they would protest. She would seethe quietly to herself and tell them to pick them up anyway. Their mother otherwise maintained a friendly relationship with Kirk and always tried to steer her sons' attention away from the ever-present headlines. Even so, the question for Michael and Joel to jostle with was: who would be their stepmother?

It seemed to have become a choice between the fiery, flighty and stunning Pier Angeli, whom they did not know, or the attractive but professional Anne Buydens. Kirk had been saving himself for the former, but he was kidding himself that something would come of it. During his nine-month sojourn in Europe, he had failed to notice that Pier was tripping here and there with an assortment of male companions, including a young Italian boy of a similar age, then Dean Martin, later James Dean ... Finally, she went into a rushed and unhappy marriage to singer Vic Damone.

There were few dissenters in the circle surrounding the two sides of the Douglas family that any permanent relationship between Kirk and Pier would have led to discomfort, if not disaster, all round, not least for Kirk's sons. Certainly, Pier's own life disintegrated into a catalogue of alcohol and drugs, with which she eventually took her own life.

Anyway, the issue was resolved for the Douglas family by the spring of 1954, when Kirk realised that his crush on Angeli was making a fool of him. By then, Anne Buydens had been divorced and had quite obviously fallen in love with the star she had once refused to help. When he finally came to his senses, they dashed off to Las Vegas and were married on 29 May 1954. The development was a key, settling factor in the lives of all members of the clan Douglas, present and future.

For one thing, Anne forced on her husband's life a stability that had been missing for half a decade; she was more forceful in a tactfully managerial sort of way than Diana had been. Kirk Douglas was still a fast mover, had a hundred balls in the air at any one time, devouring scripts over breakfast, going to work, coming home, playing tennis, swimming, jogging, going out for dinner and falling asleep reading another script. Anne managed to slow him down so that he really did find some good family time, as well as helping to redirect a career that showed ominous signs of going in the wrong direction.

Michael took to Anne pretty quickly, and the situation of the Douglas boys was made easier by the fact that their mother also liked their new stepmother. The two women became good friends, so there was no question of divided loyalties. That the two sides of the family enjoyed a remarkable friendship was evidenced when Kirk came to make his next picture. Within a few months of his marriage to Anne, Kirk had taken his first major steps towards running his own production company (a move to be followed by many other top stars, including Elizabeth Taylor and Richard Burton and later Warren Beatty). His first film as an independent actor-producer was *The Indian Fighter*, in which Kirk himself would star, along with Walter Matthau, who had recently arrived in Hollywood from New York to make his screen début in Burt Lancaster's *The Kentuckian*. Anne worked as casting director, her involvement notable for two reasons: it was she who chose the unknown Italian beauty Elsa Martinelli, a model with no previous acting experience, as Kirk's female co-star, and it was she who suggested that Kirk's ex-wife Diana should play one of the leading supporting roles.

Diana had arrived back in California in the hope of reviving her own career. She had brought the boys with her, and they were enrolled temporarily in a public state school. Diana had to test for the role first, and there was one other problem: the film would be shot on location in Oregon and Diana did not want to take the boys from their new school.

Anne offered to look after the boys while they were filming. At holiday time they all went to Oregon to watch Kirk and Diana Douglas – as she was listed in the credits – working together for the first time. Kirk made it a family affair by putting Michael and Joel in front of the cameras for a couple of bit parts which actually ended up on the cutting-room floor. But for both it was a first introduction to moviemaking. 'It was typical of Kirk,' said Anne, 'that he should include Diana in his first major production. She had been with him through the tough times and it would not need a psychiatrist to identify that he had a sense of loyalty and responsibility towards his family that bordered on a guilt complex. I think it was also a throwback to his own father's lack of loyalty.'

The Douglas sons' own introduction to a semi-permanent life in Los Angeles was traumatic. Though their father's life had been anchored by his marriage to Anne, they themselves faced a difficult period. They had visited the West Coast often, of course, to stay with their dad, who surrounded them with the trappings of movieland: swimming-pools, limos and the good life made possible by his wealth and his need to show them a good time. The boys were faced with perpetual movement, from one side of the country to the other, around the world and back again. As Michael once said: 'I had jet lag at the age of nine.'

Now it was different. Their confrontation with the reality of a public junior high school, even one in West Hollywood, after the cloistered halls of all-boys private tuition in Manhattan was nothing less than a culture shock, especially for Michael.

Because of his advanced abilities and educational standards, Michael found himself shunted up from fifth to seventh grade overnight, an eleven-year-old boy in a class full of thirteen- and fourteen-year-olds. It was a little fast for him. He had never been exposed to that kind of schooling. Back in New York, his had been a stiff and rigid English-type school. He found himself facing the novel experience of mixed classes. There was the usual boisterous rough and tumble, gangs which he had never encountered, 'and the first girl I ever kissed had her mouth wide open!'

Diana realised the problems. Michael was taken out of the state school, and for the rest of 1955 went from the one extreme of a liberal system into the strictest school discipline of the Black Fox Military Academy in Los Angeles.

In November that year he and Joel were presented with another situation which in some families might have given rise to later jealousies – though not in their case – when Anne gave birth to a son, Peter Vincent (the second name being associated with the picture Kirk was working on at the time – the acclaimed *Lust for Life*, the story of Vincent Van Gogh, which was another milestone in Kirk's career). Eighteen months later, the Douglas clan was completed when Anne produced a second son, Eric, and it is worth recording that in spite of the age difference and growing up apart, the four boys – Michael, Joel, Peter and Eric – eventually became bonded by a healthy brotherly relationship which was forged in part by the clenched-jaw firmness of their father.

* * *

By the end of 1955 Diana Douglas had become disillusioned with Hollywood once again and had decided to return to New York. Michael wasn't sorry. He was never happy with the harsh discipline of the military academy, and his twelve months of schooling in California had been an unsettling experience.

However, the final piece of the Douglas family jigsaw was about to be put in place, which in turn would have a deep and calming influence on Michael's adolescent years. Back in New York, Diana renewed her friendship with William Darrid, a theatrical promoter and talented writer who was to give George C. Scott an early opportunity on Broadway in his production of *The Andersonville Trial* (Scott, too, later emigrated to Hollywood and became a star).

Diana and Bill Darrid were married in December 1956 and set up home in Westport, Connecticut. Here, at the age of twelve, Michael went back into the private educational system, first at the Deerfield Academy in Massachusetts, and then in Choate, a co-educational Ivy League preparatory school in Wallingford, Connecticut, the Alma Mater of Adlai Stevenson and John F. Kennedy.

Whatever talents Michael possessed for a future career, in whatever direction, lay dormant. He was a game but undistinguished footballer, played trumpet in the school orchestra and turned in a steady but unremarkable academic performance. He edged his way through puberty to his mid-teens with no outstanding merit on his school record. As he got older he became a boy of quiet temperament. He admitted later that he was an 'introverted and uptight kid' who possessed no particular ambition towards either following his father into acting – which Kirk had positively discouraged through the years – or any other career.

Michael's home life was, throughout, comfortable and settled. Bill Darrid, his stepfather, became a respected and easy-going guide in his teen years, more so than his real father and unlike the stepfather in many maritally split families. There was never any animosity among the adults, no great rifts or pulling at the

37

emotional ties from one to the other. Bill and Diana, Anne and Kirk all became the best of friends, exchanging visits, staying at each other's homes and providing an environment that was perhaps as good as it could ever be in the circumstances.

Kirk continued his high-profile life as his films, some brilliant, some less successful, kept him at the top of the Hollywood tree, though that in itself was a constant battle, a struggle that Kirk said he would never wish to impose upon any of his sons.

The anguish and insecurity of remaining a major star is a familiar story in every Hollywood tale. But for Douglas senior there was more to it, more to sustain, because of the strong imposing characters he had created on screen, those larger-than-life images that were invariably of his choosing and creation, as the producer and motivator and then the actor.

In those formative years in Connecticut, the media portrait of Michael's father was as dominating as it ever was. At the time, Kirk's commitment to serious, challenging movies was counterbalanced by swashbuckling roustabouts, best exampled by his own productions of the controversial anti-war drama *Paths of Glory* followed by the brutal but highly entertaining epic *The Vikings*.

Then came such classics as Stanley Kubrick's *Spartacus* and the moving cowboy fable *Lonely are the Brave*, both produced by Douglas's own company. These two films demonstrated other facets of Kirk's character, his passion for the written word and his integrity, for he insisted on hiring the blacklisted writer Dalton Trumbo to do the screenplay for both movies.

Both landed him in deep trouble over that most sensitive of issues of the age, communism. The Senate subcommittee's anti-communist hearings had left an open wound, a festering sore on Hollywood's rump. The Cuban missile crisis and the rise of the American New Left had also aroused political tensions which would eventually explode into a crescendo of protest and violence over a wide range of issues, from civil rights and inner-city deprivation to the war in Vietnam.

What still haunted the film industry and media commentators was not so much the spectre of communism but the mood and force of McCarthyism, which in a way was now revived in a more potent manner by the fiery rhetoric of Fidel Castro and the CIA's disastrous attempt to topple him in the Bay of Pigs débâcle.

Kirk Douglas's contribution to this scenario may be viewed as mild with the passing of the years. At the time it caused a good deal of hostility. In school, the effect of his father's actions reverberated towards Michael like a small tidal wave. There was a personal connection, too, because while holidaying with his father he had joined him on the set of *Lonely are the Brave* and worked as a part-time gofer.

The newspapers were full of it. One critic complained that Trumbo's script for *Spartacus* was 'truly Marxian', while the bitchiest of all the gossip columnists, Hedda Hopper, implored her readers: 'Don't go to see it – it was from a book written by a Commie and the screen script was written by a Commie.'

The American Legion, that most right wing of organisations whose hero was John Wayne, flashed an urgent message to all its 17,000 branches – 'Don't watch *Spartacus*' – simply because it was written by Trumbo. John Kennedy, then president, went quietly to a local cinema to see what all the fuss was about.

Kirk Douglas feared no one and had never done anything specifically designed to 'please'. He went with solid, single-minded determination after the characterisations that allowed him the screen presence that few other actors of his generation could match. He had learned to live with the tag of being 'hated'.

Whatever messages Michael may have personally derived from the achievements – and brickbats – accrued by his father, by then in the middle of the most prolific and successful period of his career, are difficult to assess even by the subject himself. 'Goddammit, he *was* Spartacus,' Michael would say. 'How could I possibly live up to that man?'

And if young Michael had followed his father to a psychiatrist's couch at the time, it might well have been shown that he was reluctant to even try to live up to the image, that he even consciously fought against it. Kirk's career zenith meant that his contact with his sons was sparse through the late 1950s and early 1960s, when he was doing three pictures a year.

This was the period that saw the beginning of his prolific letter-writing to the boys: 'Dear Mike—' would be followed by a description of where he was and what he was doing, written usually in a trailer or a hotel room somewhere on location, which might be in any part of the world. This contact through letters helped Kirk maintain his ambition not to let his sons feel abandoned by their father.

He would use his letters to encourage the boys, or admonish them: stop being brats, be kind to your mother, pay attention to your school grades, try harder, and so on. If they had done anything that he disapproved of, reported by their mother over long-distance telephone calls, out would come the paper and pen: 'Dear Mike—' or 'Dear Joe—'. Inevitably he would remind them: 'Just remember this . . . I was born poor. What I did, I did for myself. I had nowhere to go but up.'

He would tell them they had to do well at school, because he wanted them to be lawyers or doctors, not actors. Kirk recognised that of all his sons at that age, Michael showed least signs of ambition. Michael himself saw it too. 'I got to be captain of the ninth-grade football team, and after that it was downhill all the way,' he said wistfully when, in later life, he acknowledged that he had been rather slow off the mark.

Michael's explanations often seemed to carry a coolness about his father and his father's lifestyle, not so much in bitterness but more as a reaction to all that Kirk stood for, as a Hollywood icon, as a father and as a man.

Michael has talked frankly about his thoughts in the early days of his own rise to fame, long before he'd made it big himself. Although his own feelings of the era seem devoid of any political interest, his words bear hallmarks of resentment, feelings of mistrust of the Hollywood system and an indication that, as a young man nearing adulthood, he did not want that Hollywood kind of life: 'My dad acquired the big mansion with fences around it, and fences around himself. He could never take it easy. He drove so hard that he turned people off . . . and I never want to do that . . .'

The disparity between the fictional screen life and reality has destroyed many Hollywood children. A succession of them through the years has been blighted by the larger-than-life images of parents on the screen, having world-famous people sitting around the dinner table, always being followed by fans, reporters and photographers, so that in the end the circus became normality itself.

Such a lifestyle was invariably combined with the handing out of cash and kind to offspring to compensate for the lack of parental presence in family life. The stories of tragedies and disturbances among major Hollywood dynasties abound. It was less evident in the Douglas household, because Kirk never gave freely of his money and the anger that he expressed on screen was also apparent at home.

Even so, that hefty image of *Spartacus* was fresh on the hoardings, peering down on the Douglas family everywhere they looked as Michael passed quietly and unremarkably through his final years towards graduation. Jibes like 'Son of Spartacus' seemed to roll off him like water off a duck's back, but perhaps subconsciously they left a scar. When the time came for the next stage of his education, he showed no particular leaning towards a profession. He talked vaguely of becoming a lawyer – which would have pleased his father – and then surprisingly passed on a place he gained at Yale.

Instead, he headed back to the West Coast, intrigued by some attractive-looking brochures for the University of California at Santa Barbara which showed surfers and bikini-clad girls having a good time on the Pacific Coast of the Sunshine State. Michael admitted that one of his motives was the fact that girls outnumbered boys at the university by three to one!

4

Banana Road

The time and the place were right – or wrong, depending on one's point of view. Had he followed his parents' wishes to become a lawyer, Michael Douglas would have gone to Yale, committed himself to a higher education more rigid and disciplined than the one he had chosen and might have ended up as a lawyer earning at best a comfortable living.

He went west, more in search of pleasure than fame or fortune, and flew into the epicentre of the new wave of liberalism, soon to be epitomised by Dr Timothy Leary's infamous call for youth to 'Turn on, tune in and drop out'.

Michael did all three long before Leary had come forward with his recommendation to the campuses of America. The year was 1963, and the nation was on the brink of a decade or more of tearing itself apart. The Beat movement had come and gone. The strange talk of the hip kids of the late 1950s and the avant-garde personalities of the early 1960s were slowly giving way to a more cynical view of life. Rock groups, headed by the Beatles, the Beach Boys and the Rolling Stones, and influential solo artists like Bob Dylan, began dealing with harsher realities than earlier rock bands.

These were stirrings of a more restless youth, successors to the generation of rebels inspired by Marlon Brando in *The Wild One* and James Dean in *Rebel without a Cause*. These rebels of almost a decade earlier looked curiously old-fashioned and were barely remembered by teenagers of the 1960s.

The West Coast of America was where it was at. Bob Dylan had just released his album *The Freewheelin' Bob Dylan*, Jack

43

Kerouac was rediscovered, road movies were becoming the rage at the drive-ins and the poet Allen Ginsberg was daring the campus kids to fight the establishment, asking: 'Are you going to let *Time* magazine run your lives?'

The first beginnings of a mass shift among young people were being signalled, and San Francisco, as numerous songs of the era would tell us, was where they would gather. The explosion of the hippie era in the city was a couple of years away, as Michael Douglas, that autumn, moved towards the hub of the action a few miles down the coast at Santa Barbara.

After the disciplines of his private school education, it was akin to being let out of detention. The freedoms and the West Coast liberalism in views, dress and style provided ample diversions to the real task at hand, which was to work. 'I suppose it was the girls,' he admitted. 'They were so gorgeously distracting.'

Kirk was not in Los Angeles to supervise his first-born son's excursion into college life. He barely saw Michael for several months, and there was some sort of coincidence, even irony, in the fact that he was engaged upon a project which would eventually bring fame and great fortune to Michael himself. This diversion into the story of *One Flew Over the Cuckoo's Nest* is an important preamble to what followed later.

One Flew Over the Cuckoo's Nest was Ken Kesey's first novel and had failed to attract much attention when it was published in 1962 – except, that is, from Kirk Douglas, who read it and immediately visualised both stage and screen dramatisations. The story is now familiar, through the film made by Michael much later, starring Jack Nicholson in the role of Randall P. McMurphy, a rebel in a mental hospital. Kirk contacted Dale Wasserman, who had written the first script for *The Vikings* and later the original draft script of *Cleopatra*. In exchange for the theatre rights, Wasserman agreed to write the stage play.

Kirk astounded his associates in Hollywood by turning his back on several current film deals worth a million dollars or more in favour of returning to Broadway to star in a play of the book, taking the lead role eventually made famous on screen by Nicholson.

In a way it was an ego trip by Kirk, and a dangerous one at that. The risks were obvious: a major movie star putting his reputation in the hands of the killer critics of New York, many of whom already disliked him. He was warned by several who had tried the same theatrical comeback in the past that the critics would give him hell. They were right.

After a try-out in Boston which attracted rave notices, Kirk took the play to Broadway, opening on 14 November 1963. He was back on the Great White Way and celebrated with euphoric glee, until the reviews came in at midnight. They were appalling, bad enough to kill the project stone dead. Kirk soldiered on to dwindling audiences over the Christmas holiday and New Year, and finally closed the play on 25 January 1964. He returned to Los Angeles, tail between his legs, declaring that he would never set foot on the Broadway stage again.

There was one more coincidental event that followed the *Cuckoo* flop which again would affect Michael's screen revival of it later. Early in 1963 Kirk and other Hollywood personalities had been encouraged by President Kennedy to become roving ambassadors spreading a message of goodwill from America through visits overseas. Kennedy was now dead, but the idea of the goodwill missions still prevailed. Finding himself free of commitments earlier than he had planned, Kirk took off for Europe and Asia at the beginning of February 1964 for a two-month tour arranged through the US State Department. It was one of several such trips, and during one a couple of years later – which took him behind the Iron Curtain – he visited the Prague Film Faculty, where he met the thirty-one-year-old writer and director Milos Forman, who, five years later, managed to get an exit visa for America.

During the visit Kirk had discussed his most recent project with Forman, who expressed great interest. Kirk said that when he returned, he would send Forman a copy of Ken Kesey's book for which he still owned the screen rights. There the matter rested ... for another decade, when they would all share a multimillion dollar windfall.

* * *

Michael Douglas was witness to this major failure of his father. His own life at the time was nothing to write home about, either. His tutors despaired of him, and his interest in the academic side of life was reflected by his grades, which were as bad as they could be. Michael had thrown himself wholeheartedly into the local scene; he loved the beach and the freedoms of the West Coast and had decided that there was nothing in life so important to him at that time as life itself.

By mutual agreement, he flunked out of college at the end of his freshman year on the understanding that he might return a year later when he had 'matured'. In fact, the absence lasted almost eighteen months.

He was drifting aimlessly and without a definite path to follow. He returned home to Westport, Connecticut, where he dabbled in building himself a hotrod, joined a local car racing club and took work in a local gas station at which he earned the title of Mobil Man of the Month. 'Big deal,' Kirk retorted. 'So what are you going to be for the rest of your life – a gas station attendant?'

His parents viewed Michael's lack of direction with dismay. If ever there was a moment when Michael seemed in danger of suffering from the Hollywood son syndrome, it was now. The possibilities of him sliding towards some drug-induced disaster or mishap were never far from Kirk's thoughts. Although Kirk had constantly said he never wanted any of his sons to follow him into the film business, he decided that Michael should be at his side for a while.

Towards the end of 1964 Kirk was heading back to Europe, to England and then on to Norway, to star in *Heroes of Telemark* with Richard Harris. He took Michael along, and had him listed as an assistant director. Kirk quietly gave instructions that his son should be worked until he dropped, and Michael ended up running around doing all the menial tasks no one else wanted to do.

After only a short break, Kirk assigned Michael to accompany him for work on his next picture, *Cast a Giant Shadow*, with John Wayne, Frank Sinatra, Angie Dickinson and Yul Brynner, which was to be filmed almost entirely on location in Israel. This time, Joel – by then a sturdy six-footer – went along too as Kirk's bodyguard. Michael was engaged as a production assistant, and also did some stunt driving in a couple of scenes.

For almost a year he was plunged into the midst of major filmmaking with some of the top stars around. The experience was not especially new to him nor, it seemed, was he particularly impressed by it, although clearly it had crystallised his thoughts for the future.

When they returned to America, he had to report back to Santa Barbara and resume his studies or face the prospect of being drafted. Back on the campus he had to 'declare' a major in his junior year, in other words to nominate which course of studies he would take. He chose English and the theatre.

Even so, he did not resume his education with any real vigour, nor had his father's tour of Europe instilled in him any determination towards a career. But he was not alone in his aimlessness. Life was like that on the West Coast at the time. The next couple of years became something of a blur, Michael's mind expanded on acid or in the clouds from good-quality marijuana, some of which he cultivated in Kirk's back yard until his father discovered it and banned this enterprising cottage industry.

Kirk was not particularly averse to drugs himself. He had smoked marijuana for years and snorted cocaine on occasions, but could not risk having his two eldest sons hauled up before the local judge for what was still an offence likely to be punished by a prison sentence.

Virtually from his return to Santa Barbara, Michael Douglas fell into the mould of 1960s West Coast youth – if you remembered it, you weren't in it. And he was most definitely in it. Jack Nicholson, then a struggling young actor doing Roger Corman quickies, succinctly summed up the times: 'We all listened to Dylan's *The Times They Are A-Changin'* and *Mr Tambourine Man* and analysed the words. We argued about the meanings and drew our own conclusions, but it didn't matter what it meant because everyone was so stoned they couldn't remember the words, anyway. That was it, babe. I mean, this was the scene we were all at, to use the then terminology. And it was terrific. Terrific.'

In April 1966 Kirk and Anne were off on their travels abroad, for a goodwill tour of Eastern Europe. By then, the hippie movement centred on San Francisco was in full swing. Commentators spoke with alarm about the march of freedom and said the youth of America appeared to be abandoning traditional values to embark on journeys into the unknown by way of pot, LSD and magic mushrooms.

There was great discussion at the time about the upsurge in drugs. Major literary and showbusiness figures on both sides of the Atlantic supported the legalisation of pot, and at the famous Human Be-In at Golden Gate Park in San Francisco, Allen Ginsberg, now converted to Buddhism, blew on his conch shell and declared that every person over the age of fourteen should try LSD at least once. Flower power, psychedelia, free love, make love not war . . .

At the time, Michael agreed.

Communes and group living – and loving – were all the rage, and Michael found himself drawn to them. In that spring of 1966 he moved into a counter-culture colony which had settled in a group of old buildings in an area known as Mountain Drive, a secluded spot on Banana Road, high in the hills of Santa Barbara.

'There were, I suppose, between 100 and 150 of us at any one time,' recalled David Garsite, one of the former inmates, interviewed in 1994 when he was in his 50s, on his fourth wife and doing 'this and that' in Las Vegas. 'The age-group was pretty diverse, from college kids – which I was – to fortysomethings who had dropped out. That was the thing then, of course, and we lounged around playing Dylan and Beach Boys and Rolling Stones. We were of the "smile on your brother" brigade – you know, from the Jefferson Airplane hit. We never cut our hair, grew straggly beards and the girls walked about topless. I have this vision of Michael Douglas in torn jeans and velour shirt – you could tell he was Kirk's son even then – flashing around on his big motor cycle, with his long hair trailing in the wind, and a blonde with the most fulsome bosoms you ever saw riding behind him. We grew our own pot and imported some, especially the fine Mexican grass, when we could afford it. There was LSD in abundance and a pot of mescaline on the stove. We freaked out and had nightmares about our pricks being cut off, that kind of stuff. It was like a scene from some Roman or Greek epic, acted out in modernity. We used to lie around naked, swim in our pool, which was more like a swamp, tread grapes to make our own wine, put on our own plays and talk abut Vietnam, the draft and civil rights. There was an abundance of casual sex, and a few children were born as a result, which in hindsight was pretty irresponsible. But generally we did nobody any harm and the only racket was the music and the occasional screams from someone on an acid trip gone wrong. Most of us survived to return, at some point, to the harshness of reality and earning a living. Or perhaps the truth was that we just got bored with lying around pickling our brains with acid and scented smoke. But that was then. Now is now. It's so different, no one who wasn't part of it could possibly understand it today.'

Kirk didn't understand. He came looking for Michael one day and found him in his seedy, sparsely furnished shack with no plumbing. He screamed blue murder, called Michael every kind of cunt and said that he had spent 'half my fucking life trying to get away from that kind of existence' and now here was his idiot son taking it up for pleasure. Jesus!

He failed to add, 'What are the neighbours going to say if this gets out?' But doubtless that was in his mind. Scandalous publicity was easily built on lesser situations involving the children of famous people.

As Garsite said, no one who wasn't part of such an existence could appreciate it. Although the hippies of the San Francisco area had already had a bad press, somehow Kirk Douglas's son managed to stay out of the headlines.

Michael kept up his campus studies, while life in the colony was relaxed and carefree. He would say that he learned much from the life there, particularly a sense of loyalty to friends and a communal trust, led by a spiritual searching and a sensitivity about life that was so vastly different from the Mammon personified in Hollywood.

Money and materialism were not the motivations of the 1960s, and, although he would acquire ambitions for both later on, at the time the goals were spiritual and drugs were part of the philosophy, along with Indian mysticism and meditation which he involved himself in regularly. The activism of the 1960s also engaged his interest and provided another platform of contemplation to which he returned virtually as soon as he began his professional life.

The counter-culture movement was born out of that hippie era and eventually provided a decidedly more serious edge to the cult of just dropping out: politics, protest and peace marches, demos, campus sit-ins and a general mistrust of authority became standard, and Michael Douglas was heavily involved in those too.

The draft and the shadow of Vietnam loomed large, as they did across the entire student population of America. Michael and his friends would sit around for hours discussing how they could beat it. All kinds of schemes were devised, and Michael himself decided that he had no intention of being drafted into that war; he would skip off to Canada if it became necessary. He told Kirk, who said he understood. In the event, it didn't happen. When Michael eventually went for a medical, he was disbarred from military service because of a previously undiscovered floating vertebra.

The scene at Banana Road provided everything he wanted at the time – drugs, sex, a strong feeling of attachment . . . Above all, perhaps, the colony life surrounded him with freedom and a surrogate family which, for the time being, were all he wanted.

5
My Friend Danny

The summer holidays of 1966 saw Michael Douglas back in Connecticut, where he was drawn to the Eugene O'Neill Theater Center in Waterford. Even as a student majoring in drama and the son of a famous actor, he was offered no greater job than unpaid backstage hand and general dogsbody, with the promise of a small part in one of the plays. It was there that he first met Danny DeVito, then a would-be young actor who was to become his lifelong friend and associate.

Michael and Danny were an unlikely pair. The diminutive but tough DeVito, five foot nothing in his stockinged feet, came from a fairly typical sharp but comfortable New Jersey upbringing. His father ran a pool-hall and a variety of other businesses, including a little bookmaking, and was sufficiently well off to send Danny to a prep school, away from friends and relatives who had fallen to the fashionable vagaries of drink and drugs.

Unlike Michael at that time, Danny was very serious about acting. His father, noticing a theatrical streak, had encouraged him to study in New York. Like Michael's own father, Danny possessed sufficient determination and talent to win himself a place at the American Academy of Dramatic Arts, where he became a grade-one student (a fact barely acknowledged in the early roles in which he was cast, as in the television series *Taxi*; as he was constantly being told, major parts for a man of his build would never be in abundance).

As their friendship developed, DeVito's own ambitions for the theatre and film became an early influence on young Douglas, helping to crystallise his own thoughts on a future path.

DeVito arrived at Waterford to perform in a play written by a tutor from the academy which had been selected for a summer showcase of work by new playwrights. The O'Neill Center was housed in a former mansion set in twenty acres of grounds. The barns and garages were turned into sleeping quarters, and local people provided additional accommodation in their own homes. The Playwrights' Conference was founded the previous year out of locally raised funding, and authors came from all over America to have their work presented and discussed.

Danny DeVito found himself assigned to the same barn/dormitory as Michael Douglas. They struck up a rapport straight away, but not through some intense discussion about the meaning of Chekhov. 'Oh, sure, I arrived there expecting to meet a load of actors sitting around bullshitting, and there were plenty of them,' DeVito says in remembrance of that first meeting. 'But then there's Michael Douglas and a bunch of guys shifting wheelbarrows full of dirt and concrete and sawing timber. Being from Jersey, I know about that stuff. So I came outside and that's how we met.'

The friendship was instant and they became a common, if not slightly comical, sight, dashing around on Michael's motor cycle, their long hair flowing in the wind. They were both considered hippies among the Waterford summertime gathering of more intense theatrical types. They liked to get high on headier stuff than beer. They were also both drawn by what Douglas described as 'a sense of admittedly attenuated immigrant roots'. It was a bonding that went back generations to the togetherness of Italians and Jews in neighbourhood struggles.

When the holiday stint at Waterford ended, DeVito went back to New York to struggle on and Michael returned to Santa Barbara with a touch more determination than he had possessed at the start of the summer. Off the campus, life continued in the Mountain Drive colony, which DeVito himself was soon to experience.

A few weeks after their meeting, he arrived in Los Angeles in desperate hope of winning a role in the 1967 film version of

Truman Capote's faction novel *In Cold Blood*. Armed with a letter of introduction to director Richard Brooks, Danny landed at Los Angeles airport and telephoned Michael to apprise him of his mission.

DeVito suggested that Michael should immediately cut class and jump on his motor cycle and ride like hell down the Pacific Coast Highway to meet him. Michael thought DeVito would be better advised to catch a bus, which he did, and the three-and-a-half-hour journey to Santa Barbara remains a jokingly sore point between them.

Danny was a sight to behold. The tiny figure turned up at the commune in a floor-length coat and white sneakers, looking more like the psychotic killer he was hopeful of playing in Hollywood. Danny didn't get the part, but would never forget his introduction to life in the offbeat hippie commune, where the naked and nubile lounged around their swamp blowing grass in the hot Californian sunshine – which even for a New Yorker was an uncommon experience.

Michael's own involvement with the commune continued for some months. Eventually, as he became more taken by the serious prospect of becoming an actor, he began to drift away from his laid-back companions. He began to tire of the life when the drugs, the change of scenery in bed and dashing around on his motor cycle became the norm rather than the adventure.

The novelty of nudity and dropping acid began to wear thin. 'I reckon the ideal of the commune sort of petered out as a natural cycle,' Michael recalled. 'Eventually, you just got sick of lying around cramming drugs down your throat. I enjoyed the drugs experience because – and this sounds corny – it made you feel like somebody. Don't ask me who. I could be anyone because I had been there. New England. Europe. Hollywood. I could change with the wind. Reality was a complete stranger.'

Other aspects also turned him away from the communal existence: people were soon discovering they could make a lot of money by dealing in drugs. The West Coast became heavily populated by con artists, fleecing young people and moving them on to harder drugs or using the hippie scene simply to hide from the law or the draft.

By then, the realisation was dawning that in the last stages of his educational life he would have to buckle down to work. His parents were still hoping that he would yet choose a respectable profession. But the man who professed he never wanted to be like his father did the opposite – to use his own word, he 'slunk' into acting.

Kirk Douglas had three key reasons for wanting to keep his sons out of the business. The first was the stark economic statistic that, at any given time, eighty-five per cent of actors in America were unemployed.

Secondly, although Hollywood had provided him with a remarkable opportunity – or, as he and other stars would say, the reverse was true – he would not wish the place on his worst enemy. Like Gable years earlier, he regarded the hierarchy collectively, and largely without exception, as bastards.

Thirdly, and perhaps most important of all, he wanted to shield his sons from what he believed to be the most debilitating experience of all for people who made it in the business: what he saw as wanton, often wilful, hurtful and destructive criticism of the work of actors, whether on stage or on film.

The critics have been the bane of artistic life since time immemorial, and Douglas senior had suffered at their hands as much as anyone. He reckoned that, in a single sentence, critics who were neither constructive nor objective could ruin an actor and shatter his confidence. There were instances in Kirk's past where critics' words were burned on his memory and would remain there, quotable, forever, not least the battering he received from the critics for his stage version of *One Flew Over the Cuckoo's Nest*. It hurt him so much that the cast had taken a full-page advertisement in *Variety* to tell the critics what they thought of them; Kirk still lost the battle, and the play closed. Since then, he had hawked the film rights around every movie studio in Hollywood and had failed to find a backer.

He said he did not want his boys to have to face what he had been through on that score.

54

Kirk, who could always sound off with a well-chosen piece of psycho-talk, came up with another well-quoted one-liner about the need 'for parents to remember what it's like being an adolescent'. He himself was bitterly disappointed by his own father's failure to applaud the way he got on in life or to praise his work as an actor. But when Kirk first saw Michael in a play he promptly ignored his own feelings on two counts – as a critic and as a parent.

It was during the obligatory period of reading Shakespeare that Michael took a smallish role in *As You Like It*. He invited Kirk and Anne to the college theatre at Santa Barbara for the performance and afterwards sought his father's views on both the play and more particularly his own performance in it. 'You were terrible,' said Kirk, and marched off muttering that the whole idea of Michael's becoming an actor was plain stupid.

There was, it was said by the father much later, a particular reason for that criticism, delivered in a way that might have been written in a newspaper after an opening night on Broadway (and which was apparently well deserved). Kirk earnestly hoped that by hitting him hard, Michael would rid himself of thoughts of becoming an actor and turn to studying law. If anything, Kirk's ploy had the opposite effect.

Michael went ahead with renewed vigour. Doubtless there was an incentive swirling around in his brain, like 'I'll show the bastard'. And by the end of that very year he was voted best actor of 1967 for his performance in *Candida* at the UCSB.

Michael was a star on the campus not merely for his stage performances, either. He was a leader of one of the guerrilla troupes that mushroomed in the late 1960s, darting around the campus, perhaps invading a class-in-progress and faking some kind of accident or shooting, then, with the full attention of the students and tutors, making a speech about the terrors of Vietnam.

In the summer of 1967, back at the Playwrights' Conference in Waterford, Douglas took his first major roles outside the UCSB. He joined the resident troupe which performed most of the new plays brought in by writers eager to have their work produced, taking the lead in the anti-war play *Summertree* by a new young writer named Ron Cowen. The play was an examination through flashbacks of the life of a young man forced into uniform and who becomes a Vietnam casualty.

Like much of the work showcased at Waterford, it was a new play which was also considered to be an excellent social observation of the times. It was a feather in Douglas's cap to be cast in the lead, but the benefits were greater than that – being thrown into a variety of new work after short preparation during these August excursions to Waterford provided invaluable experience for actor and writer alike.

Douglas roomed with Ron Cowen at Waterford and their association on that play led to other collaborations, including an off-Broadway production of the play which did not include Douglas in the cast and a later film which did. Another association was formed that summer at Waterford when Michael was cast opposite Brenda Vaccaro, a young actress destined for a long stay in Douglas's life, though all of these developments from the summer engagement lay in the future.

Michael returned to Santa Barbara that autumn seriously contemplating a future in acting, even though terrible bouts of stage fright made him throw up almost as soon as he came off stage. Until then, acting might still have been just a student fling to be discarded in favour of a career in one of the professions.

He added to his student accolades – and his enthusiasm for a career in the performing arts – during the following semester by being voted best director at UCSB for his presentation of John Guare's biting one-act social satire, *Muzeeka*.

That year, also, he received his BA degree from the University of California, his family present to witness a graduation that at one time seemed a most unlikely possibility. He moved immediately to New York to continue his dramatic training, taking an apartment which he shared with Danny DeVito on West 89th Street. He secured a place at the Neighborhood Playhouse, appearing in workshop productions of Pirandello's *Six Characters in Search of an Author* and

Thornton Wilder's *Happy Journey to Trenton and Camden*.

In November he moved on to join Wynn Handman at the American Place Theater, where he faced new challenges in a more demanding setting. But in terms of being a qualified, professional actor, Douglas had much to learn, and he knew it.

The speed at which he found decent roles outside the normal route of off-Broadway and neighbourhood theatre was surprising, and seemed to have more to do with who he was than with his ability.

His first big break came early in 1969, after one of those casting calls for which New York is renowned. He was cast for a role in a CBS Television Playhouse production of Ellen M. Violett's moralistic drama *The Experiment*, to be televised nationwide on 25 February. It was a pivotal role of a scientist who compromises his liberal views to accept a lucrative job with a major corporation, a role meaty enough for him to show off his talents to a wider public and to face some serious reviewers for the first time – and with a decent reaction.

Prestigious television critic Jack Gould wrote in the following day's *New York Times*: 'Michael Douglas turned in a remarkably lucid and attractively relaxed performance.' Gould could not let the moment pass without reminding his readers of the Douglas parentage, adding: 'He could easily go as far as his father. He has a promising knack for intuitive versatility.'

His début on the small screen also brought him instant recognition and notice by the public and reviewers but not, it would seem, by the director who would later cast him in his first major screen role.

The comparisons between himself and his father were bound to be made. He expected it, and Jack Gould's comment was fair enough. His performance in the television play was also sufficiently convincing to give his career a boost when he was summoned by a casting director to audition for another CBS project, *Hail, Hero!* This was the first major film planned by the television company's newly formed film unit, Cinema Center Films, which would make low-budget movies for the big screen with potential for television later.

However, Michael's screen test failed to bring any response whatsoever. Director David Miller, who auditioned him, did not even know who he was at the time, which was odd because they had met seven years earlier.

Michael's agent, apparently without his client's knowledge, telephoned Miller and gently pointed out that he had just auditioned the son of Kirk Douglas. Miller and Kirk had crossed paths on a previous and famous occasion when Miller directed Kirk in *Lonely are the Brave*. The two men argued from start to finish over interpretation. The movie was a particular favourite of Kirk's: it was produced by his own company, he gave one of the best performances of his career, won rave notices in Britain and the film became a cult classic. But Kirk and Miller did not part on the best of terms.

Miller, who first rose to directorial fame in the 1930s, had directed only two modest and unsuccessful movies in those intervening years since working with Kirk. He badly needed a success, and the CBS film production project was itself on the brink of foundering. No past troubles would stand in the way of his commercial judgement. He undoubtedly saw in Michael someone who might boost his movie, not so much as a startling new actor – Michael wasn't, not by any stretch of the imagination – as from the publicity Michael would bring.

Miller could have taken his pick from a pool of young acting talent at his disposal. Instead, he awarded the role to Michael Douglas. Kirk was not alone in expressing surprise. At the time Kirk was recovering from a throat infection and satirically scribbled on a pad when told his son was to star in a Miller picture: 'I'm speechless!'

The movie was based upon John Weston's timely and controversial anti-war novel of the same title and had Douglas in the lead role of Carl Dixon, a pacifist attempting to defend his beliefs to his conservative parents and testing them to himself. There were a number of such stories around at the time, and the screen version was no less tedious than most.

Miller's move in hiring Douglas was a wise one. It was just about the only thing about the picture that attracted any

A picture that encapsulates the professional life of Michael Douglas . . . he has kept on running (in this case for the film *Running* which he made in 1979) with grit and determination (*Hulton Deutsch*)

Michael's mother, Diana Dill, pictured on the cover of *Life* in 1943 which sent Kirk in search of her

Happy family, but not for long. Diana and Kirk separated when Michael was five and brother Joel was two

A new stepmother, Anne Buydens with whom Kirk eloped and married at the Sahara Hotel, Las Vegas, in 1954 (*Syndication International*)

And then there were four . . . Michael, then fourteen, in family portrait with his brother Joel and two stepbrothers, Peter, five, and twelve month old Eric (*Yardley Collection*)

The scions of famous fathers, Michael Douglas and Diedre Flynn, daughter of his father's old friend Errol. They met when he was making his first movie, *Hail Hero*, in 1969. Diedre, then pursuing a career as a stunt-artist, was Michael's stand-in (*Syndication International*)

A scene from that first picture, *Hail Hero*, in which he starred with Arthur Kennedy— and which vanished without trace (*Yardley Collection*)

His first long-time love, the Oscar nominated actress Brenda Vaccaro whom Douglas met while he was a student. They lived together for almost five years until they parted at the end of 1974 (*Syndication International*)

Appearances in five movies at the beginning of the 1970s failed to kickstart Michael's career. Only when he joined Karl Malden for the new TV cop series *The Streets of San Francisco*, did he begin to get noticed. He stayed with the show for 104 episodes (*Yardley Collection*)

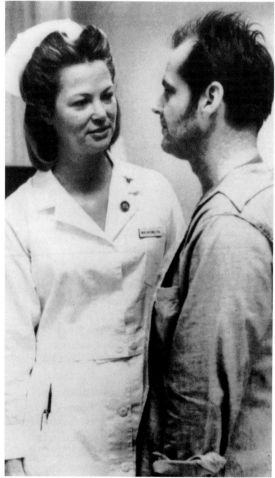

The movie that launched Michael Douglas into the big time—but his face is not in any of the photographs: *One Flew Over the Cuckoo's Nest*, starring Jack Nicholson, Michael's lifelong friend Danny DeVito and Louise Fletcher. It became one of the biggest box office successes of the 1970s and made millions for all concerned (*Yardley Collection*)

(*Yardley Collection*)

Oscars galore for *One Flew Over the Cuckoo's Nest*, including one for Douglas himself, pictured here at the ceremony with Milos Forman (best director), Louise Fletcher (best actress), Jack Nicholson (best actor) and Saul Zaentz, co-producer (*Hulton Deutsch*)

Confounding those who said it was a one-shot wonder, Douglas did it again, producing *The China Syndrome* and this time he was among the stars, along with Jack Lemmon and Jane Fonda—another box office smash (*Yardley Collection*)

At a party to launch *The China Syndrome*, he introduced the world to his new wife Diandra who found herself the focus of much unwanted attention. They had married within weeks of meeting at a party given by President Jimmy Carter (*Hulton Deutsch*)

Though a hugely successful producer, his career as a screen actor remained decidedly low profile and the 1980 movie *It's My Turn* in which he starred with Jill Clayburgh, did nothing to improve his goody-goody image (*Yardley Collection*)

publicity. *Hail, Hero!* was not a great picture by any means, and Michael's performance, though sturdy, was marred by his obvious inexperience. Even so, he managed to hold his own among decent company, which included veterans Arthur Kennedy and Teresa Wright, and collected a batch of reviews which could have been much worse, ranging from 'admirable' to 'confused'.

Michael was naturally sought out immediately by the media, promoted by the publicity department of CBS and some mischievous hints that tensions existed between Kirk Douglas and son. Michael showed considerable restraint both in commenting on his association with Miller and in handling the inevitable questions – which he would face in profusion for the next decade or more – about the problems of being his father's son, the young man in the shadow, and so on. He merely conceded that having a famous father 'gets you parts because the publicists will capitalise on who you are'.

In later years he showed a marked reluctance to discuss *Hail, Hero!* and would merely say that he felt he had been 'exploited'. Perhaps so, but then there's some truth in the old Hollywood adage about who's exploiting whom? Even before the fate of his first picture became adjudged at the box office, he was signed to star in the next CBS Cinema Center Films project which bore the unfathomable title of *Adam at 6 a.m.*

Thinly plotted and unprovoking, the film script by the husband-and-wife team Stephen and Elinor Karpf had Douglas playing a rebellious young college professor in the grip of West Coast counter-culture who returns to his roots in Missouri. The renowned New York critic Judith Crist described his portrayal as 'finely individualised'. Little else was written about it, and the movie quickly slid into the late-night TV zone, never to be heard of again.

It is debatable whether Michael had done his career any good by appearing in these two movies, but the money had been respectable for a young man only just out of college, and at least he was working and getting experience.

The money also enabled him to keep up his half of the $150-a-month rent on the apartment on West 89th Street he still shared

59

with Danny DeVito. Their continuing friendship, DeVito says, was something of an anchor for both, though it was never based on professional interests and they seldom had long or meaningful conversations. They didn't go to plays together and rarely discussed who was playing what on Broadway. 'We just enjoyed each other's company and basically set out to have a good time – girls, clubbing, and we laughed a lot,' says Danny.

They were still a slightly hippie pair, though the term was already dying out, and they were often mischievously cynical of their more serious colleagues. Neither of them had much time for the uptown party circuit to which Michael's name and pedigree would have assured them an entrance. In the year after Michael's arrival in New York, they became a familiar duo in the downtown clubs and jazz spots of Lower Manhattan.

When they occasionally ventured into the domain of the smart set, they deliberately set out to have a private joke at the expense of the chattering classes. A typical stunt involved DeVito accompanying Michael to a party in one of Madison Avenue's more snobbish locales wearing a pair of oversized stage teeth and imitating a hunchback. They both watched as the rejection of DeVito by the snooty crowd turned to admiring interest when Michael lied that his companion was to star in a new Richard Brooks movie.

From such escapades they would take off, back to their favourite areas of Manhattan, towards Greenwich Village and SoHo, cruising the downtown streets in DeVito's old Chevy car which Danny, barely visible over the steering wheel in spite of a thick layer of cushions, drove with complete confidence. 'He used to scare me to death,' Michael admitted, 'ticking the sideview mirrors of the double-parked cars, never moving a muscle, never easing off.'

Increasingly, however, Michael's sights were being turned towards the West Coast, away from New York and Broadway. In the months since his arrival, and between films, he had taken a number of small roles in neighbourhood and off-Broadway productions and was disappointed when he was rejected for a New York production of Ron Cowen's *Summertree*, in which he had starred on the first try-out of the play at the Waterford Playwrights' Conference in 1968.

Summertree was set for a run at the prestigious new Lincoln Center, and Michael read for the part. Having showcased it for Cowen as well as being a close friend of the author, it seemed he had secured the role. First he had, then he was called back for a second reading and lost it.

Enter Kirk Douglas stage left. There were discussions about the merit of the play and Michael's disappointment at not getting the role. Kirk toyed with the idea and, almost as an aside, suggested they might make a movie out of it. At the time his own career was sliding towards the doldrums and the calls were getting fewer.

Though Kirk was still busy, the pace had slowed, and his last three movies *A Lovely Way to Die, The Brotherhood* (both 1968) and *The Arrangement* (1969), fared only moderately. The latest, *There was a Crooked Man*, in which he co-starred with Henry Fonda, would face derision from some critics when it was released in 1970; Pauline Kael in *The New Yorker* lambasted it as 'commercialised black comedy nihilism [which] seems to have been written by an evil two-year-old'.

A younger generation of actors had appeared on the scene, a great new wave of talent sweeping in during the late 1960s – actors such as Burt Reynolds, Robert Redford, Dustin Hoffman and Gene Hackman. Hollywood itself was on the verge of the most monumental changes in its history, with the throwing off of self-censorship and a moral code which had pretty well kept the lid on explicit sex and violence for mass-market movies, finally giving way to the influence of directors like Arthur Penn and Roman Polanski.

With gaps appearing in his own schedule, Kirk was increasingly looking towards generating his own productions. He decided, in the good Jewish tradition, that with Michael bent on becoming an actor – which Kirk had finally accepted – he was 'going to do something for his son – put him in a big movie, make him a star'. The thought that he might generate some income for himself must also have been part of his motivations.

61

That, at least, was the plan.

But the end of the free-love era had also brought with it some social changes that were reflected in attitudes across the globe and would affect the style and content of both movies and theatre in the 1970s. World events forced the pace, and particularly those in America, which was being torn apart by internal issues, from the war in Vietnam to civil rights.

That explosion of social disturbance had seen the assassinations of Robert Kennedy and Dr Martin Luther King; the upsurge of Black Power and the police shootouts with Black Panthers; the Vietnam war, claiming its 40,000th American victim; fever-pitch anti-war demonstrations and the symbolic burning of draft cards; draft dodgers escaping to Canada; massive public demonstrations for peace in every major western city; and two million acres of defoliation in South Vietnam by the beginning of 1969.

Overseas, there were the Paris student riots, the Biafran conflict and scenes of devastating suffering and starvation; Yasser Arafat became head of the PLO and enlisted thousands of young people into his army; Muammar Gadaffi threw out the Libyan monarchy and installed himself as his nation's leader and hero of terrorist factions everywhere; the streets of Ulster became a battlezone with troops, fire-bombs and unbelievable scenes of street fighting; Jan Palach, a twenty-one-year-old Czech student set fire to himself in Wenceslas Square to protest at the Soviet invasion of Prague.

And, soon, the American National Guard – in a repetition of the horrific violence ordered by Chicago's Mayor Richard Daley only a few months before – used bayonets and teargas to disperse anti-war demonstrators at Kent County University, Ohio. Two nights later, in the grounds of the same university, four students – two of them girls – lay dead, shot by the bullets of fellow Americans in the National Guard.

All of this violence, all of this blood and gore, all of this inhumanity and human sacrifice was being conducted in the corners of living-rooms everywhere, as television stations broadcast on-the-spot coverage of such events.

Liberalisation was beginning to blossom. The old Hollywood code of conduct and the ratings system of U, A or X movies were scrapped. In London stage censorship ended in December 1969 and the nude musical *Hair* was enjoying packed houses. *Myra Breckinridge*, the sizzling exposure of sex in Hollywood by Gore Vidal, had just made its first appearance in London, along with Norman Mailer's *Armies of the Night*, about the invasion of the White House by pacifists and hippies protesting at the war. John Lennon and Yoko Ono allowed the world's media into their hotel suite in Amsterdam for their bed-in, a honeymoon to epitomise the advantages of love and not war.

For those in the midst of these events, there was in addition to the tension and the menace a certain air of unreality. Drugs provided the wherewithal for the suspension of reality – a route so desperately sought, for instance, by those young men in American uniforms in far-off Vietnam. As young people were being encouraged, if not forced, to raise the stakes of involvement – by the pressures of the wars, police brutality, terrorist causes and assorted hostilities elsewhere – violence suddenly became a part of the youth movement as a feeling of impending doom heightened.

Michael Douglas recognised the changes. He reckoned that the 1960s represented a mood of spiritual discovery and well-being, led by music reinforced by widespread drug use. But he realised the warmth of that scene had gone. Cynicism had taken over; the mood of youth and protesters at large altered dramatically, coincidentally as he began to make his way in his father's world.

6
San Francisco Nights

Hollywood was in turmoil when Michael returned as an actor, rather than as a student and a visitor to his father's house. The times, as Bob Dylan had predicted, had changed in the interim. A product of the 1960s, Michael had participated in the mood of the previous decade with laid-back vigour and had pretty well loved every minute of his adventures, carefree and promiscuous, lighthearted and lightheaded.

The sterner mood that now prevailed was apparent all around him.

The Age of Aquarius was over. It ended, as the American writer Joan Didion said in her 1979 essay 'The White Album', with the explosion of bloody violence in the Tate/Bianca massacres ritually performed by Charles Manson's drug-crazed gang the previous August. 'The tension broke . . . the paranoia was fulfilled,' wrote Didion.

Kirk and the Douglas family, as good friends of Roman Polanski and his wife Sharon Tate, were caught up in the aftermath as the media began a massive and incisive assessment of Hollywood life and the effect of its movie output on society at large.

In fact, the analysis of the film industry had begun earlier, in the wake of Polanski's bloody satanic rituals in *Rosemary's Baby*. Warren Beatty's film *Bonnie and Clyde* had also caused upset: *Newsweek*'s Joseph Morgenstern joined the outrage voiced by several other leading critics in branding it 'the most gruesome carnage since Verdun and, for those who find killing less than hilarious, the effect is stomach-churning'.

Although Morgenstern later recanted and re-reviewed the film on its artistic merit, the debate over the boundary-breaking content of explicit sex and violence in movies was under way. *Time* magazine ran a cover story investigation labelled 'The New Cinema: Violence, Sex and Art', in which a cabal of New Wave independent moviemakers, including Beatty and directors Arthur Penn, Mike Nichols and Roman Polanski, were put under the microscope. Thus, when the media was confronted with the gruesome murder of Roman Polanski's wife Sharon Tate and their friends, the media let rip against Hollywood itself.

Responsible magazines and newspapers, opinion-formers in the international news arena, devoted yards of column space to the developments in the movie capital of the world. *Newsweek*, in reporting events at the Polanski house, wrote: 'Almost as enchanting as the mystery [of the killings] was the glimpse the murders yielded of the surprising Hollywood sub-culture in which the cast of characters played. Hollywood gossip about the case is of drugs, mysticism and offbeat sex and, for once, there was more truth than fantasy in the flashy talk about town.'

The *New York Times* published a 2000-word article on the current mood of Hollywood, running alongside it a photograph of Sharon Tate dining with friends, most prominent of whom was Kirk Douglas. According to the *Times*, the Polanskis were part of a Hollywood set whose philosophy was 'Eat, drink and be merry, for tomorrow your agent may not call. They exuded a magnetism that people just wanted to be near.'

If the list of mourners at Sharon Tate's funeral represented, by implication, a cross-section of that set, then Kirk Douglas was included, along with Warren Beatty, one of Polanski's closest friends, and Steve McQueen, James Coburn, Yul Brynner and Peter Sellers.

At the same time, movies themselves were making headlines as the age of the anti-hero dawned with the arrival of Jon Voight and Dustin Hoffman in the 1969 movie *Midnight Cowboy*, that brilliant Oscar-winning evocation of living by your wits in or near the gutters of New York. It was a film that, like Beatty's *Bonnie and Clyde*, pushed out several boundaries, largely sexual, and just about killed off once and for all the Hollywood code of practice which insisted on one-foot-on-the-floor bedroom scenes with no naked bottoms or genitalia in sight. Twenty-one years later, the circle was completed, allowing Michael Douglas to perform the most vivid, explicit and lengthy sex scene in Hollywood history in *Basic Instinct*.

But it was Jack Nicholson, in another of the trend-setting 1969 movies, *Easy Rider*, who really gave a new edge and meaning to the term anti-hero. Cagney and Bogart had been given the label years before. Nicholson's interpretation in the movie he made with Peter Fonda and Dennis Hopper was something else and promoted him overnight to number-one hero of the counter-culture movement. *Easy Rider* was born out of an idea by Fonda and Hopper, a story of free love and excessive drugs and American society at large, in a way reflecting the views that Michael Douglas held at the time. As Hopper said in the film: 'Don't be scared. Go try and change America, but if you're gonna wear a badge, whether it be long hair or black skin, you'd better learn to protect yourself.'

The bottom line, however, spoke volumes to the commercial masters of Hollywood. The movie cost a paltry $400,000 to make and was, in 1969 terms, a blockbuster, grossing $40 million at the box office, one of the largest profit-to-cost ratios ever recorded.

This fact was not lost on Hollywood and its older population. As Henry Fonda succinctly put it in conversation with Kirk Douglas one day about the success of his son Peter as producer of the movie: 'That little bastard – he and some other young punks have put together a movie out of nothing and have made more money from that piece of crap than I have made in a whole lifetime in Hollywood.' It hadn't gone unnoticed by Kirk, either, as he began to put together a production deal for his son as the star of the film version of *Summertree*.

However, while Cowen's play had been applauded for its anti-war content and social observations when it was written as a play in 1968, it had quickly dated. It was tame by comparison with similar character studies that had emerged since, like *Midnight Cowboy* and *Easy Rider*. And Michael Douglas was no Jack Nicholson, either in appeal or, more important, acting ability.

Though Jack Nicholson became an 'overnight' star and won an Oscar nomination for his appearance in *Easy Rider*, he had been in Hollywood for fourteen years and had appeared in twenty movies, albeit mostly Roger Corman horror quickies and biker tales aimed at the drive-in market. But they were his schooling, where he learned to act. Michael may have had the advantage of media interest, but he lacked the charisma that surrounded the likes of Nicholson or Warren Beatty, who was famous before he made his first movie, or Robert Redford, the latest sex symbol. Worse still, he lacked the experience and the acting tuition. Alongside some of his contemporaries – and even his friend Danny DeVito – his CV looked slender and unconvincing.

Douglas had only his name – bolstered at the time by the return of his mother Diana Dill to acting and currently appearing in a popular television soap, *Love is a Many Splendoured Thing* – and was frank enough to admit: 'Being the son of a famous film star might give you a start, but it does not necessarily equip you for anything, least of all for becoming a star in your own right.'

That statement was made in hindsight. At the time he and his father had great hopes for *Summertree*. They must have done, or Kirk would not have spent so much time – almost a year – trying to get a deal in place and risking his own money through his film company Bryna (named after Michael's grandmother) for the script development before managing to secure distribution and production backing from Warners. From the moment they decided to try to get the project off the ground to the time the picture appeared in the cinemas was more than two years – and a lot would happen in the meantime to affect the film's commercial potential.

On a personal note, there was a major development that came out of the making of *Summertree*: Michael became involved with his co-star Brenda Vaccaro, and he settled in for the longest relationship so far in his life.

Brenda was almost five years older than Michael, and came from a similar background. Her father was a first-generation Italian immigrant who had made a pile of money; her mother was an actress. Brenda herself had gone through the only route that seemed open to actresses since the old Hollywood studio contract system collapsed – getting her face recognised by modelling. She was already pushing thirty when she secured her first big break in films.

John Schlesinger picked her from a thousand faces for the role of the rich and slinky woman who takes a shine to Jon Voight in *Midnight Cowboy*, a part which brought her attention at last, not least from inquisitive magazines. She and Michael were eventually discovered to be cohabiting. They did not hide the fact, even though in the early 1970s famous people were still shy of making such admissions. The old phrase of 'living in sin' remained part of the social vocabulary and sufficient for the gossip writers to contact his father to ask whether or not he approved of such an arrangement.

It seems preposterous to 1990s readers, after two decades of the gradual, creeping process of the exposure of private lives once left to scurrilous magazines like *Hollywood Confidential*, that Kirk was being asked for an opinion on the living arrangements of his twenty-five-year-old son. Kirk said he approved, and quoted the old adage of wed in haste, repent at leisure.

He reckoned there was no reason in that day and age why two people who believed they loved each other should not live together before marriage to make sure of their feelings; a bold statement for the times. His younger son Joel, he pointed out, had been far less promiscuous than Michael, had rushed into marriage with the girl he thought he'd spend the rest of his life with and ended up divorced.

Workwise, Brenda was busier than Michael. After *Midnight Cowboy* she had been signed for three movies in rapid succession, including the Douglases' own *Summertree*. Michael, on the other hand, had nothing pressing. *Summertree* would not be released until the early spring of 1971, and by the end of the post-production process Kirk Douglas was experienced and honest enough to know that his movie was not going to set the world alight.

However, towards the end of 1970 Michael continued in the

anti-war theme ahead of the publicity for *Summertree* by seeking, and winning, the coveted role of Jerry the Naz in the George Talbot play *Pinkville*, which was scheduled for a six-week run at the American Place Theater, just off Broadway.

There were advantages in such an engagement: the play would provide him with some much-needed theatre experience, especially since it was part-musical and called for him to sing several numbers. It would not tie him down to a long run, and would not confront him with either rows of empty seats or the threat of closure after a mauling by hostile critics. In the event, his performance was widely praised.

The American Place was an intimate, in-the-round theatre run on a subscription system, which ensured full houses and a guaranteed and specified run for any play staged. There was a spin-off with the publicity he attracted for the forthcoming release of *Summertree*, and the whole was a topical exercise: *Pinkville* is the story of a young American who is turned into a wartime killer.

Michael had a speech at the end which was ironically and accidentally in tune with the times. He had to say: 'So what if a few gooks get killed. They've killed 50,000 of our guys. We ought to wipe them all out.'

Similar statements were being made in real life as another piece of American self-analysis began to unfold with the opening of the court martial of Lieutenant William Calley, who was accused of murdering 109 Vietnamese in the infamous Mylai massacre. 'I shall be proud,' said Calley, 'if this trial shows the world what war is really like . . .'

While Michael's appearance in *Pinkville* brought in some timely publicity interviews in the run-up to the release of *Summertree*, the Calley trial overshadowed all fictional stories about the war. The case had inspired a severe bout of apoplexy among Americans, torn as they were between the doves and the hawks. The court martial reached a guilty verdict and imposed a death sentence on Calley in March 1971, just as *Summertree* went on general release. The true story outweighed mere fiction to the extent of virtual obliteration.

America's crescendo of discomfort with the war that President

Nixon had pledged to end barely left a place for plays and films about young American sons caught up in it. The nightly scenes of horror on television were enough to make futile any cinematic attempts to discuss the rights and wrongs, the whys and wherefores of the conflict. And so the great expectations of the Douglas clan for a movie that would hit a nerve at exactly the right moment in American history were overtaken and quashed by history itself.

Almost fourteen years had passed since Kirk had made his own anti-war statement with *Paths of Glory*, one of the earliest productions of his Bryna company. The film was still remembered, but, once again, there could be no real comparison between him and Michael Douglas in *Summertree*.

Written and directed by Stanley Kubrick from the novel by Humphrey Cobb, *Paths of Glory* was a strong and bitter tale, filled with nerve-racking intensity and some of the most vivid trench scenes ever filmed. The movie was populated by characters writ large. It was superbly performed and photographed and became, overall, a powerful piece of cinema history.

When comparisons were made, *Summertree* fared badly, and so did Michael. Critical reaction was mediocre, especially to the faltering direction of Anthony Newley, and generally fell under the description 'tedious'. The only weight was provided by Jack Warden and Barbara Bel Geddes, but overall the play itself could not sustain a full-length feature-film treatment.

Michael's performance was competent but lacked compassion. It could have been performed better by any one of a thousand young actors around at the time. That essential ingredient for star status which Michael and his father had hoped for when they set out on the project was missing. If his father had hoped that his son would become a 'big star', he had seriously overrated the potential of his movie and the audience appeal of his son.

Michael realised it too. After filming *Summertree* was complete, he and Brenda Vaccaro spent some time at the small holiday ranch he owned in Vermont and then took off to Europe for an unmarried honeymoon. Michael knew by then that he had moved too quickly in his attempt to get into the mainstream of movie-acting. He had showcased his talents as leading man in two pictures with a third upcoming, but he had failed to attract the interest of anyone.

Even before *Summertree* was premièred, there was some indication that Michael was extending his options when he made a move towards producing films by forming his own production company, Bigstick Productions. He toyed around with a couple of shorts on his return from holiday and talked vaguely about making a movie out of *One Flew Over the Cuckoo's Nest*, which had been recently and briefly revived off Broadway.

His acting career was already going in the wrong direction, which became abundantly clear with his output in 1971–2. He made two more forgettable forays into film work, first in a made-for-television movie aptly titled *When Michael Calls*, in which he played a supporting role to Ben Gazzara and Elizabeth Ashley, and then in the lead of a Walt Disney production, *Napoleon and Samantha*. The prestige of a Disney film, albeit for children, failed to translate to a box office success, and the movie was notable only for Buddy Baker's music, which won an Academy nomination, and for the introduction of a ten-year-old child actress named Jodie Foster.

After that – nothing. He was forced to consider television work which, in 1972, still carried something of a stigma for Hollywood actors. For years the mainstream film studios had banned their contract actors from appearing on television; but with the employment prospects of so many now looking bleak, some major names of the silver screen were being won over to the small screen.

'It had to happen,' said Charlton Heston, who cut his teeth in early television drama before going to Hollywood. 'The old studio system, which was finally laid to rest in the 1960s, was criticised by all and sundry for enslaving actors and forcing them into movies they never wanted to make. But the advantages were also very evident – it provided countless young actors and upcoming writers and directors with experience, especially in the B-movie output. Everybody had a turn to bat. By 1970, that was all gone and to a degree television was offering a replacement.'

At the time the producer Quinn Martin was one of the leaders in the field of quickfire television series. That bold sign-off voice that marked the end of every show – 'This has been a Quinn Martin Production' – became as familiar as cornflakes at breakfast in the late 1960s and the 1970s. Michael thought long and hard when the opportunity came to work for Martin. 'In all honesty, I was reluctant,' he recalled. 'I somewhat arrogantly thought I had this image to live up to. But then I said to myself, "Hey, wake up. They're not exactly knocking your door down with movie offers." In fact, there were none.'

First Michael took a role in a series called *Medical Center* and then appeared in the top-rated Martin show *FBI*, which he was called for as a last-minute replacement for a supporting actor who had dropped out. One thing led to another. It was his good fortune to be around at the very time Martin was planning a new police series, entitled *The Streets of San Francisco*, and his agent pushed his name forward. 'Michael had stuck in my mind after that *FBI* episode,' Martin said. 'He had a kind of presence that we were looking for in the role of sidekick to the star, Karl Malden. He was tall and good looking. He had to be good but – let's be honest about this – not overpoweringly so. Karl was number one, after all. So I called him in. I told him frankly that he was one of a number of actors under consideration, and probably not even the front runner at that point. I said I thought he had the potential for a great future but he needed experience. He needed the solid grounding that hard work – and it is hard – a series would give him. I reckoned that in five years' time, after a long run in a television series, he would be mature enough to get some feature roles.'

When Michael arrived at Martin's office, Karl Malden was there too. The meeting went well and, though Martin tested a number of other actors, he eventually settled on Michael Douglas – a decision aided by Malden's own liking and support for the son of his old friend. They went into production almost immediately with a two-hour pilot; it was shown in 1972, and did so well in the ratings that the series was up and running – and set for a long-term future. Even so, Michael remained nervous about it.

Some snooty looks were cast in the direction of both Malden

and Douglas for going over to television. Michael would admit that he would wake up in the middle of the night arguing with himself. 'If I go into television, I'm finished. That's it.' Then he would try to set down the alternatives and find he was staring at a blank page.

The series turned out to be especially important to Michael Douglas. It can now be identified as a career-shaping period of his life, better than anything he had experienced so far. Working alongside Karl Malden was like being provided with his own personal tutor in the craft of acting.

Malden was one of Kirk's earliest friends in the business. They'd met in summer stock around New York in the late 1930s when Kirk had newly graduated from St Lawrence University. Malden went on to join that rare breed of screen people who deservedly won the title of 'actor's actor'. He was one of the major exponents of The Method, learned at the Actors' Studio in New York; other actors grounded in The Method included Marlon Brando, John Garfield, Maureen Stapleton and Montgomery Clift.

Malden worked with some of the great innovators in the theatre and cinema in the late 1940s and 1950s. When one of his own mentors, the director Elia Kazan, reproduced his smash-hit Broadway production *A Streetcar Named Desire* for the big screen, Malden, already a star of half a dozen decent movies, won an Oscar for Best Supporting Actor for that year of 1951 and established himself as one of America's leading character actors.

In a career punctuated by many superb roles in more than fifty films, notably *On the Waterfront, Baby Doll* and *Hotel,* Malden's distinctive sharp and hurried style, coupled with his absolutely rigid professionalism, was an open textbook to an emerging talent like Douglas's. In fact, it was just what he needed.

Malden, known as a generous actor who was as concerned about the work of his colleagues as his own, never put on the big-star treatment that might be expected of an actor coming from the major league of Hollywood into a television series. His relationship with Douglas was, from the outset, the best Michael could have hoped for. Malden was the star of the show, but he allowed Douglas the space to develop his own character. The role Michael created was that of Malden's partner, Lieutenant Steve Keller, fictionally billed as the youngest man to achieve that rank in the San Francisco force. 'We were partners in every sense of the word,' said Douglas. 'The role written for me was not just that of a sidekick, who drove the boss and answered his telephones. I was the precocious college-educated student of criminology, while Karl's character never went beyond high school and learned his job on the street. It allowed a good deal of creativity on my part and Karl respected that, and never tried to crowd me.'

Malden insisted upon a meticulous study of the local scene so that they could establish a true empathy with the local police. Michael himself did many of his own stunts and much of the driving, careering like a racing-car driver up and down the hilly streets of America's most recognisable city. He treated the sign 'San Francisco Welcomes Careful Drivers' with the same kind of disdain as Steve McQueen in *Bullitt*.

Malden knew he was in for an exciting ride during the very first episode. They were doing a scene at the top of Nob Hill. The light was fading and the director was calling for action. Michael and Malden jumped into their car and put the flashing light on the roof. Michael screeched off. As they went over the top of the hill, all four wheels of their car left the ground; for a second or two the vehicle was airborne. Malden's head bumped the roof. He looked murderously across at Douglas and screamed: 'Jesus . . . that's not driving. Is that what you call driving?' Douglas thought he was going to be fired.

The pilot was such a success that the series went into production immediately. For the first season, running for seven months, the action was filmed on location in San Francisco, then the whole team moved back to Hollywood. To complete an episode each week required an almost impossible back-to-back schedule of fourteen-hour days of live filming and then even longer periods of studio work, virtual round-the-clock shooting for five days to get fifty-five minutes of television in the can.

Douglas had experienced no such pressure before. He was to learn much across the whole spectrum of filmmaking. There was certainly no time for nerves. The madcap pace was such that for the second season Quinn Martin decided to move the whole production unit into San Francisco itself. A special studio was built in an old warehouse close to Telegraph Hill, and the actors and key production people had to sign a seven-month residency clause so that they were permanently on hand for the duration.

Malden moved into a small residential hotel on Nob Hill, his wife Mona commuting regularly between there and the Malden home in Beverly Hills. Douglas, whose salary was upgraded to account for the residency, took an opulent apartment at the top of Russian Hill; it had extensive views over the Golden Gate, with Alcatraz visible in the distance, and was within earshot of the fog-horns that are a feature of San Francisco Bay.

Brenda came to visit twice a week when she could or he would fly back to Los Angeles late on Saturday night and return on the last flight on Sunday. She did not want to move to San Francisco, naturally, because of her own career commitments, and she remained in Los Angeles in the large house they shared in Benedict Canyon. Their separation was to be the source of constant bickering between them. She did not care much for San Francisco; the place had obvious attractions to the visitor, but Brenda was quite adamant: 'I'd die if I had to live there. It's too provincial.' The physical demands of the city were also not to her liking. Though the arrangement was good for Douglas's career, it played havoc with his lovelife.

The Streets of San Francisco became one of the great success stories of television in the early 1970s with an average audience in America alone of 25 million viewers for each episode. The series was also a precursor to many other cop series. It was sold around the world – and twenty years later is still being rerun. The face of Michael Douglas, until then largely unknown, became instantly recognisable across the globe.

Much of the success of the series could be attributed to Malden himself, not merely for his acting prowess. He was one of the most diligent and disciplined film people in the business, and was a stickler for his homework, a part of the preparation for a role that came from his training at the Actors' Studio. Even after the series had been running for months, he was continually updating his performance, focusing on style, language and mannerisms. He and Douglas were regular visitors to the real-life police department, sometimes going out on patrols; Douglas himself once went on a hair-raising undercover mission.

It was Malden who suggested to Quinn Martin that Michael should be allowed to take a lead role in some of the episodes. Michael also directed a couple of episodes. 'He was very ambitious,' said Malden, 'and I say that in the best sense of the word. He worked very hard at every aspect and was mopping up the atmosphere. He was also never afraid to listen to advice.'

By then, the production unit had developed into a team of people who spent their lives together for two-thirds of the year. Michael was a popular member of the crew, noted for his daring stunts, which were not always scripted or planned. Once, during the 1974 season, he rescued stuntman Robert Butler, who had been accidentally hit while filming a powerboat chase. Butler was badly cut and unconscious. Michael dived into the water fully clothed and kept him afloat until he could be brought aboard a boat and taken to hospital. 'He saved my life,' said Butler. 'No question about that.' Michael received a presidential award for bravery.

Off duty, he was similarly adventurous, much to the chagrin of the producer. He had learned to fly, went skiing in winter, took sailing lessons in the bay and bought a Lotus sports car which he raced in local meetings until one day he spun out of control at Willow Speedway and crashed the car. Life was hectic, but at a price: it gradually took a toll on his private life.

As the team began its third season, and settled in for another eight-month spell, Brenda's visits became less frequent. Whereas Michael had once compensated for their days and weeks apart by arranging trips, like renting a Cessna and flying her to a local resort for a weekend, she now found him often tired after a gruelling production schedule. She would fly in from Los Angeles, join him at the apartment and spend the next eight hours watching him snore.

She described their relationship as having dwindled to that of a long-married couple, but without the bonds of permanency derived from living together. He was also seeing other women. Discussions about her moving to San Francisco for at least part of the filming season had long been discarded, with dismay on Douglas's part. Eventually, he began to look elsewhere.

By the end of 1974, the relationship was hanging together by a thread, and the next season of filming would see it end. 'I think the warning signs had been around for some time,' said Vaccaro. 'We should have split long before we did. But there was a reluctance by both of us to call an end to it. We had been through a lot together, at a particular time in our lives when the support and encouragement of a partner really mattered.' They both needed the support and encouragement at the same time, but Douglas, at this moment in his career, obviously needed the presence of a woman who would always be around.

It was a selfish attitude, but he found his own work so self-consuming and self-involved that he lacked the patience to have a career-minded partner. The split in some ways mirrored the tensions that had caused the break-up of his parents' marriage.

Vaccaro's disenchantment coincided with developments in her own career. This was set to reach a new peak when she was cast to star, ironically alongside Kirk Douglas, in Howard Koch's production of *Once Is Not Enough*, based upon Jacqueline Susann's steamy novel of the same name. Billed as an erotic follow-up to Susann's devastating *Valley of the Dolls*, which was about the pill-popping antics of Hollywood women, this story too was close to home – about the daughter of a movie producer corrupted by his circle of friends, and filled with fashionable sexual novelties. Vaccaro's performance would eventually win her an Academy Award nomination.

By then, her five-year sojourn with Michael was at an end and, as often happens, the break came at the moment of a major change in Douglas's own life. Long-held ambitions were about to be realised in a manner that he could barely have imagined possible.

7
Cuckoo's Nest

The hopes of Kirk Douglas to get a film deal for *One Flew Over the Cuckoo's Nest* had long ago been transferred to his son. 'Kirk was heart-broken about it,' said Paramount executive Charlie Fellows. 'He could never understand it. He was a big star who owned what he considered a very dramatic property yet he couldn't get anyone to touch it. He became obsessive about it, and kept asking, Why? Why? Personally, I think in the end everyone had heard the story of Kirk and his Cuckoo and it was sort of dismissed before it even got to the stage of being considered.' In his frustration, Kirk had let it be known that he would sell the rights for $150,000, so that it might be made without him, but there were no takers.

Michael had been living with his own ambitions for the project for four years. When his acting career seemed to be going nowhere at the start of the 1970s he had formed Bigstick Productions in the hope of bringing *Cuckoo's Nest* to the screen. He had worked on the project, off and on, for almost three years, just as his father had done.

Between the two of them, the hoped-for movie had been put on ice so often that it had frostbite.

There was some nagging litigation from Dale Wasserman, who had written the play for Broadway and considered that he was entitled to part of the film deal. When that was resolved, separating ownership of the film rights to the book from ownership of the play by Wasserman, Michael was clear to have a shot at bringing the project to the screen. He, like Kirk, had total faith in the movie idea. The play itself was still being

79

performed around the country, in spite of Kirk's own bad experience, and ran in San Francisco for almost five years.

Three years after making a tenuous agreement with his father for the rights, Michael finally started to make the pieces of his well-thumbed jigsaw fit. He made the momentous decision to quit *The Streets of San Francisco* after the 1975 season, having notched up 104 episodes, and to concentrate wholeheartedly on *One Flew Over the Cuckoo's Nest*.

Most biographical accounts of well-known personalities identify a particular all-important turning-point, that mythical fork in the road. This was Michael's. Oblivious of what lay ahead, he was setting out on what became one of the most remarkable and little-known behind-the-scenes sagas of modern Hollywood history. As such, the story deserves a more detailed look at how he finally brought the movie into being.

A big party was held to mark Michael's departure from *The Streets*. Karl Malden was especially sorry to see him go, probably aware that the series would not go on much longer. 'The series had evolved so that there were three stars,' said Malden. 'Myself, Michael and San Francisco itself. Michael had been a superb partner in every respect.' Malden remained *in situ* for another season, but by then he too had had enough. Apart from that, there comes a time when interminable car chases over the brows of hills in San Francisco no longer excite; also, some other action-packed police series, like *Starsky and Hutch*, were already by then on the stocks.

Michael had enjoyed a rewarding life in television, but Malden knew he wanted to try to make his comeback into the film business, giving it one last big heave with his father's film rights. Michael would, however, find no easy route to a production contract, and work on *Cuckoo's Nest* overlapped his last two seasons with Malden. He, too, discovered a reluctance on the part of major studios even to look at his proposals as he canvassed them for backing, largely because of the subject-matter. The replies were very similar – 'Who wants to laugh at pathetic mental patients?' – to the kind of reaction Kirk had been getting for the previous ten years.

Some studio executives remembered that Kirk's play had flopped, and any research by a studio's script executive would have turned up all of those devastating reviews of the Broadway opening: 'tasteless in the extreme' . . . 'preposterous proposition for the theatre' . . . 'embarrassing and appalling'. The lack of interest that Michael faced was also much to do with the difficulties that pervaded Hollywood at the beginning of the 1970s.

The industry was battling against falling cinema audiences and rising production costs. Changes in attitudes and in society at large had also moved on at such a rapid pace in the previous few years that even the trend-setters had been overtaken by events. Movies like *Easy Rider* and *Midnight Cowboy*, which had been singled out by the pundits as pointers to the age of the anti-hero just five years earlier, had become as dated as yesterday's news.

The anti-hero was still in vogue, but only viable in more sophisticated, more extravagant situations aimed at attacking the establishment, and corrupt governments at large, rather than one aspect of it, like the Vietnam war. Two of the best examples of the new anti-hero would be portrayed by Jack Nicholson, first in another classic, Roman Polanski's *Chinatown*, and then in *One Flew Over the Cuckoo's Nest*.

Jack Nicholson himself recognised that the characters he had played to that point – in *Easy Rider, Drive He Said, Five Easy Pieces, Carnal Knowledge* and *The Last Detail* – were important at the time but not evergreen. They were a gallery of flawed characters of the age, insecure dropouts, sexually delinquent and cynical, all attached to that departing swinging era, with its hippie, roadie and anti-Vietnam connotations.

The focus had changed. Sex in a 1960s context had become boring. The drugs scene was no longer news; so many pop stars had fallen by the wayside that the headlines had long ago subsided. Violence was so commonplace on television that films which depicted it would have to discover the art of the spectacular to make it an attraction to audiences, and that became a developing theme through the 1970s and on into the 1980s.

Nicholson himself had just gone on record noting a new trend emerging in Hollywood, the era of the blockbuster. Studios would lead their annual production tally with such films and allow cheaper films to fall in behind.

The moneymen and dealmakers who had replaced the moguls in the control of Hollywood's output remained nervous of content. None the less, they toyed with new extremes of sex and violence in the early 1970s, pushing forward to a new era of boundary-breaking productions, such as *The Last Tango in Paris*, in which Marlon Brando and Maria Schneider performed tricks designed to shock, especially that which involved a half-pound of best butter.

Similarly, Coppola's *The Godfather*, with Brando again, introduced a new dimension to the use of 'artistic' violence. It was one of several prime movies of the time designed to lure the fans back into audience-depleted cinemas.

The background to these developments was self-evident. In 1973 *Variety* reported that between 1969 and 1972 the major studios had lost $600 million between them. Annual attendances had fallen from 4060 million in 1946 to 820 million in 1972. Packaging big names in highly hyped films was taken to new extremes. By the mid-1970s the major distributors were loath to back a film without a star partnership.

Such a response was not necessarily the solution. One of the most expensive was the packaging of Burt Reynolds, Gene Hackman and Liza Minnelli in *Lucky Lady* (the studio had to wait a year until they were all available); the film was not a success. The studios jostling with one another to sign big names meant bigger and bigger cheques for that clutch of actors currently enjoying popularity. The seemingly astronomical salaries paid to Taylor and Burton were made to look like peanuts. Top actors, basking in this new-found independence, were also getting very choosy about scripts.

What hope of finding a backer for his project had a thirty-year-old would-be producer who was already classed in some of the more cynical quarters of Hollywood as a failed movie actor?

For Douglas it was like being trapped in an overgrown maze

in the dark; blind alleys came upon him in abundance, rejection became a way of life. 'I wished him luck, naturally,' said Douglas senior, 'but, frankly, at that time I did not give him a cat in hell's chance of pulling it off.'

Kirk was right. Michael had to beat the system to produce one of the classic, multi-award-winning films of the 1970s, a movie which is impossible to ignore in any retrospective of cinematographic history. He did it by actually going outside the system, both in his quest for backers and in the filming of the movie itself. A lot of luck and a good deal of coincidence also played their parts.

Michael began by scouring all his father's old files, listing the names of every single person who had shown any interest in *One Flew Over the Cuckoo's Nest*. The name of Saul Zaentz popped up; with other probables getting fewer and fewer as he ticked them off on his list, he decided to get in touch.

Zaentz was the head of Fantasy Records at Berkeley, California, one of the most successful of the smaller independent labels that grew in the 1960s producing bands like Creedence Clearwater. He was also located in one of the hotbeds of the counter-culture movement and the place where, not long before, troops had opened fire on campus students. Memories took much longer to fade there, and the attitudes of protest lingered. That is why *Cuckoo's Nest* ran for so long as a play on the West Coast.

Zaentz had a hankering for movie involvement. As they chatted, with Douglas giving him the hard sell about *Cuckoo's Nest*, Zaentz felt he could do business with Michael. He came back a few days later brimming with enthusiasm and offered far more than Michael had anticipated – a partnership in a production deal.

Most important of all, Zaentz had the ability to guarantee personally initial finance for the picture, which Douglas had budgeted at $2 million – small beer among the heady figures in the big studios at the time, but still a sizeable sum of money to put at risk.

Even with the hurdle of finance overcome, Douglas faced problems with the film at almost every turn, from getting the right script to finding top actors willing to play mental patients.

The book, though written in 1962, still fuelled controversy on several fronts, especially regarding the treatment of mental patients with lobotomies and electric shock therapy and the prison-like institutions in which the patients were housed – all of which author Ken Kesey had portrayed from his own experiences in a mental hospital.

Michael Douglas and Saul Zaentz worked together for months on their production plans. Since neither had ever produced a film before, success rested on their determination to succeed and on Michael's own experience drawn from *The Streets of San Francisco*.

It was Saul's idea to commission the original author to write the screen version of his novel. Ken Kesey was still a hero in Berkeley. Kirk Douglas, on the sidelines, warned that Kesey was a burned-out 1960s person who had done nothing of merit since. There had been a good deal of unpleasantness after Kirk's Broadway production of *One Flew Over the Cuckoo's Nest* involving lawsuits and rows about who owned what. The mention of Kesey as the potential writer of the screenplay did not fill him with confidence.

The first time Kirk had met the author was on the opening night of the play on 14 November 1963. Kesey, a farmer's son, flew to New York from his home in Oregon and arrived at the theatre with a glazed look, which Kirk put down to drugs. Kesey had had a long involvement with illegal substances and served a prison sentence for drug possession. Tom Wolfe wrote *The Electric Kool-Aid Acid Test* about him in 1968.

Michael and Zaentz did not heed Kirk's warnings; later, they wished they had.

Kesey was brought to Los Angeles. It was explained that he would have a percentage of the film, whether he wrote the script or not. Kesey said he would write it, and they shook hands on the deal. No contracts or papers were drawn up because Kesey said he did not believe in agents and lawyers. Some weeks later he submitted the draft, and Michael had to tell Saul that it just did not work. Kesey had retained the hallucinogenic voiceover narration of the Indian character, as in the book, and had added some bizarre and horrific scenes.

Kesey felt strongly that they should adhere to his vision of the film and would not budge. Douglas and Zaentz flew to Oregon. Kesey appointed a friend to represent him in the discussions, which developed into a messy row. The author threatened to sue; eventually, he did. They returned to Los Angeles and commissioned another script elsewhere.

The selection of a director was equally important. Their vision of the movie needed a particular kind of treatment to bring out the humour of the book, so that audiences would laugh with, and not at, the pitiful characters it was based upon.

Coincidence came into play in their search. Kirk Douglas, it will be recalled, had met Milos Forman in the early 1960s when Forman was a thirty-one-year-old scriptwriter and director with the Prague Film Faculty of the Academy of Dramatic Arts.

Kirk had been so taken with Forman that when he returned home he had sent him a copy of *One Flew Over the Cuckoo's Nest* to see if he was interested in the proposed film project. The package was never delivered to Forman, probably because it had been opened and destroyed by the communist regime. There the contact rested without further progress.

Unaware of this background of the undelivered parcel – as indeed was Forman himself – Michael and Saul began casting their net for a director. 'He *has* to be exactly the right one,' said Michael Douglas. They interviewed several. Some did not want to do it, others seemed reluctant to even venture an opinion as to how they would tackle it. Eventually, they turned to Forman.

In the years that had elapsed since Kirk Douglas had met him, Forman had made a name in his home country with films like *Blondes in Love* (1965) and *The Firemen's Ball* (1967). He showed a remarkable ability at lampooning authority, so much so that the Czech fire brigade went on strike in protest. Soon afterwards, Forman left his young family in Prague and headed for the United States. By another coincidence, Forman's first film in the US was *Taking Off*, a hippie story of runaway teenagers co-written by Michael's old friend from his Waterford days, John Guare, which he dealt with in a light and cheerful vein. Guare recommended him, Forman was approached and joined the planning at an early stage.

The next hurdle was the selection of actors and actresses. Michael Douglas found another set of doors being slammed in his face as star after star turned him down flat.

The key to the success of the picture was signing the right actor to play Randall McMurphy, a cheerful anti-authoritarian imprisoned for rape who is transferred to a mental ward for observation, then leads his fellow inmates to revolt until he himself is finally subdued by the dreaded electrotherapy.

Kirk hankered after the role he had created in the theatre. Michael had to be blunt: it needed one of the new young stars who would bring more youthful appeal for the audiences, especially as Michael's vision of the play would veer towards the anti-government attitudes of society in recent times.

Who would it be? They anguished over it for weeks. Several names were in the frame, but those judged to be the best candidates – Marlon Brando and Gene Hackman, with an obvious eye on box office appeal – had little hesitation in saying no. Burt Reynolds, though a major box office attraction after *Deliverance*, was discussed but ruled out for lacking the menace that the part required.

Finally, Michael said: 'What about Nicholson?'

More talk. More anguishing. Was he right for the part? Was he available? He had just finished *The Last Detail* and was currently working on *The Fortune* with Warren Beatty for director Mike Nichols. For all his recent success and acclaim, Nicholson was still not considered a mainstream actor. His was not a name to immediately come to mind when discussing the top ten male stars of the time, nor was he even considered an A-list actor by some of the more establishment directors and producers.

Jack was a free spirit, perhaps the most free in Hollywood then and now; was and is very much his own man, chooses the off-beat, the ultimate portrayer of spit-in-your-eye irreverence off screen and on, creates his own interpretations, never reads for directors until he's got the part, never screen tests – 'Take it or leave it, I don't give a shit!'

They were all the reasons why he was right for the part. When the movie was made it seemed that no other actor could have got the role so right, but there were a number of questions at the time as to his suitability. Eventually, he was approached, and Michael learned of another coincidence.

'It's funny,' Nicholson told him. 'When the book first came out, I tried to get an option on the rights and was told Kirk Douglas had bought them.'

Forman, Douglas and Nicholson became instant comrades. Nicholson's interest in and respect for European directors and Forman's admiration for some improvisation scenes he had Nicholson perform for him convinced everyone that a certain magic between them was developing. Nicholson kept in touch with pre-production work and marvelled that Douglas and Forman saw more than 900 actors from whom they were selecting their relatively small cast of a dozen primary actors.

Forman said: 'We told Nicholson we were going for the best we could get. He agreed. Some actors don't like that because they could be outclassed in such a movie where the actor is one of a group, but he said straight away that good actors would enhance his own performance rather than detract from it.'

That, at least, was the plan. The movie ended up with no other famous name in the cast list. Five major actresses turned down the other major role of Nurse Ratched, the formidable controller of the mental ward where all the action takes place. As Nicholson later commented, all five have been kicking themselves ever since.

Among them were Anne Bancroft, Jane Fonda – 'I'm fed up with people telling me how good Jack Nicholson is' – Faye Dunaway, who had starred with Nicholson in *Chinatown*, Geraldine Page and Angela Lansbury.

It was one of the best female character parts around, but there was an 'attitude' towards it among the women actresses who were approached. Most of them perceived the role as running against the mood of the times, when the women's liberation movement was coming into its own. Nurse Ratched was a

87

battleaxe character who represented the very authority that the film was taking a swing at. Leading ladies of the moment did not apparently care to portray an evil bitch.

Louise Fletcher had no such qualms. She had made two movies up to that point, and Milos Forman remembered her from the first, Robert Altman's *Thieves Like Us*. He called her in to read; they virtually signed her on the spot.

Danny DeVito's inclusion in the cast was established even before Nicholson and Fletcher. He was not an actor who would have readily come to mind if Michael Douglas had not been involved. He had virtually no Hollywood pedigree, just a few bit parts, the last in Kirk Douglas's own production of *Scalawag* in 1973.

But Danny and Michael had made a pact. Whoever got there first would call in the other. Michael made the call.

DeVito was exactly right for the role of the happy psychotic Martini, a role that launched him headlong into a busy film career. The film was also the start of his close friendship and working relationship with Nicholson; he appeared with him in three films, including Nicholson's own *Goin' South*, *Terms of Endearment* and – when DeVito himself was a big star and a director – in *Hoffa*. He would also team up again and again with Michael.

In their perfectionist search for the right people, Douglas and Forman looked long and hard for an actor to play the large Indian chief who was supposed to be deaf and dumb until McMurphy got him to talk. They scoured the countryside and the Indian communities and found him in Mount Rainer National Park, where the plain and ordinary Mr Will Sampson was working as an assistant warden. 'Suddenly, two men appeared on horses and offered me a career in the movies,' said Sampson later. 'I thought they were kidding.'

They weren't, and he too became a minor celebrity, appearing later in a string of movies, including *The Outlaw Josey Wales*.

The final problem was in finding a suitable location. Douglas and Forman wanted to film inside a real mental hospital, but every one they approached rejected their offer of a financial donation, fearing they might be drawn into damaging publicity over the controversial nature of the book. They ended up going to the hospital where Kesey had set the story, based on his own experiences, in Salem, Oregon. The hospital's director had loved the book and understood what had motivated Kesey to write it.

8
Oscars Galore

In his very first production of a movie, Michael Douglas established a pattern that he would adhere to in all his future productions. He was as much the author of the film as its manager. Once filming was under way he left his director to get on with the artistic side, but he saw every aspect of the film through to the end. This was much the same behaviour as that other successful actor-impresario Warren Beatty, who at the same time was producing *Shampoo*, and similar to what producer-director Steven Spielberg was doing with *Jaws* in the same year. Both those blockbuster movies of 1975 were aimed to be sure-fire box office success; commercialism oozed out of the scripts, the development and the promotion.

One Flew Over the Cuckoo's Nest was altogether more risky. Although it was the type of film that crossed all social barriers, making the movie and predicting the measure of success or failure – in other words, would it make or lose money – was like sailing out to sea in a dense fog: the horizon was simply not visible. Furthermore, compared to Beatty and Spielberg, Douglas and Zaentz were relative amateurs. The collaboration between Douglas, Zaentz and Forman was a feisty one. They shouted a lot. According to Zaentz, they were all novices, thrusting around in a business they knew little about in practical terms. Forman, very much like Polanski in some respects, ranted at the other two in his thick Czech accent: 'You don't know nothing, you two. You are so stupid. Let's go eat.'

Zaentz recalls that they argued constantly, often shouting so loudly they scared those around them. 'We fought like hell,' Zaentz

91

said, 'but the thing is that all of us remember it happily. Mike worked his guts out. There is a very considerate side to him. He went out of his way to do nice things without publicity. I also felt that he was trying to prove something to his father.' They did everything wrong, but it turned out right – including filming on location in a mental hospital.

Their story dealt with the topical and vexed question of 'curing' mental patients with electric shock treatment. On the face of it this was hardly a crowd-puller, especially when weighed against Beatty's sexy *Shampoo* and Spielberg's shark horror *Jaws*.

In Douglas's film, audiences were to be given a more realistic view of life in a mental institution than anything that had gone before. The telling of it needed an actor like Jack Nicholson, with his underlying twinkling sense of humour to lift the story from an abject, depressing tale. Aided and abetted by a cast of similarly talented people, Nicholson kept the film bouncing with his sympathetic humour almost to the dramatic end, when he is himself immobilised by the shock treatment.

The film was a dramatic observation of the convicted rapist, McMurphy, who had convinced the authorities that he was mentally disturbed in order to avoid heavy prison duties. At the same time, Nicholson had to hint to the audience that he was feigning insanity and then also show that he had a very definite mental disorder of which he was unaware.

He arrived at the institution as the epitome of a man who has spent a lifetime baiting the establishment.

Once inside the ward, where a controlled calm prevailed, he pitted himself against the hospital bureaucracy in the person of Nurse Ratched, who daily supervised the administration of tranquillising medication. Naturally, McMurphy resisted and began his own one-man rebellion, leading his fellow inmates into riot, escape and a party with imported drink and prostitutes.

McMurphy's personality, as portrayed by Nicholson, was magnetic and destructive, both of himself and fellow inmates. He was the complete anti-hero.

The alleged concern of several of the actors who were originally approached was that the film might upset a number of people.

More likely, they turned down the roles because the subject-matter would do nothing for their own image. Nicholson has never shown the slightest concern about image; nor did he in this case.

Egged on by Douglas and Forman, Nicholson attacked his part with his usual methodical tenacity, analysing the implications, dissecting the character, measuring its demands and psychological tones. As he read the script, he underlined key phrases in his lines and numbered certain words to signify beats and phrases. Michael Douglas had been installed at Oregon with his crew and the rest of the cast when Jack turned up to begin work after a skiing holiday with Roman Polanski.

Jack had never previously met any of the actors, who were already mingling with patients. Douglas had given the hospital superintendent, Dean Brook, an outline of the film's characters and asked him to find patients whose profile fitted the play, so the actors could hang out with them.

This had been going on for five days when Nicholson arrived. Jack came in at the end of rehearsals for one of the group therapy sessions in which inmates participated. When they broke for lunch and sat around the table, Jack was obviously uneasy. He suddenly banged down his fork and walked out.

Michael Douglas followed. 'What's wrong?' he asked.

'Man, these guys don't quit. I'm eating lunch and these guys don't break character. What's going on here?'

Douglas calmed him down, explaining that the people around the lunch table were not all actors. Most of them were inmates. There were 582 patients, most of them classed as criminally insane. With Douglas and Forman on hand, Nicholson had talks with the chief of staff, with nurses and patients. He was shown all around the hospital and personally persuaded the hospital's medical chief to let him watch patients undergoing shock treatment.

He went into the maximum security ward and was already sitting in the hallway when the patients were brought out of their rooms. They included a number of especially violent cases, including several murderers. They all thought he was a new patient, and most were anxious to engage him in conversation.

One was a handsome blond man who had killed a prison guard three weeks earlier with twenty-eight stab wounds. Nicholson went to lunch with them and continued his conversations, with hospital staff never too far away.

Part of the deal that Douglas had made with the hospital superintendent was that, during filming, the inmates would be employed in the technical departments wherever possible to give them extra money and provide a sense of responsibility. As a result, an arsonist who had tried to burn down the hospital a year earlier was working with the painters, a murderer was employed with the electricians and a couple of child molesters were scene shifters.

Some inmates also appeared in background scenes. Dean Brook himself had a walk-on part. Although he later ticked off Michael over certain inaccuracies, he felt it 'a great honour to do a scene with Jack Nicholson, who is an absolute genius in getting across the character of McMurphy, a sociopath of whom there are plenty around. Jack's performance typified them.'

Filming in Oregon was to cover a period of eleven weeks. Nicholson's partner at the time, Anjelica Huston, came to join him on location. She wished she hadn't: she found him so immersed in the role that he was increasingly difficult to live with. Nicholson explained: 'Usually I don't have much trouble slipping in and out of a film role, but in Oregon I didn't go home from a movie studio, I went home from a mental institution, and there's a certain amount of the character left in you that you can't get rid of; you are in a mental ward and that's it. It became harder and harder to create a separation between reality and make-believe because some of the people in there look and talk so normal. You would never know they were murderers.'

In fact, Nicholson became so engulfed by the institutionalised life he was acting out that Anjelica started to get worried. His behaviour towards her when he came home at nights got worse as the days went by.

Eventually, she challenged him: 'Can't you snap out of this? You're acting crazy.'

He could not. Anjelica packed her bags and flew back to Los

Angeles, complaining: 'I am no longer certain whether you are sane or not. I'll see you when you come back into the real world.'

Michael Douglas took the trouble to apologise to her for the difficulties she was experiencing with her lover. 'If it's any consolation,' he said, 'this movie is going to be a smash. I've never been more impressed with any actor in my life.' Saul Zaentz added his praise: 'I can think of only one other actor to compare him to, Paul Muni.'

There was no doubt that the way Nicholson had taken the movie to heart helped turn it into the raging success it became. Milos Forman was an excellent director, but Nicholson was doing a lot of it himself. The rest of the actors, inspired, fell in behind him; without exception, they gave the best performance of their lives. Louise Fletcher, like Nicholson, was self-motivated, fired not merely by the screenplay but by the atmosphere of the whole production.

It was an emotionally exhausting picture for the actors, and one that formed an incredible bond of friendship between them. Nicholson said: 'It was the most intense thing I ever worked on.' There were personal tragedies, too. Half-way through filming, Billy Redfield, who playing the character nicknamed Hard-On, was diagnosed as having leukaemia. He told Forman and Douglas that he was desperately ill and did not have long to live, but he begged them to allow him to carry on. He died six weeks after the film was completed.

And there was fermenting anger from Ken Kesey. Just before the Academy Awards ceremony the following April, he arrived in Los Angeles bearing writs for damages over the unused script, complaining publicly that he thought that Douglas and Forman had sacrificed the radical nature of the book for the sake of commercialism. 'They took out the morality,' he complained bitterly. 'They took out the conspiracy that is America.'

He broke a habit of a lifetime and sought the advice of lawyers, who filed a suit claiming five per cent of the film's gross and $800,000 punitive damages. Douglas pointed out that he had already assured Kesey of a cut. The author settled for a two-and-a-half per cent slice of the gross, which would turn out to be a very considerable sum.

But there was plenty of money to go round: the film was breaking box office records.

Columbia worked out a slow release in the autumn of 1975, allowing the movie to build up to a nationwide release towards nomination time for the Academy Awards. The strategy proved exactly right. *One Flew Over the Cuckoo's Nest* picked up an astonishing nine Academy nominations for the 1976 ceremony, equalling the tally of some recent expensive blockbusters like *The Godfather*:

BEST PICTURE: Michael Douglas and Saul Zaentz
BEST ACTOR: Jack Nicholson
BEST ACTRESS: Louise Fletcher
BEST SUPPORTING ACTOR: Brad Dourif
BEST DIRECTOR: Milos Forman
BEST ADAPTED SCREENPLAY: Lawrence Hauben and Bo Goldman
BEST CINEMATOGRAPHY: Haskell Wexler and Bill Butler
BEST FILM EDITING: Richard Chew, Lynzee Klingman and Sheldon Kahn
BEST ORIGINAL SCORE: Jack Nitzsche

The award ceremony was on 29 March 1976. Kirk and his wife were at home watching the proceedings on television. It was a bitter-sweet occasion in one respect – Brenda Vaccaro, Michael's long-time companion, was in the running for an award. She was nominated Best Supporting Actress for her role in *Once Is Not Enough*, in which she had co-starred with Kirk Douglas; hers was the bright performance in an otherwise mediocre film.

Jack Nicholson and Michael Douglas sat together, vying with each other for the worse case of nerves. The technical awards came first – and they did not pick up one of them. Jack was saying: 'I told you, I told you.'

Then, their luck changed. One by one they counted off the *big* five Oscars: Best Adapted Screenplay, Best Director, Best Actress,

Best Actor and finally Best Film. The official history of the Academy points out that it was the first time any picture had picked up four major awards since *It Happened One Night*, starring Clark Gable and Claudette Colbert, forty-two years earlier.

A couple of personal dramas were played out at the ceremony, more poignant than what usually surrounds the Oscars, and which made Douglas and his comrades shed a few tears. Louise Fletcher gave her acceptance speech partly in sign language, for the benefit of her deaf mother watching at home, telling her: 'I want to thank you for teaching me to have a dream. You are seeing my dream come true.'

Milos Forman, meanwhile, had sent for his two sons from Prague. They arrived at Los Angeles just twenty-four hours before the presentations, speaking no English. 'I had not seen them for five years,' said Milos, 'and we were strangers to each other that evening. But they had learned to recognise the name of the film, and could say "Cukusnest". Then the film was mentioned in the category for Best Supporting Actor, and they thought it meant I had won, and they cheered as George Burns, who won the section, went up to collect his Oscar. I had to tell them to cut it, and they looked at me as if I was making a bad joke. After we had lost the first four nominations, Petr fell asleep and Matej concentrated on his bubble gum. I realised that if I did not win, they would wonder what they had come over for. Finally, I won my Oscar and was filled with fatherly pride. I told my sons they could have anything they wanted. "Anything?" they asked. I nodded and Petr blurted out, "We want to see *Jaws*." Oh, well . . . !'

Reaction to the film was wildly enthusiastic. Actors, film buffs, producers and reviewers alike were all completely stunned by the tumultuous audience response when the film opened, scenes that were repeated across the land.

It was not merely the lighthearted moments that brought such stirring participation; even the most soberingly dramatic moments, as when McMurphy tried to strangle Nurse Ratched to death, were received with cheers and applause. For that reason alone, while praising Nicholson and Forman's direction, reviewers sounded many notes of caution. Stanley Kauffmann in *The New Republic* noted quite adamantly that the film was warped, sentimental and possibly dangerous. Pulitzer prizewinner Roger Ebert, one of the most influential critics in America, is still of the view that Nicholson and Forman milked the film so that it became a simple-minded anti-establishment parable. 'I think there are long stretches of a very good film,' he says, 'and I hope they don't get drowned in the applause for the bad stuff that plays to the galleries.'

But this was reviewer-speak. The movie was a classic exercise in meticulous – and not accidental – casting and direction, a movie which drew on Nicholson's considerable powers as an actor to such a degree that the audience was enabled to have total suspension of disbelief. The film never seemed like a performance of actors acting; it was more like real characters being filmed in natural surroundings.

The film added another important notch to the reputations of Forman and Nicholson and launched Michael Douglas into orbit.

9
Enter Diandra

When such remarkable success comes virtually overnight, give or take a month or two, Douglas's life had to change. He was also at that age of breaking thirty when men are known to want their lives to change, personally and professionally. All around him, people were saying that he had proved himself as a producer and they expected him to quit acting and concentrate on making movies. There was a queue at his front door, with directors and dealmakers offering scripts jostling with big-name interviewers from the glossies dashing to get the lowdown on how he pulled off his great coup.

For once, the media people weren't asking questions about what it was like to be Kirk Douglas's son. Now they were asking Kirk Douglas what it was like to be Michael's father. Kirk recalls his reaction with a degree of fatherly pride which glossed over the periods of his son's life when they did not get along too well:

'Well, yes, if I'd known what a bigshot he would become, I'd have been nicer to him when he was a kid. It's also odd . . . As a boy Michael did not like my world very much, which was perhaps a reaction against me and my surroundings and, yes, it's true I thought and hoped he would make a good lawyer. Then he takes my play and turned it into a phenomenal movie. I was a little disappointed that I didn't get to play the McMurphy role, but I can't complain – the picture grossed nearly $200 million and I had a piece of it. I made more money out of it than I did on *Spartacus*. I knew this movie would be a lesson for him, if nothing else . . . and it was. From my own point of view, I would willingly have sacrificed the money to have played the role of McMurphy.'

Publicity was important. Michael made himself available to pretty well all who asked, talking freely about his ambitions. The movie made on the cheap in a state mental hospital grossed $185 million, and later the television and video rights took the figure over the magical $200 million. That meant a profit of $120 million after all the post-production costs had been added to the original minuscule budget.

Kirk's share was a reported $15 million. Michael became a multimillionaire virtually overnight. So did Jack Nicholson. He was also on a percentage deal, so he too collected well in excess of $2.5 million. Invitations from film festivals and foreign distributors flooded in, as did requests for interviews as the movie opened across the globe.

Michael and Jack decided to take themselves to the world, launching into a year-long jaunt of promotional travels with every kind of pleasurable extra thrown in. It became a notorious event. They were like-minded, easy-going individuals who discovered an instant rapport and very similar interests, professionally and off duty. They had liberal views and tastes born out of the same era, liked the same kind of movies and music and the same kind of girls.

Douglas had already acquired a surprising image as a Mr Nice Guy among the media people, in striking contrast to the label given to his father. Nicholson, too, was very approachable, though when stardom was established he strictly limited his contact with the press and hardly ever appeared on television chatshows, a rule he has stuck to down the years.

When Jack made friends, they were generally friends for life. He was a down-to-earth man who kept a bowl full of dollar bills on his coffee-table to signify his suddenly acquired wealth, ever mindful in the early days that it could just as easily blow away. He also had a collection of pot pigs, presumably indicating his continued empathy with 1960s thinking. On all counts, Michael Douglas concurred.

As they went from stop to stop, they would check the mounting box office returns and chuckle. 'Ah, well,' Nicholson would say, 'another day, another fifty grand.'

They allowed themselves the time to have a ball: women, the finest champagne and the best grass money could buy. Michael had been short on sexual activity of late; he made up for it on the tour. Even Nicholson, Hollywood's most renowned boulevardier after Warren Beatty, was ready to admit on their return: 'We had a blast – I couldn't keep up with Michael. Oh, and by the way, he has a penchant for the bizarre.' Stories filtered back, and Anjelica Huston became very angry indeed. Soon after Jack came home, she decided that what was good for the gander, etc., and decamped to London with Ryan O'Neal for what was the first of several partings during her seventeen-year relationship with Nicholson.

There was no one who worried about what Michael got up to, except the gossip columnists, and they didn't really matter, Michael was basking in success as a producer, not as a charismatic actor like Nicholson. To the wider public he managed to remain fairly anonymous in spite of the vast publicity the film achieved.

Anyway, the tour was supposed to be strictly to promote the film and they made certain that it was scandal-free, at least as far as the newspapers were concerned. Behind the scenes and in their private rooms, it was one long party. 'Well, I was single at the time,' Douglas says defensively. 'And I was determined to savour the experience in the most decadent of ways. True, it did get a bit excessive, and people close were worried what I was doing to myself . . . but it was fun, and it was meant to be. I knew it could not last and never intended that it should.'

Their world tour took them to England, Sweden, Denmark, France, Germany, Italy, Japan and Australia, where Jack pulled out to return to Hollywood to begin a new film, *Missouri Breaks*, with Marlon Brando.

Douglas went on alone to South America, calling at Brazil, Venezuela and Mexico, and did not get back to Hollywood until the autumn of 1976. There was already talk among the pundits that he had made so much money out of *Cuckoo's Nest* that he would quit acting for good and concentrate on producing movies. Michael would soon show that this rumour was without foundation, but first there was a personal matter that attracted

101

his complete attention for the next six months.

He had never been a particularly overt supporter of any political cause since his younger days when he, like everyone else in his circle, was opposed to the Vietnam war. But all around Hollywood there were actors who campaigned for presidential hopefuls, notably Warren Beatty, Robert Redford, Jack Nicholson and others who became involved in George McGovern's 1972 campaign; later, Beatty became deeply committed to the presidential bid of his good friend Gary Hart.

In the 1976 campaign, Californian liberals had been less than enthusiastic in backing the unknown senator and peanut farmer from Georgia, Jimmy Carter. Lew Wasserman, head of Universal/ MCA, eventually threw his weight behind Carter midway through the campaign, leading the fundraising and general morale-boosting effort locally which gave Carter's chances a considerable leg up in California.

Thus, when Carter became president, he recognised this show of support by inviting a number of people from the world of entertainment to his great inauguration gala in Washington on 19 January 1977. Jack Nicholson and Michael Douglas were among the many who received an invitation by virtue of supporting Wasserman's fundraisers.

The jamboree was a typical Washington bash, if slightly subdued. The Democrats had won, but Carter was an unknown quantity. They arrived on Inaugural Eve for the do at the Kennedy Center, Jack as usual hiding behind a pair of black shades from his extensive collection and Michael sporting a bushy beard and longish hair.

The hall was crowded with hundreds of people from every walk of life and profession along with a smattering of Washington socialites. One of them appeared like a vision across a crowded room. It was as 'corny' as that, Douglas admitted, when he first caught sight of Diandra Luker, then a student at Washington's Georgetown University School of Foreign Service, studying for a diplomatic career and fluent in five languages. She was tall and slender, a very beautiful young woman wearing a stunning white dress.

They made eye contact. He excused himself from his party and manoeuvred his way towards her, introduced himself over some hors d'oeuvre and made small talk. She had never heard of him, or the fictional cop Steve Keller, because she never watched television and seldom went to the movies. Perhaps it was a put-down or perhaps true. She rather imagined he was an artist or a writer; Douglas did not immediately disabuse her of this notion.

Diandra considered Douglas's conversation distinctly vigorous but also 'ridiculous', as they spoke on quite different levels of awareness, which she also found 'intensely interesting'. As they talked, she identified him immediately as an ageing hippie whose subject-matter harked back to the time she was a child.

Diandra was nineteen and he was pushing thirty-three, but this was no impressionable-young-girl-meets-famous-movie-star situation. For one thing, he wasn't a famous movie star. They continued their conversation long enough for him to feel that he must not let this girl out of his sight. When she said she was going on somewhere afterwards with her date and other company, Michael said he would probably see her there.

That, she said, was unlikely because it was a private club. Was he a member? No, he wasn't, but he would have no difficulty in gaining admission. He had Jack Nicholson with him. She wished him the best of luck and hoped she would see him later.

She didn't. The club was for members only, he wasn't a member and he couldn't get in. But he had gleaned sufficient detail from their conversation to track her down the following day, and discovered her telephone number. He also made some inquiries and found she was a young girl-about-town who had strong connections in Washington's political and social circles.

Her father, who died when she was a child, had been an American diplomat. She spent her early years abroad, notably in Majorca, where she was raised, and in mainland Spain. She had spent time in Paris, London and Madrid, and had been to boarding-school in Switzerland and America. She describes her childhood as a fairy-tale existence; she lived in a Moorish castle called Miramar, rode horses, went swimming, knew Robert Graves, who lived nearby, and the Spanish artist Joan Miró.

Her mother, who like Michael's mother had British connections, was an archaeologist who also travelled extensively. 'I was never treated like a child,' she recalls. 'I often spent time with my mother's friends, archaeologists, writers and artists, and if I matured quickly it was because of my surroundings.' She had been at Georgetown for three years before she met Douglas.

Michael telephoned and they agreed to meet for dinner. They arranged to meet again the day after, intending to look at Washington's sights; but it rained and they ended up in his hotel bedroom. 'He literally stole her away,' says Jimmy Webb, Douglas's good friend of many years.

Douglas was proverbially smitten, totally and utterly. He soon told Nicholson that he was going to ask the girl to marry him. Nicholson could not believe it. Michael said he could not believe it himself, and nor could anyone else in his circle. Not long before, he had said that he did not feel ready to commit himself to monogamy; he would never get into anything that he could not end by walking out of the door. (This philosophy was similar to Nicholson's, after his early divorce from his wife, and Beatty's, who both seemed set for perennial bachelorhood).

Now, suddenly – and for once the word is totally apt – Michael was talking of getting married. He proposed two weeks into the relationship. She said she would consider it but that they had to give it time.

No one really believed it would happen, but the whirlwind courtship whirled faster and ended when they married on 20 March 1977, two months to the day after their first dinner together. The wedding was held at Kirk's and Anne's house and was a relatively quiet affair for Beverly Hills, a mere two dozen friends and relations. Jack Nicholson and Warren Beatty were his supporters, and other guests included the Gregory Pecks and the Karl Maldens.

They took a house in Beverly Hills, and Diandra signed on at the University of California at Los Angeles to continue her studies. It was not an uncommon sight to see Douglas dropping her off and collecting her from school. Diandra was mature enough to know that if their relationship were to succeed, they would both have to make changes. Michael said he knew that, too, although perhaps the severity of the adaption to the Hollywood lifestyle was far greater than Diandra realised.

Though a young woman of the world, she had been surrounded by her mother's intellectual friends and colleagues during her upbringing. And in recent years she had lived among the somewhat cloistered halls of Georgetown, which produced entrants into establishment circles and where the formality of introductions still prevailed. Few in the social set she had departed could believe her new life was happening, least of all her mother.

The sight of the likes of Jack Nicholson, in crumpled suit and dirty sneakers, saying, 'Hi, babe, howya doin' ', or the excessively charming and self-preening Beatty – 'You are the most gorgeous creature I have ever met' – was a culture shock.

The Hollywood style was totally alien to her previous nineteen years, as indeed was life in that great urban sprawl of Los Angeles, which people either love or hate. After the initial excitement of the novelty had worn off, she fell into the latter category.

Neither had she any concept of the goldfish-bowl syndrome, life lived under the constant scrutiny of the media, the gossip columnists and the ever-watchful gaze of the most bitchy village-like community of Hollywood. With her new husband currently enjoying both fame and fortune, attributes that invoke ire and envy among those in that false and hypocritical hothouse, she stepped straight into an overwhelming crescendo of interest.

Diandra was Hollywood's newest princess in one of the most famous film dynasties, and she was 'shocked' by it all. There was simply nothing 'normal' about it. She was unsettled from the start, and it would show in the somewhat nomadic nature of their early life – to which was added a degree of uncertainty about Michael's own future.

He was already pushing ahead with plans for a new movie by then, inspired by a screenplay that would, in the event, require almost as much tenacity as it took to bring *Cuckoo's Nest* to the

screen. To produce one of the most successful movies of the decade
was one thing; to return to his first love of acting was another.
After completing *Cuckoo's Nest* Michael had set up an office in
Los Angeles for his own production company. For the time being
he seemed to be going down the route of becoming a full-time
independent producer. His attitude was that if an acting role
came along, well and good, but he was not overtly active in seeking
one, and nor were directors falling over themselves to offer him
anything. The production route for an actor of his standing was
no easy ride, either. Traditionally in Hollywood, actors aspiring
to become producers have not been given a great deal of support
by the studios, who still remembered the words of that foul-
mouthed Columbia mogul, Harry Cohn: 'The lunatics are trying
to take over the asylum.'

There was a cabal of up-and-coming young moviemakers,
almost all from the excellent film faculties of the University of
Southern California or the University of California at Los Angeles.
This thrusting new crowd included Steven Spielberg, George
Lucas and Francis Ford Coppola, who were grabbing the big-
budget productions. Meanwhile, directors like Martin Scorsese
(*Mean Streets* and *Taxi Driver*), Polanski (until he had sex with
a minor and fled US justice), Brian De Palma (who had just scored
a big hit with *Carrie)* and a small collection of others had cornered
the market in subterranean explorations. But, generally, directors
were hirelings who would have a percentage of a deal if they
were lucky.

Any independent producer had to put together a package of a
property – i.e. a good story – a screenwriter, an established
director and at least two major stars to get the backing of a mainstream studio. That is what Michael Douglas ultimately sought.

Even established actors who tried to produce found no route to
getting finance. Kirk himself could attest to that. So could Warren
Beatty, one of Hollywood's few successful actor-producers. He
had to kiss Jack Warner's shoes to charm him out of a paltry
$1.7 million for *Bonnie and Clyde*, took four years to bring
Shampoo to the screen and an obsessive ten years before he
managed to get a print of *Reds* in 1980.

The rewards for successful movies could be tremendous. Beatty made an estimated $40 million out of his four most successful movies, *Bonnie and Clyde, Shampoo, Heaven Can Wait* and *Reds*. But because of the time spent on wheeling and dealing, his output was considerably less than, say, his pal Nicholson's – twenty films in thirty years compared to Nicholson's fifty-plus.

Michael also faced another problem. The old Hollywood saying 'You're only as good as your last picture' was paralleled by another thought: if you have one major success, you are a failure if you don't match it the next time around. After *Cuckoo's Nest* people were asking him: 'What are you going to do? How do you top this?' Or they would say: 'It's all downhill from here.'

He heard it so often that he sometimes thought that he had gone as far as he could. 'Well, it's all been fabulous, thank you and good night.' The big decision always was: 'What do you really want to do?' The well-known booby trap for moviemakers was trying to second-guess what audiences wanted. The old moguls guessed instinctively; but they also got it wrong, often, and their mistakes were generally covered by the enormous output of the big studios.

In the 1970s these 'guessers' were not the moguls, who no longer controlled the studios, but a large body of commissioning executives and financiers. Mistakes would be pounced upon and ridiculed. Michael's reaction was a gut one: to go with what interested him. He reckoned that if he were working on a project for three years, he didn't want it to be a picture that bored him: 'All those steps in pre-production, doing your homework, having that script sold, choosing the director, haggling with agents for the actors, getting your locations straight – all that is so important. And then the shooting and post-production and distribution. You can't let up at any time. That's a huge endeavour, so you have to be in love with the project, and you've got to know what you want to do just to keep interested.'

He had another white-knuckle, roller-coaster ride ahead of him. Screenplays and manuscripts came flooding through the door. He dismissed most. They came, by and large, from fortune-hunters and owners of every worthy, dull, dark and boring property in existence – save for one that caught his eye. It was an original screenplay by Michael Gray for what became *The China Syndrome*, a thriller based on a fictional disaster at a nuclear power plant.

It hit the mark for Douglas as exactly the type of project he wanted. In many respects it was similar to *Cuckoo's Nest*, in that it carried an anti-authority message and centred on a subject which touched the masses, who were growing nervous about the safety of the nuclear energy industry. While lessons from the past and observations of his father's work never allowed him to forget that a popular filmmaker must provide entertainment, he was also looking for stories that had a point of view or something thoughtful to say. He described this as the difference between reading a forgettable pulp novel and a classic that haunts you.

Michael recognised at once that *The China Syndrome* was going to be a controversial picture, dealing as it did with a current social problem, not in the past like a picture about Vietnam after it was over or about the Depression, like *The Grapes of Wrath*. Michael set up a meeting with Michael Gray and was surprised by his opening line. He said: 'You know, this is going to be a race.' Douglas asked why, what race? Gray replied that it was going to be a race to get the picture out before a major nuclear accident. Douglas did not say as much, but thought he was being over-dramatic. In the event, it would be a close-run thing. The real-life nuclear meltdown at Three Mile Island happened twelve days after the picture was released.

Michael began immediately to put together a package of stars and costings to present to would-be backers. At this point a glazed look came into the eyes of those he approached and the doors started slamming again. Michael booked in for another long haul, and it was almost three years from the time he first took the script on board to getting the movie completed.

That development lay in the future. For the time being, an acting role that appealed to him had been offered by Michael Crichton, prolific novelist, director and screenwriter. Douglas admired Crichton's work. At the time, Crichton had two scripts going into production and would direct both. The first was *Coma*, based upon Robin Cook's successful novel of the same name; the second was as writer-director of a screen adaptation of his own novel *The First Great Train Robbery*, which would star Sean Connery and Donald Sutherland.

Michael was wanted in *Coma* as second lead to the star, Geneviève Bujold, who portrayed a doctor who suspects that patients are being put deliberately into a coma so that their organs could be sold for the growing business of spare-parts surgery. The movie would be billed as a Hitchcockian suspense-horror thriller.

The addition of Richard Widmark and the cool Elizabeth Ashley (plus an unknown bit-part player, Christopher Reeves) failed to inject credibility to a script that lacked the ability to match the description in the publicity handouts. Douglas received a mixed bag of reviews, some praising his quiet sensitivity, others dismissing him without much comment. Michael himself admitted that 'making *Coma* was really uncomfortable for me'. He hadn't acted for almost two years.

By then, *The Streets of San Francisco* was off the air, so he'd had no public exposure except as a fairly anonymous (as far as audiences were concerned) producer. He discovered a re-emergence of his camera-shyness. He found himself 'taken aback on *Coma* and part of it had to do with the role I was playing'. Geneviève Bujold did all the investigating, leaving him with the back-up lines like 'Come on, honey. What is it?' He had had a lot of practice on the television series at standing around doing nothing except look interesting, but while he was happy to play second fiddle the film's dialogue often made him wince. He had to do one scene forty-five times because he could not remember the medical lines.

Even so, his performance made an impression on production executive Sherry Lansing, later to become one of Hollywood's most powerful women. She reckoned he had a combination of sexuality and vulnerability that would 'turn him into a mega-star'. A few years later, she was instrumental in seeing that prediction finally achieved in her own production of *Fatal Attraction*.

109

For the time being, however, Michael Douglas, actor, was on no one's A-list.

He continued in his search for backers for *The China Syndrome* and found none. Even Saul Zaentz did not want to come to the party this time. 'True, I asked him,' said Michael, 'but I think we both, for different reasons, had to go off on our own.' At the time, Zaentz had his own problems. He was producing an expensive, innovative and complicated cartoon version of Tolkien's *Lord of the Rings* which did not do well (though he redeemed himself with his next film when he teamed up again with director Milos Forman for the Oscar-winning *Amadeus*).

Michael was on his own. Had it not been for his comfortable bank balance he may well have contemplated his future with more tension than he did – especially now that they were to be three.

Diandra was pregnant, expecting their first child in December 1978. That became another reason, for her, why they should move out of Los Angeles to healthier, more peaceful climes. Anyone living and working in Hollywood who is surrounded by friends doing the same thing simply cannot stop talking shop: who's doing what for whom, what deals are being pulled off where and for how much; the lives of actors, producers, directors, and to a lesser degree writers, revolve around such gossip – that, for the most part, is all that there is.

Everyone in that town is always on the verge of a major deal. It is the one thing that has remained constant in Los Angeles down the years. For those not especially interested, the whole topic can become an incredible bore.

For this reason and because of the pollution – that great blue haze of smog was more prevalent in the non-environmentally friendly 1970s – Diandra and Michael decided to move to his old stamping-ground of Santa Barbara. After a period of intense motherhood after the birth of their son, she transferred from the University of California, Los Angeles, to the University of California, Santa Barbara, to continue her studies for her degree. With no financial pressures to concern him, Michael often stayed home to play house-husband. The home they chose was to become their anchor for the future, a place of retreat and replenishment in difficult times, of which there were an abundance ahead.

They bought the first house they were shown, a Spanish Colonial Revival villa, high on a hill overlooking the ocean and barely a mile from where Michael used to live in Banana Road. Their impulsive decision scared them at first. The house needed a great deal of work. Outside, it was unimpressive and needed architectural attention; inside, it was overdone. The next three years would be spent refurbishing, at a cost, including the price of the property, that ran eventually to $10 million.

It was a task that fell to the control of Diandra, because, very soon after they acquired the property, Michael's filming took him back to Los Angeles and elsewhere for months on end. Diandra graduated from university in the midst of the work and spent much time with architects and builders.

She had a very clear vision of what she wanted. 'I wanted to drive through the gates and see this other world. I've always had a need to create environments that are a refuge, going back to my childhood in Majorca. It was important to me that nothing looked temporary.'

She personally sketched out her design for the driveway and the architects brought plans to remodel the front. They pulled down existing structures and refitted an impressive set of double arches. The rear was similarly remodelled, turning a small patio and pool area into a superb garden layout visible from the house through french doors, and installing a huge set of steps which made use of the natural incline of the property.

The interiors were restyled with the help of a leading Los Angeles designer and co-owner of an antique shop, and the rooms were filled with fine Baroque furniture and paintings. 'Over the years,' said Diandra, 'the house had been buried beneath a veil of decoration which we stripped away to create an elegant country house of a kind you might find in Spain or northern Italy.'

She transformed the property into a magical place, he said, to which he couldn't wait to invite his friends. It became the scene of many relaxed parties for 200 people or more, with live bands.

111

Otherwise, it was Diandra's house in every repect – started at a time when she was also pregnant. Michael's contribution to the work became minimal, especially when he at last began to make headway with his plans for *The China Syndrome*.

10
Exploding Myths

The package looked attractive, but getting *The China Syndrome* made into a film became another saga, with as many twists and turns as the plot itself. As he made his approaches, Douglas reckoned that he might actually have been hampered by the success of *Cuckoo's Nest*. He detected an underlying resentment towards himself: he was considered by many of the powers that be to be a 'second generation' throwback who had struck lucky once, with his father's help; they were not about to gamble on its happening again.

He was not part of the much-favoured film-school crowd who had a great deal of camaraderie and exchange of ideas and worked with one another, and also had an entrée to the people who mattered in the big studios. They considered they had worked hard to make it on their own and through their own artistic merits, whereas the likes of Michael Douglas were considered to have been handed their opening on a silver platter.

This was true only to a very limited degree; helping hands in the background simply did not exist. More often, as we have seen, being who he was was a hindrance, and he would say that there were very few people in Hollywood who did not have a certain amount of hostility towards him.

Whereas he had side-tracked Hollywood completely to get *Cuckoo's Nest* under way, he was now confronted by a string of problems which showed that he had perhaps overestimated his potential. 'I kept smelling my armpits,' Michael recalled with some bitterness. 'Jack [Nicholson] and Milos Forman were getting all kinds of new offers and my phone wasn't ringing. A lot of people I spoke to were real buddy-buddy, then they stuck it to me. I have a long memory and I like to carry grudges. I'm going to remember my friends and I'm going to remember those who weren't.'

He had a good story in *The China Syndrome*. Michael Gray, author of the screenplay who also had a track record of a couple of well-received documentaries, wanted to direct the film. Michael knew from the outset that this would be difficult; because of the nature of the film, backers would almost certainly want a name director. But he put that problem to the back of his mind and went on trying to find a buyer.

Jack Lemmon agreed to star in the film. Lemmon had previously been involved in the anti-nuclear movement, was a vociferous spokesman on environmental issues and was one of the few seriously radical voices among Hollywood's more senior professionals. He had also narrated a controversial NBC television documentary series in which one episode, entitled *Plutonium: An Element of Risk*, caused a furore in the early 1970s.

Michael got in touch with Lemmon more by accident than good judgement. He had gone into the William Morris Agency with his script quite early on in the preparations and asked star-minder Lenny Hirsham to suggest an actor to play the plant engineer, Godell, a thirty-two-year-old man.

'Does the guy really have to be thirty-two?' asked Hirsham.

'Why? Who do you have in mind?' Douglas inquired.

'Jack Lemmon.'

'Terrific . . . but will he do it?'

A two-minute telephone call to Lemmon established that he sure as hell would. Douglas sent him the script. Lemmon enthusiastically came back and asked Michael to put his name against the role of Godell, the key character in the story, obsessed by the thought of a potential meltdown in the power plant where he worked. 'It was a terrific screenplay,' said Lemmon, 'and I wanted it to get made. It was the sort of role I had been seeking for a decade or more and I wanted to be part of it – so I stayed out of work for a whole year to do this little mother. It would scare the studios shitless, of course, but Michael went on with his preparations regardless.'

Michael himself was going to play the producer of the documentary film crew that goes to the scene, and he wanted Richard Dreyfuss to play the cameraman. Dreyfuss also expressed his interest. Michael finally put together his package, budgeted at a moderate $3.8 million.

Months of inactivity followed as Douglas tried to establish a market for his property. By then, Dreyfuss was involved in *Close Encounters of the Third Kind* and was just about to begin filming *The Goodbye Girl*, for which he won an Oscar. He was, as they say in Hollywood, hot, and his salary was rocketing by the minute. In the end he had doubled his original asking fee to $500,000 and had priced himself out of the movie. He would later say that he set a high price deliberately because he did not want to work with Michael Gray.

Robert Redford was contacted. Douglas offered him the script and the starring role alongside Lemmon. Redford did not call back, but sent Douglas a curt letter: 'As an actor I am looking for something different than the character in *The China Syndrome*.' He was out. Nicholson also passed.

In the meantime Douglas had made contact with Jane Fonda, another of the second-generation clique so disliked in some quarters of Hollywood. Fonda had passed through several phases in her career, first as an *ingénue*, followed by her flirtation with the French New Wave cinema during her marriage to Roger Vadim, and at the time was in her anti-establishment mode, married to left-wing activist Tom Hayden and campaigning with vigour and commitment for issues ranging through civil rights, feminism and corruption in high places.

After her earlier deep and outspoken involvement with the anti-war movement, the FBI and the CIA had accumulated extensive files on her activities.

An executive at Columbia had suggested that Douglas should contact her. Having presented his script, he was told that she too was working on one of several known film projects about the nuclear issue. Douglas telephoned Fonda in London, where she was filming *Julia*. She told him she was developing the story of

Karen Silkwood, the woman who was contaminated by radiation while working at a plutonium processing plant in Oklahoma in 1974. Silkwood died later in a mysterious car crash on her way to meet a newspaper reporter; later, her estate won a multimillion dollar settlement for damages from the plant operators.

At the time Fonda's project was held up by legal disputes over rights to the story – which she lost – and the film was eventually made by Mike Nichols in 1983 (Meryl Streep received an Oscar nomination for her title role).

Douglas outlined the story, emphasising the controversy it might cause, and told her that Jack Lemmon was waiting in the wings. Jane said she liked the sound of the screenplay, and asked for a copy with a view to merging their interests. The talk around Hollywood after she'd lost the Silkwood battle was that she would use some of her scenes from that story in the Douglas film.

Many more weeks passed before they finally met. By then, Fonda was back in Los Angeles filming *Coming Home* with Jon Voight, one of a clutch of social message movies around at the time; this one was set amid the remnants of her old hobby-horse, the Vietnam war, and would win her and her co-star an Oscar each for Best Actor and Best Actress of 1978.

Douglas arranged to meet her and her film production partner, Bruce Gilbert, for lunch. That day, they more or less agreed to join him in the venture – though one glaring flaw had to be rectified. An additional part would be written for Fonda since there was no female lead.

She and Bruce had an idea for developing a new character as a television news reporter, based on some articles Jane had read by Robert Scheer about the impact women reporters were making in the international arena of television news.

Jack Lemmon would have to be told. Lenny Hirsham at William Morris was given the task. Lemmon describes the call: 'Lenny said straight out "What if the Dreyfuss part was to become a girl?" My first reaction was to get angry. "Jesus F. Christ," I said. "That's fucking typical of Hollywood to try and jazz it up with a love interest." Lenny then finished his sentence: "Jane Fonda . . ." I said, "Holly shit, yes." So Jane came in and we became a co-production with her IPC company.'

A new script was drafted. Four months later they were able to go back to Columbia, where Jane had a production contract for the cancelled Silkwood story. They made a powerful combination – the two radicals, Fonda and Lemmon, plus Michael Douglas – sufficiently powerful, in fact, to submit what was then known as a 'pay-or-play' deal.

Basically, this meant that they offered the picture with all the elements in place. The studio would then agree to finance it, but if, for some reason, they did not go ahead and make the picture the production company and the stars would still get paid, which more or less forced the studio to proceed. Columbia accepted, but by then the costs were mounting.

Jane and her production company would require a slice of the profits and a substantial fee for her appearance, with the script rewritten to develop a part for Jane. These factors, and increased production costs, almost doubled Michael's original budget. But with the weight of Fonda behind him, Douglas was at last seeing signs of movement, though not without further complications.

Michael Gray, who had wanted to direct, was side-lined. 'Suddenly,' he complained, 'a very workable budget was escalated to two billion dollars.' The figure was an exaggeration, but it meant that the studio would not approve a first-time director in such a costly production. It was a major disappointment to Gray, since he had spent more than three years working with Douglas and was personally deeply involved in the nuclear issue. Gray was bitter. He reckoned Fonda had just walked in and taken over, and had reworked the original script to make it more acceptable to a mass audience. 'She may have been a radical in her private life, but she was quite conservative in terms of the movie,' Gray complained. 'Professionally, she was a Hollywood conservative.'

Douglas himself wisely accepted the view that if the movie was to stand a chance commercially, it had to have mass appeal and be sold as a thriller, not some quasi-documentary on the nation's nuclear industry. Even so, the choice of replacement director by Fonda and Douglas hardly supported Gray's claims;

it was not a name in the A-list of directors, nor was he among the Bs and Cs either.

The man they selected was the offbeat writer-director James Bridges. His selection was undoubtedly the high point of his career. He had made only three movies. He wrote and directed the low-budget *The Baby Maker* in 1970, an overwrought surrogate mother tale, followed in 1973 by *The Paper Chase*, a superior comedy-drama which earned its maker an Oscar nomination, an Oscar for one of its actors, James Houseman, and spawned a television series.

Lately, he had written and directed *September 30, 1955*, an autobiographical and rather disappointing tale centred on the death of James Dean, though it earned him cult status.

Columbia had doubts about Bridges' experience. They hesitated and offered other suggestions. Fonda and Douglas stood their ground, which was eventually to the film's credit. Even so, the matter was not cut and dried. What Douglas had not anticipated was that Bridges himself would turn them down – three times. However, he was eventually persuaded to join in, and the film was finally up and running.

Next, they had to seek the co-operation of nuclear power companies, for both research and location shots. Here, Douglas knew he was walking into a political minefield. As he went public with his plans for the movie, he discovered that his office telephone had been bugged. He was never able to establish whether it was commercially or politically motivated.

He first went to Oregon, where he had received enviable assistance with *Cuckoo's Nest* from the state medical board and the local mental hospital. Once again, the state authorities agreed to assist by giving him access to their Trojan nuclear power plant. In fact, his crew were met at the airport by a helicopter from the plant. It was a grey and damp day, and as they neared the plant the huge 550-foot cooling tower, arc-lights focused on it, rose eerily out of the morning mist. They were all given G-suits to wear and were taken on a complete tour of the plant, allowed to photograph the control-room and to ask as many questions as they wanted.

Several characters in the picture are based on people at the

Trojan plant. Later, in California, Pacific Gas and General Electric, which had once complained about Jack Lemmon's NBC documentary, also agreed to their visit on the assurance that they weren't 'going to kick nuclear energy in the ass'. Then, they hired a company of consultant nuclear engineers who were to advise on every aspect of the issues covered in the film.

Douglas had done his homework. All that now remained was to lay over the basic ingredients of the nuclear situation their own story, a story to interest and captivate audiences by cloaking the underlying issues as a race-against-time thriller. And this is exactly what *The China Syndrome* turned out to be, a marvellous thriller.

The movie was still judged by many as a political film, and the starring trio made no effort to hide their personal views about nuclear power. In fact, the whole publicity campaign for the movie would be geared to their personal appearances and comments on the issue.

Columbia's pre-release planning was meticulous – 'as good as I have ever experienced,' said Douglas. It began with a couple of preview screenings before invited audiences made up of members of the public. They were given preview cards asking how they would describe the picture to a friend – an anti-nuke picture or an entertaining thriller? Most opted for the latter.

The publicity campaign was mostly designed to promote the film. But it was also meant to offset the anticipated reaction from the nuclear industry and from political lobbying, especially in view of Jack Lemmon's personal experience with the documentary series. 'It was like a presidential briefing,' Jack Lemmon recalls. 'A publicity executive drew up a list of all the hard-ball questions a hostile press might ask, and the three of us would sit for hours while he threw the questions at us. It was that organised, more like a rehearsal for a play. And I'm glad we did, because the questions were tough, especially from the newsmen with a right-wing bent who had been amply supplied with all kinds of material from the power companies to show how inaccurate claims of a possible meltdown really were.'

Three weeks before the film opened, a $1.5 million television advertising campaign was launched. This had a hint of Orson Welles' famous radio introduction to his *War of the Worlds*, with images of disaster but without saying it was an upcoming film. In the second week, the ad showed clips from the picture, without naming anyone. Finally, the week before release, the commercial blasted out the name and stars of the picture. The three stars also began a round of publicity interviews on a scale that had not been seen in Hollywood for years.

The campaign concentrated on half a dozen major cities. Newspaper, radio and television people were brought in from the surrounding towns and cities. One day would be allocated to television interviews, another to newspaper interviews. Three interviews would run on three different days, one with each of the three stars given in separate rooms.

The film was given a massive coverage which blanketed America as Columbia moved towards releasing the movie into 700 cinemas. Coverage ranged from sympathetic to sheer hostility; one conservative columnist must have seriously regretted this paragraph: 'Jane Fonda has invented nuclear fantasies about melting cores in the interests of satisfying her own greed.'

Reviews, by and large, were excellent, and, far from being branded a Jane Fonda anti-nuke essay, the film was generally appreciated as a movie which was, above all, entertainment: a well-produced, excellently acted and well-crafted film.

Michael Gray's original story remained the underlying theme, with characters added and upgraded to accommodate Jane Fonda's role as a television reporter. There were a couple of fairly obvious allusions to the Karen Silkwood story, particularly when a car was forced off the road by pro-nuclear 'bad guys' and vital documents stolen. The story itself was said to be based upon actual occurrences in nuclear plants. But *The China Syndrome* develops into a thriller based upon personal values and relationships. The element of suspense comes not from the threat of what could happen in a nuclear accident but from the reactions of the characters.

Jack Lemmon played Godell, a supervisor at the plant in

southern California. He lives alone, and lives for his work. He is also firm in his support for nuclear power. Then, during an earthquake, he believes he felt an aftershock deep down in the core of the plant. His theory is that the water which cooled the plant would drop to a dangerously low level.

He believes that the accident could lead to the advent of the 'China syndrome', so called because in theory the overheating would cause a meltdown in the nuclear pile so powerful that it would burn a hole in the base and on through the earth, and keep on burning until it hit China. The reality would be a disastrous explosion which would release radioactive contamination over a massive area.

By coincidence, the accident happens as a television crew is filming a mundane feature on the plant. Michael Douglas plays the cameraman who covertly films the panic among control-room staff; Jane Fonda is the reporter who tries to get the story on the air.

Fonda's bosses bow to lobbying by the power industry and refuse to show the feature. Lemmon, meanwhile, has been investigating his theory of the aftershock deep in the core and discovers that documents relating to X-ray tests have been falsified. The film becomes a thriller, with Lemmon assisting Fonda and Douglas to expose the true extent of the accident.

James Bridges' direction was well paced, bringing his audience to the cliffhanger finale without allowing nuclear technicalities to mar the entertainment. He found working with Douglas 'a terrific experience'. Even allowing for the back-slapping, Douglas was obviously meticulous in separating his two roles of actor and producer. He would perform to Bridges' direction on the one hand; then, wearing his producer's hat, admonish Bridges for lingering too long on a particular scene.

Both the direction and the actors' individual performances were the key to the movie's success. Neither cast nor director fell into the trap of wanting to be seen as anti-nuclear campaigners, more as characters just doing their jobs. The performances of all three stars were so good, and the film itself filled with breathtaking action, that an occasional glibness in the script could be forgiven.

Though none would merit the attention of the Academy Award nominations, Fonda was in finest fettle in her role.

Lemmon similarly played one of the most complex and memorable characters in his long and distinguished line of screen creations. Douglas himself was also first rate as the loud-mouthed bearded anti-establishment cameraman.

The China Syndrome notched up respectable box office returns in the first two weeks after opening, grossing around $15 million in the US alone. Douglas and his associates had now had a fair bashing by the right-wingers for being over-dramatic and for attempting to scare the public on what some writers criticised as the most tenuous of plots and exaggerated portrayals.

Some power companies even organised a mailout to film critics across the nation, warning them that *The China Syndrome* was irresponsible. That was all acceptable. The crew had expected criticism and attempts to flatten the movie by over-zealous critics and the pro-nuclear lobby.

Then the ultimate in life matching art occurred. Douglas was relaxing at home in Santa Barbara on 31 March 1979 when all hell broke loose. His wife Diandra, who had herself been particularly interested in the film and had actually played a bit part 'for the fun of it', was out shopping but was sent dashing back to the house when she tuned in to the car radio.

'Did you hear the news? Did you hear?' she called out breathlessly to Michael as she came in.

'No, what?'

'There has just been a flash on the radio. A nuclear power plant has exploded in Pennsylvania.'

They turned on the television and the story of the atomic leak at Three Mile Island unfolded, almost an exact parallel to the story Douglas had just told in *The China Syndrome*. The words of Michael Gray, spoken when he first gave Douglas the screenplay almost four years earlier, flashed into his mind: 'It will be a race to get the picture out before there is a major accident.'

The similarities were uncanny, even down to a line in the

picture in which they turned to each other and said: 'If an accident happens it could destroy an area the size of Pennsylvania.'

A potentially explosive bubble of hydrogen gas inside a crippled reactor at the Three Mile Island power station at Harrisburg, Pennsylvania, threatened a nuclear disaster of massive proportions. If the reactor exploded, large amounts of radioactive contamination would be released over a wide area. The problem was apparently caused when the flow of cooling water failed to function, and the plant operators compounded the error by taking the wrong corrective measures.

The result was that part of the core was left without sufficient cooling water and the exposed nuclear fuel began to go into meltdown – just as it had in the film. The authorities advised that pregnant women and children should be evacuated from the area immediately. The potential disaster was superseded in its scale only by what actually happened at Chernobyl in 1986, when a nuclear plant explosion killed 31 people and caused 120,000 to be evacuated.

'It was scary,' said Douglas of Three Mile Island, 'and though I am not religious I would say that it was the nearest thing to a religious experience that I have ever had. I was as scared as hell as these images kept flashing on to the screen from Three Mile Island which mirrored what we had done in the film.'

After the initial reporting of the Three Mile Island accident, the news media very quickly focused on the Douglas film. The cast was drawn inexorably towards the controversy they had hoped to avoid. Columbia was besieged by requests from television stations seeking clips of the movie to inject into television news programmes, thus merging fact with fiction.

At cinemas where *The China Syndrome* was showing, audiences were met outside by reporters and questioned about their views on what had happened in real life. Dozens of requests came in for fresh interviews with Fonda, Lemmon and Douglas.

Columbia became so concerned that the movie would get caught up in the aftershock of Three Mile Island that it called a hasty conference of all concerned and decided on a publicity blackout so it would not be seen to be exploiting what had happened. The studio asked all three stars not to co-operate with the news media and to generally play down any connections between the movie and events at Three Mile Island.

Lemmon and Douglas agreed. Douglas postponed an appearance on Johnny Carson's *The Tonight Show* and Lemmon cancelled an appearance on a CBS special about Three Mile Island. Fonda, however, was Fonda. She gave a press conference which she prefixed with a statement that the opinions she gave were personal and were not given as a member of the cast of the film. She reiterated her long-held views about the safety of nuclear power and the potential disasters in every major plant.

She went as far as to say that if the movie had not been made, the nuclear industry could have buried the incident without the brouhaha that followed in its wake – because *The China Syndrome* became the required viewing of every reporter sent to follow up the story, and the focus of every television programme that came in its wake.

The China Syndrome was a commercial and critical success, eventually grossing close on $95 million. Douglas himself believed that the Three Mile Island disaster actually worked against the film, because audiences had seen on television all they wanted to know about nuclear disasters.

Still, all concerned enjoyed a substantial payday, though again the film failed to establish Douglas as what Hollywood would term a bankable leading man, despite plaudits from the critics. He had been involved in the production of two of the top ten films of the 1970s, but audiences and casting directors do not react to such statistics.

For an actor, it's sex appeal that counts. It always was and probably always will be the prime essential of any actor's stock-in-trade. *The China Syndrome* had not even a hint of sexual chemistry, so his persona was decidedly low key on that front. He still wanted to be considered an actor first and a producer second. Nothing he had done so far had really convinced anyone of that, and there seemed a curious disparity between the two aspects of his work. He was a successful producer but only a moderately successful actor, which remained the case even after *The China Syndrome* appeared in the theatres.

This aspect of his life and work was further confused by a film he made during the weeks of post-production work on *The China Syndrome*, that period between the completion of filming and release into the cinemas. He was still involved in the last stages of filming when his agent sent him a script for a low-budget movie entitled *Running*. This was being produced by a Canadian-based company and financed in part by the government-backed Canadian Film Development Corporation. It was written and directed by Steven Stern and taken up in Canada, where lucrative tax benefits were available to moviemakers.

Michael was Stern's first choice because he looked like a runner. But there was another motive. The producers wanted a star who was as appealing to television as to cinema audiences. They were negotiating a joint production deal with ABC-TV which, mindful of his appeal in *The Streets of San Francisco*, signed up as soon as Douglas put his name on the contract. The television showing was guaranteed not to go out until two years after the movie was released, and it meant that, with a distribution deal from Universal, the film was in the black even before it was completed.

Douglas's share of the proceeds was not huge, but he was attracted to the story: of a man who fears he is one of life's failures and attempts to make something of himself in one last-ditch effort as a marathon runner. He reckoned the script moved him to tears, an emotion sadly not shared by audiences when the film came out.

He had five months after the completion of *The China Syndrome* to prepare himself before filming began in Toronto. He started running eighty miles a week to get himself into shape; he shed eighteen pounds of flab accumulated during his last five years of Hollywood living, and cut his smoking from two packs a day to a more moderate amount.

Michael's training verged on the fanatical. The producers were talking in terms of the movie taking off on the strength of the upsurge in the jogging craze and the forthcoming 1980 Olympics. Michael believed them; he was as unaware as everyone else at

125

the time that the Moscow Olympics would descend into a political furore, with Britain and the US pulling out.

But that was not a factor which affected the film's success or failure. It was a flop in the cinema. Whatever merits Douglas saw in the script did not transfer to the screen. The film served only as mildly interesting to jogging and running enthusiasts through some quite decent action scenes in which Douglas looked quite authentic as a long-distance athlete. Few critics even bothered to review it, and *Running* was nominated by one magazine to be placed in its list of the worst movies of 1979.

His credibility as an actor, enhanced by his performance in *The China Syndrome*, was left somewhat dented in Hollywood when *Running* was released in the winter of 1979. Unlike some of his best friends in the business, he had been unable to establish any pattern to his career as an actor. After ten years of saying that acting was his true forte, as an actor he had only one movie to his credit which could seriously be considered worthwhile.

An interesting pointer to the way he was viewed by his audience, and certainly by the pundits, at the time was given in an interview he did for *Cosmopolitan* just before *Running* was released. The writer Dennis Hickory travelled up to Toronto to meet Douglas on the set. He was able to provide an intriguing portrait of Douglas which sums up the difficulties he was having with his image.

Hickory found Douglas a thoroughly decent chap, as did most who interviewed him, and a refreshing change from the monosyllabic responses of some major movie people of the day, most notably Warren Beatty, Dustin Hoffman and Steven Spielberg. Hickory questioned whether this dynamic, sensitive young actor possessed enough of the killer instinct for Hollywood.

'Are we ready for a paragon in this scrappy business?' Hickory queried. 'Michael is so unpretentious and low-key that I worry briefly – maybe behind that boyishly pure face there lies a dull story. But luckily Michael in not ALL flat planes . . . [his] occasional crankiness came as a welcome relief.' And was it really a compliment to say that while Newman and Redford were filmland's most gorgeous jocks and Stallone and Travolta (at the time) its most appealing Latin lovers, Douglas might be regarded as the thinking woman's sex symbol. That really only meant one thing: boring.

If Kirk had been in the business of handing out advice to his son at that point – which he wasn't – he might well have advised him to do something drastic about his image . . . saucier and sexier. The thought had surely crossed Douglas's mind as he wrestled with the paradox of his work, which on one level, as a producer, was busy, exciting and financially rewarding and, on another, as an actor, was dull and going nowhere.

11

Elation to Despair

As the 1980s dawned, so did one of the most frustrating and barren periods of Michael Douglas's career. After *The China Syndrome* nothing seemed to go right, and more than once he heard that old saying about two swallows not making a summer. Sure enough, the two swallows had brought him sufficient wealth to ensure that he was comfortably endowed and did not have to worry about keeping a roof over their heads.

On that score, there were no problems. Indeed, it was the enjoyments of his family life which kept him from the depths of those well-known Hollywood feelings of insecurity when the right parts and the right scripts seem beyond reach.

He faced career troubles on both levels. The movie *Running* had failed dismally, and once again he was in the position of having nothing of note on offer. On the production front, he signed a contract with Columbia, after the success of *The China Syndrome*, which on the face of it seemed to secure his future and to put him in direct competition with Steven Spielberg for major film development money at the studio. But, as we will see, this turned out to be the worst mistake of his life.

Even before the Columbia deal was finalised, he had become involved in one more movie as an actor which would bring him only grief. It is hard to see why, after the flop with *Running*, he accepted what was basically a supporting role in *It's My Turn*, a low-key feminist movie that was heavy on enthusiasm and not much else.

There seemed to be a definite weakness in his ability to identify and reject acting work that offered him little prospect of making that big breakthrough. It was true, also, that he was simply not getting the opportunities that were going to friends he had grown up with in the business. It was a regular theme of discussion among them whenever they met.

Jack Nicholson would complain to Douglas that he had been mis-catalogued by the media and by casting people. They identified him with particular roles which made best use of his personal demeanour of nonconformity, and had so far not been offered another role that would match his success as Randall McMurphy in *One Flew Over the Cuckoo's Nest*.

Nicholson had made three movies since – Arthur Penn's distinctly odd and unsuccessful western, *Missouri Breaks*, with Marlon Brando, a supporting role playing Eugene O'Neill in Elia Kazan's version of the Fitzgerald novel *The Last Tycoon,* and his own *Goin' South,* which he directed and starred in and which found much praise at the arty film festivals but made no commercial impact whatsoever.

However, in 1979, as Douglas himself was looking around for what to do next, Nicholson was working on the movie that finally broke down all past barriers, Stanley Kubrick's horror classic *The Shining*. Michael Douglas would have welcomed such a challenge, though he was not that kind of an actor, yet, and the offers were limited to a degree by his own persona. The offer to appear in *It's My Turn* came at a vulnerable time, when nothing was on the stocks. But in taking the part he unwittingly became embroiled in an 'it could only happen in Hollywood' battle of feminist attitudes and studio mischief. How he ever let himself fall into it remains, even now, a mystery, because it did him no good at all.

The story began eight years earlier when Claudia Weill, who was making television documentaries, read a political novel by Eleanor Bergstein called *Advancing Paul Newman*, which was about two girls in the 1960s. Weill contacted the author and asked if she would consider writing a screenplay called *Girlfriends*. Bergstein said she was too busy on her second novel and would consider it later.

In the meantime, Weill slowly made herself known as a

director, mostly in television. She still hankered after a Bergstein screenplay, especially when she discovered she might be able to get a $200,000 grant to make a movie for American public television. Several years passed before she contacted Bergstein and asked under what terms she wanted to write.

This time, Bergstein said she would write an original script provided she had total involvement at every stage. Weill agreed, and Bergstein went off into seclusion in Vermont to complete her first piece of dramatic writing. She emerged some time later with the first draft of *It's My Turn,* wondering if it would qualify for the grant.

Her story, in a nutshell, is one for the feminists, involving a brilliant young female mathematician who had a live-in boyfriend and a new stepbrother when her father remarries. The stepbrother is a handsome baseball player at the prime of his career but has been forced to quit through injury. And so on.

Weill, meanwhile, had become moderately 'hot' after critical acclaim for her film *Girlfriends*. Hollywood, being short of female director success stories, virtually came with chequebook in hand – notably Alan Ladd Junior, who was at the time running 20th Century-Fox. Weill told Bergstein about the offers. Bergstein was horrified. She said she had written her screenplay for public television and did not want to get involved with Hollywood.

Weill put forward an inviting scenario: a bigger budget, major stars, expensive location filming, money no object. Eventually, Bergstein agreed. They both wanted Jill Clayburgh for the film. Clayburgh was a leading lady of the 1970s, most noted for her starring role in *Gable and Lombard* and *An Unmarried Woman*; she had been nominated for an Academy Award for her role in *Starting Over*, in which she co-starred with Burt Reynolds.

Michael Douglas was sought as the baseball player. He agreed, not so much for the script as for the opportunity of working with the gorgeous Ms Clayburgh, whom he 'admired immensely'.

All was proceeding at a pace when catastrophe struck. There was a revolution at 20th Century-Fox, and Alan Ladd Junior and most of his executive support group walked out. In the bloodletting of the aftermath, Michael Douglas and the largely all-girl team that surrounded him were left high and dry, though not for long.

By then, Michael was in negotiation with Columbia, which wanted him to take up a residency at their studio as a semi-independent producer of Columbia movies.

Meanwhile, another Columbia producer, Ray Stark, took up the option on Weill's film and everyone was happy, or so it seemed. 'It was the most gruelling movie I have ever been involved in,' said Clayburgh. 'The switch of studios caused some headaches. There were also a lot of last-minute changes, so Michael and I would rehearse in the evenings and a lot on weekends. We had very little free time.'

Weill was fairly inexperienced in the ways of Hollywood. It must have been an odd experience for a man who had produced two of the biggest movies of the 1970s to be bossed around by a woman making her first Hollywood movie. But that, really, was the theme of the movie itself – the relationship between a strong male and a dominant female.

Michael Douglas sounded a touch patronising and not entirely convincing when he spoke of working with a woman director: 'I have not had many directors come up to me and say, "You are such a dish." I was immediately spoiled, and comforted in an offhand sort of way. There is a moment in every actor's life when he sees the director, normally male, go over to the leading lady, put his arm around her shoulder and whisper, "What's wrong, darling? Let's talk." Well, I'm sorry, but guys like to be complimented too. I just loved having the director come up to me, put her arm around my shoulder and ask me if I'm OK. She made me feel confident.'

Weill spoke with some pangs of bitterness at what eventually transpired: 'I did not have a problem with it. It was Hollywood that had the problems . . . you know "Who the hell is she? What does she know?" But the whole notion of the director is fucked: the macho image, the authoritarian sort of figure. I think you have to be able to command the set, keep things moving, communicate. I think actors feel very reassured and trust you if they know you are really paying attention – whether you are a woman or not is immaterial.'

Douglas was caught in the middle of this battle, and the normal pressures of making any picture were increased, first by debates over the interpretation of the screenplay and secondly by the close scrutiny Weill received from the studio. Jill Clayburgh praised Weill's relaxed way of working but appreciated the problems that came with her lack of experience. 'She was new and we were in a big company. It was really difficult for her in that respect.'

Yet more problems arose in the post-production period at an embarrassing time for Douglas, who was then at the point of signing his own production deal with Columbia. *It's My Turn* was shot for seven weeks on Columbia's Burbank lot and one week in New York. As Weill readied her movie for in-house screening, the Hollywood whispers started. Several preview screenings were abruptly cancelled without explanation, and finally a mischievous item in Mary Beck's Hollywood gossip column set the cat among the pigeons. She claimed that Douglas hated the film, wished he'd never got involved in it and was refusing to promote it.

Executives at Columbia were naturally appalled that the movie was getting that not unfamiliar Tinsel Town treatment of 'bad-mouthing' before it was even released. Douglas stepped forward to protest. He denied that he had ever refused to promote the film or that he hated it. He telephoned Mary Beck and asked for her source. He learned that it had come from the office of the movie's producer, Ray Stark, who apparently did not like Weill's finished version.

Clearly there was some basis for the story, but Douglas said it was not for the reasons quoted. 'The whole thing was planted,' he recalls. 'It was an attempt to manipulate the situation. I called Claudia, who was shocked by what had happened. I explained that I had never said it. I was perfectly willing to do some interviews, but I had said that they should not count on me for all the talkshows. I considered I was very over-exposed in that respect after *The China Syndrome*. I am an actor, and I cannot do that after every film.'

133

He was summoned to the Columbia executive floor to explain formally that he had not been bad-mouthing the picture. Douglas and the rest of the cast were instructed not to discuss the dispute with newspapers, but studio sources reckoned that it was Ray Stark, whose company had produced the $7 million movie for Columbia, who hated the film. He recut Weill's edited version and showed it to the studio bosses. They, in fairness, also watched Weill's version – and decided they liked hers better.

Whatever the politicking that went on behind the scenes, and the politics of the film itself with its feminist overtones, in the end it mattered only to the personalities involved. *It's My Turn* was not a commercial hit, and the reviewers gave it a very mixed reception. For Claudia Weill, it was an exasperating and unnerving experience – and she never went back to mainstream Hollywood again.

For Douglas it was an incident that normally could have been brushed aside easily. But the experience went deeper than that, as it affected his career with Columbia.

At the time of the movie's release he had been installed in a suite of offices on the Columbia lot, with a secretary and a staff of four and a lucrative contract to generate new films for the studio which he would produce, perhaps act in and generally make good.

Douglas appointed Columbia vice-president and Hollywood veteran Jack Brodsky as vice-president of his own company Bigstick, a move rumoured to upset the Columbia hierarchy with whispered accusations of poaching. Douglas, unabashed, looked forward to a new era in which he would concentrate on producing. He told his friends confidently that he now expected to move into top gear and make one picture a year.

That was the plan. Indeed, the then boss of Columbia, Leo Jaffe, made grandiose statements about Douglas's arrival at the studio. 'It is a great coup for us,' said Jaffe expansively. 'We are looking for properties which we can mutually put into production under the Columbia banner.'

In reality, Douglas would kick his heels at Columbia for three years, from 1980 to 1983, without producing a single foot of film. It was not through the want of trying. He came up with a dozen or more projects. But, like a thousand and one great movie ideas before and since, they simply faded into oblivion as they passed into that selection system in which decisions are made by a succession of people until, finally, the project ends up at the bottom of someone's pile where it may remain for eternity.

There was a touch of irony in that the first project he put forward was a screenplay based upon a novel by Gloria Nagy entitled *Virgin Kisses*. Michael bought the rights for Bigstick, but failed to inspire any interest at Columbia. A million words of rewrites later, the screenplay would eventually become a film – under the title *Fatal Attraction*. That event lay seven years in the future. For the time being, Michael was becoming more and more frustrated as each month passed.

There was one other project Douglas was involved in at an early stage. It was the only one that he would see through to completion for Columbia, after he had left the studio. A science fiction screenplay called *Starman*, it was about a space traveller from another planet who accidentally becomes trapped on earth. Columbia agreed to put the movie into production, and then along came Steven Spielberg with his plans for *ET, The Extra Terrestrial*.

Spielberg was the hottest new director around, after the smash hits of *Jaws* (1975), *Close Encounters of the Third Kind* (1977) and the blockbuster about to be released, Harrison Ford in *Raiders of the Lost Ark*. Frank Price, head of Columbia production while Douglas was in residence, admitted that they had rejected Spielberg's *ET*, because they had already decided to go ahead with *Starman*.

The stories had a similar theme. But it was considered that *ET* was a picture for children while *Starman* was perceived as an adult picture, a love story with a sci-fi background. That very opinion showed Columbia's grave error of judgement.

The fact remained that Spielberg and his associate George Lucas had turned Hollywood upside-down by making pictures that appealed to family audiences, and had produced a selection of movies that became the most lucrative in the history of filmmaking. Pulp flicks, as they were termed by those envious of their achievements, they might have been, but the Spielberg–Lucas productions dominate the list of the world's most successful movies.

Spielberg's *ET* was considered competition for *Starman*. Even though they knew they had a head start on him, Columbia procrastinated for months on a start date. Defensively, Frank Price contends: 'It takes time. We had *Tootsie* in development for four years before it came out. If you're trying to make exceptional pictures, which is what Michael, all of us, are trying to do, it takes time.'

Perhaps it does. Meanwhile, *Starman* was put back time and again. A succession of directors came and went and the script went through a dozen rewrites. Spielberg, meanwhile, had put *ET* into production with Universal and completed it towards the end of 1981 in time for release the following season. To be fair, the outcome surprised everyone.

As the American Academy of Arts and Sciences' own historian points out in the review of films released in 1982: '*ET* was in Hollywood terms a true sleeper, a quietly made project of little expectation that became the biggest moneyspinner of all time, and won nine Academy nominations. It won four of those prizes.'

Columbia's only consolation to that piece of movie history was that their own major release that year was Richard Attenborough's epic *Gandhi*, which was nominated for eleven awards and took most of the ones that *ET* did not get – eight Oscars in all. It was also the year of *Tootsie*, another Columbia production which was also a major box office hit.

Even so, future projects were the lifeblood of any studio, and Michael Douglas believed that he was at Columbia to help in that department. *Starman* did not see the light of day until 1984 – long after Douglas had left Columbia. It had undergone severe surgery and umpteen rewrites to dispose of some of the more noticeable similarities to *ET*, and it turned out to be a very decent film, starring Jeff Bridges and Karen Allen. What was especially interesting was the way director John Carpenter turned it into a kind of sci-fi road movie. He also extracted some fine performances from Bridges and Allen, and their love story was one of the more memorable events for film buffs in 1984.

But Spielberg had it all covered. What came after *ET* in the sci-fi genre, and especially those movies dealing with aliens on earth, would have to be totally original, if not spectacular in the extreme, to succeed. *Starman*, for all that, fared surprisingly well at the box office, inspired a television series and secured an Oscar nomination for Jeff Bridges.

It would have fared even better if Columbia had brought it out ahead of *ET* instead of in its wake. In the event the film earned a fraction of Spielberg's blockbuster and became best remembered in the trade as the movie that Columbia turned down *ET* for.

Douglas was by then already reflecting with some bitterness on his ill-fated engagement at Columbia: 'What has happened to the movie business is market research. I will be honest and say that when I moved into my office suite on the lot, I thought that here I am, I've produced two big movies, I've got a track record – but it turns out that doesn't matter. Basically, I was just left to rot.'

Douglas and Bigstick departed from Columbia as soon as the three years were up, and he contributed little to the eventual marketing of *Starman*. He made it clear that he intended to go back to his old routine of working from a 'funky little office with one reader and a secretary', do a spot of acting and make pictures that interested him.

The glamour, glitz and enhanced reputation created by *Cuckoo's Nest* and *The China Syndrome* were dimmed by the three years of relative inactivity, and compounded by a severe skiing accident and a virus condition affecting his blood. He was off-colour for months. His prolonged absence inspired the unkindly but typical Hollywood buzz that Michael Douglas was after all just a two-hit wonder and was as good as finished. His next excursion into acting did not do much to dispel that notion.

He took on a movie called *The Star Chamber*, in which he would receive star billing as an idealistic young judge. The plot came

137

from Roderick Taylor and Peter Hyams; it looked good but was far-fetched. Douglas's judge is increasingly disillusioned with the failures of the legal system, in which he is forced to clear murderers and rapists on technicalities while personally convinced of their guilt.

Senior judges talk him into joining their secret society, known as The Group. They see themselves as modern vigilantes, and set up a system for rearresting defendants whom they believe have been unjustly freed, then retrying them and having them executed by hired assassins. It was really low-key material, hard to swallow and over-long. The production company, with which Douglas had no personal connection, tried to rescue their turkey with an expensive television campaign, promoting the *Death Wish*-style vigilante theme. The campaign didn't do well.

Why had Douglas accepted the part in the first place? Hope springs eternal, perhaps, especially when the alternatives are limited. Perhaps, at the time, that was his mark as an actor – that kind of movie, that level of success. Certainly, his acting career remained under a darkening cloud; if it had been left to outside forces, it would have languished further.

12
Separation

The months of frustration during Douglas's sojourn at Columbia came as a blow to both his pride and stability, professionally and personally. The pressures brought change in several directions, some welcome, others not; the latter came in the area of his marriage. It was placed under great strain for many months for several quite distinct reasons, leading ultimately to a ten-month separation from Diandra and his son Cameron.

As he headed towards his fortieth birthday, that great milestone when a man gets to think about his relationships and ambitions, his life was in disarray. At the turn of his previous decade, at thirty, he had had the energy and vitality to succeed with *One Flew Over the Cuckoo's Nest*. Now, at the beginning of that other new era when life begins, the desire, if not the need, to alter his whole style and approach became very evident.

On the work front, where he had been diving in and out of possibilities that came to nothing, he had salvaged a project which consumed his time and thoughts. 'He had a property called *Romancing the Stone* that he could not get off the ground at Columbia,' said his Bigstick vice-president Jack Brodsky. 'When we put it to the studio, they said they would do it with Burt or Clint. Neither Burt nor Clint wanted to play, so the studio said No. At the time Michael did not put himself forward for the role because he was pretty certain that Columbia would not wear it. He was no big draw in the business, and he knew it. If Michael was going to be that kind of a star, have that kind of appeal, he had to change himself – you know, the image. He had to switch from the earnest, sensitive, socially concerned roles and worthy redeeming films and become a sex symbol – that was it. He didn't especially like it, but his new situation demanded it.'

He needed to become active again, to pull off another spectacular stunt that would make Hollywood sit up and look, and to put himself into the cinemas as a major star. His determination verged upon desperation.

His career, and the effects it had on him personally, in his pursuits and the way he ran his life during that barren period, collided with his marriage like a train hitting the buffers. His age played its part: a man's desire to look around and examine his lifestyle and direction becomes threatening to long-held positions.

The looseness of his work ties at Columbia had allowed him dangerous free time, which might be spent along the boulevards with Nicholson or other friends, chasing adventure and excitement.

Diandra had despaired as these pressures began to build up during the last year or so of heel-kicking at Columbia. What lay ahead, during the succeeding eighteen months, was totally different, where her own loyalty was tested to the limit to the point where she felt she could not put up with the situation any longer.

She knew the problems; she had already experienced plenty that she did not like in Douglas's life of contrasts. One of their closest friends at that time recalled: 'The way Michael's career went seemed to throw them into a kind of maelstrom of extremes. There was a period when he was home a lot, and deeply involved with his son's early years, followed by a situation where they passed like ships in the night. When he got moving again, he barely took a breath, and in a way it was no different for him than it had been for ten years or more – big highs, and then deep lows. A young marriage has to be very strong to bear that kind of pressure.'

For Diandra personally, the novelty of being a movie wife had long ago subsided to sufferance. Neither she nor her husband ever wanted to be part of the Hollywood social crowd that Michael had despised in his childhood and youth. Diandra stayed pretty much in Santa Barbara, and their few friends locally were generally outside showbusiness. The work remodelling their home was complete, and she had little to occupy her time.

As Michael's work had become more permanently based in Los Angeles with the Columbia deal, they had run a separate home there, though she was keen to stay in the hills of Santa Barbara whenever she was able. 'It had become a logistical nightmare,' Michael recalled. Even so, Diandra was not happy. She found it difficult to grow in the Hollywood environment. It still rankled that she was surrounded by people in only one profession – 'like being surrounded by dentists for the formative years of your life' was how she once described it. There were a number of rows. She tried to be philosophical: 'Everybody has problems; every marriage goes through bad times.' Kirk's wife Anne was rather less forgiving, siding with Michael: 'In Europe men would never put up with such behaviour from wives.'

After the initial fascination of watching her husband at work, doing so no longer captured Diandra's imagination or interest. The trade talk was endless, the jargon relentless. It was of 'treatments' and 'properties', 'vehicles' and 'grosses' – the terminology for having an idea, book or play written up into a workable script, and assessing the potential box office appeal which might or might not make you a star and make you rich. Such talk, the life blood of producers and actors, was the topic of every conversation when groups of them met. The work itself was no more likely to retain the interest of a person on the side-lines.

As every wife of every filmmaker knows well, watching a picture being made from behind the cameras, on set or on location, can be no more exciting than watching paint dry, and can be quite embarrassing if your spouse is among those involved. A day's filming may be twelve or fourteen hours long.

On set in a studio, conditions are often cramped and hot, and invariably tense. Location filming, far from being glamorous, is more often than not in some godforsaken, fly-blown outback where wooden shacks pass for four-star hotels and all food and drink has to be imported.

141

If the director is in a particularly pernickety mood, a whole day's filming may be devoted entirely to the shooting of just one three- or four-minute scene, done over and over and over again. Those not directly involved will have begun to yawn with boredom even before lunch. Then there are the opportunities to stray from the fold; Hollywood psychiatrists had long ago identified and excused this as a common release for stress and insecurity for those people thrown together in the intensity of filmmaking. There is, too, the more common element of lust.

Diandra also had her own strong ambitions, which did not include either sitting around a film location or being housebound. Her course at the University of California at Santa Barbara was completed soon after the birth of their son, and she had her own academic and personal interests in political studies. The opportunity to fulfil the aspirations of her youth, when she imagined herself following in her father's diplomatic footsteps in international politics, no longer was possible.

In Los Angeles she had involved herself in a couple of local causes including groups opposed to American military involvement in Nicaragua. She and her husband became founder-members of a committee of concern to inform people about South American issues. They also had a part-interest in a publishing venture.

Such pursuits were welcomed by Diandra, but they were certainly nowhere near satisfying or mentally taxing enough for an academic young woman who could hold forth with confidence and authority about political situations around the world. She felt stifled. The realisation that she was heading nowhere except towards the age of thirty was equally disheartening.

As one of their friends observed, if Michael was ever short of a plot for a new movie, he had the ideal 1980s situation right there in his own house: the well-educated wife whose career and aspirations were frustrated by the overpoweringly ambitious husband who was going nowhere to the point that they began screaming at each other, only to be calmed down by a patriarchal father (Kirk) holding his grandson in his arms as a reason why they should not fight.

The marriage hit its stormiest seas while Michael was involved in the early stages of producing *Romancing the Stone*, with Kathleen Turner and Danny DeVito, and a mutually agreed separation ensued. 'I think they would always be seen as opposites, though oddly enough they weren't,' their friend recalled. 'There was an age-gap, certainly, but they were both highly intelligent people with similar interests. Neither of them went into the marriage with their eyes closed, although they did not really give themselves time to stop and think about the pitfalls, of which there would be plenty.'

Michael explained that their parting was a form of evaluation to discover what was going on in their lives and in their marriage. He recognised the difficulties faced by any marriage of film people: long periods of work-induced pressures, followed by a long period of togetherness when he was at home and waiting for the next project.

Some kind of balance between the two extremes was needed but had been virtually impossible. 'What we attempted to do,' he said, 'was to try to catch the situation in our marriage before it got ugly, and I suppose we succeeded to a degree. There is nothing wrong with the term separation, so long as it is for that purpose. I think we both of us had to discover that we were not missing something in our lives together. To go deeper, neither of us wanted to go through that whole dating scene again. I think we were striving to find a better balance between the times we were happy and the times we were crying. You can't be happy all of the time. Marriage, with very few exceptions, is just not like that . . .' This analysis was a distant afterthought. At the time of the separation Michael was so unhappy that he lost almost a stone in weight.

Friends and family feared that what was happening to Michael and Diandra was in many respects a rerun of Kirk's separation and eventual divorce from Diana Dill. There was a degree of expectancy from Michael that Diandra should be satisfied with her lot: financially comfortable, a superb home which she had redesigned herself, a supportive family . . . Kirk was devoted to his grandson and thought Diandra was the best thing that had happened to Michael.

As it turned out they were able to put their differences aside and resume their marriage ten months later, Michael promising greater consideration towards Diandra's needs.

This period of emotional turmoil was undoubtedly bolstered by Michael's renewed determination to do something to improve his status as a filmmaker and actor. In doing so he would show the same resolve as he did in achieving his two previous major successes. The effect this time was to change his life for good: a sea change in every respect.

Ironically, the route to his enhanced Hollywood status was unwittingly forged during the early part of his time on the Columbia lot, when he worked on two projects that were both rejected by the people in power. One was the book *Virgin Kisses*, for which he had acquired the film rights and which eventually became a huge hit. That development still lay in the future. First, he was consumed with bringing another of his early acquisitions to the screen – an original screenplay entitled *Romancing the Stone*.

Douglas's career had so far been punctuated by lengthy sagas of producing movies. *Romancing the Stone* was no less traumatic. It took him almost half a decade from the moment he first read the script to get the movie on the screen. Once again, the whole process demonstrated his terrier-like tenacity. But more than that, the story provides another instructive excursion around the insecurities, suspicion and vacillation that exist in the highest echelons of Hollywood power, where deals have to be fought for every inch of the way.

This particular saga went back to the autumn of 1979. Just before he signed his contract with Columbia he received a script of *Romancing the Stone* which intrigued him sufficiently to seek out the author. She turned out to be a thirty-three-year-old unknown writer named Diane Thomas, who was at the time working as a waitress in Alice's Restaurant on Malibu Beach. Within a week Douglas had made Ms Thomas exceedingly rich, presenting her with a contract guaranteeing her $250,000 for the screen rights.

He thought the script had a 'virginal quality' totally fresh in its construction and theme. It failed totally to confirm to normal screenplay structures, and that's what appealed to him, with scenes of comedy juxtaposed with adventure and romance. The sum total was a movie of fun. He had no doubts about it personally, though some of his closest friends advised caution, since it was well away from the mould of Douglas's earlier socially conscientious themes and his characters of a redeeming nature. In truth, that's exactly what he needed to get away from.

Columbia listened to his proposals but it took him a long time to convince the people in charge of the money that he could juggle successfully with the comedy-action-romance elements. They would say: 'What is it? Comedy or adventure? Action or romance?' They couldn't grasp the moulding of the three.

Eventually, Columbia instructed him to put together an A-list package of talent for the film. As Jack Brodsky recalls, they wanted only 'Clint or Burt' in the leading role. Both Clint and Burt turned it down; so did Sylvester Stallone. Robert Redford and Harrison Ford were also considered. But then, out of the blue, Columbia brought down the shutters on *Romancing the Stone* for a very particular reason.

Steven Spielberg had just come out with his blockbuster adventure *Raiders of the Lost Ark*. It was thought that *Romancing the Stone* was too similar, just as Columbia had also postponed Douglas's *Starman* project because Spielberg had stolen the march on them with *ET, The Extra Terrestrial*. It was true that when *Romancing the Stone* eventually appeared as a movie, reviewers mentioned its similarity to the Spielberg movie, starring Harrison Ford, when in fact Douglas had acquired the rights long before *Raiders of the Lost Ark* was filmed.

When Douglas's three years with Columbia finally expired at the beginning of 1983, *Romancing the Stone* was still firmly on the back burner, a state known in Hollywood as 'in turnaround'. This meant that it was up for grabs by any other studio prepared to reimburse Columbia for the development money it had so far invested, which in this case wasn't huge. Douglas grabbed.

Brodsky recalls that he and Douglas set up a meeting with

20th Century-Fox soon after Douglas left Columbia. They outlined the script and presented a budget with an A-list of actors at under $10 million. The Fox people sounded enthusiastic. The Douglas duo was well experienced with Hollywood 'enthusiasm' and remained nervous until Fox came back six weeks later with a production contract for Douglas's Bigstick company. The studio also offered him a contract for leading male, a decision which was to set the seal on his future.

Unlike other actors he could mention, Michael had no qualms about the fact that both leading male and leading lady would receive equal billing – something that some of the more famous names who had been offered the male part would not accept. But Douglas viewed this from a different perspective, because basically he still had no image as far as the public was concerned.

As producer and initiator of the film, he appreciated that the script was centred on the leading lady, an authoress in search of a guy who is the antithesis of all the heroes she has written about: 'I saw it as a story about the growth of a young woman as she progressed through each stage of the adventure, tackling problems the like of which she had never been confronted with in her life, including a boisterous romance. It was her story.'

From his own point of view, there was one other change: he was taking on a role that was brimming with sexuality. Though there would be no explicit sexual activity in the film, there was no hiding the flying sparks when the two leading characters got together. The male character of Jack Colton did indeed require a rugged Clint Eastwood-style portrayal, a completely new departure for Douglas.

He had hidden behind the kind of social consequence roles he had undertaken in the past for too long, almost as if he was scared of displaying any swashbuckling sexuality on screen. Perhaps this may have been a throwback to trying to get away from being associated with some of his father's more famous portrayals.

His role in *Romancing the Stone* meant he had to finally stand up and present himself as a romantic hero. He would be on show for the first time as the fit and tanned, snarling and rough chauvinistic male, with a partly hidden gentleness that gave him vulnerability. The birth of Michael Douglas superstar began here, when he cast himself as leading male. Douglas then proceeded to go through the remaining appointments with the same precision he had applied in the past.

The first key role was that of a director. Here, Douglas followed exactly the same pattern as he had with *Cuckoo's Nest* and *The China Syndrome* by seeking a comparatively new director with a modest track record but who was noted for his artistic nonconformity.

That was the case with Milos Forman, his first director, and with Jim Bridges on *The China Syndrome*. This time he selected Robert Zemeckis, a virtually unknown graduate of the film faculty of the University of Southern California. Douglas's theory was that the freshness of the Diane Thomas screenplay needed the freshness of a director pretty well untainted by standard Hollywood formulas. Zemeckis was one of the brightest of an up-and-coming band of movie directors. He was thirty-one years old and had, to that point, been involved in just two films.

The first, *I Wanna Hold Your Hand*, was a modest period comedy which he wrote and directed for Steven Spielberg. It was about a day in 1964 when a crowd of Beatles fans awaited the group's arrival for the *Ed Sullivan Show*. His next was *Used Cars*, an excellent but distasteful (and financially unsuccessful) black comedy about the antics of used-car salesmen. Apart from some screenwriting for Spielberg on his less successful movie *1941*, Zemeckis had not worked as a director for three years when Michael Douglas called and invited him to lunch.

Zemeckis was overjoyed and apprehensive. Here was Michael Douglas, who had produced one of his all-time favourite films (*Cuckoo's Nest*) offering him the chance of a lifetime, control of a $10 million picture. Zemeckis had no idea then that, as for just about everyone else signed by Douglas for *Romancing the Stone*, his feature-length directorial début would make him a star of his profession. He went on to direct the ultra-successful *Back to the Future* trilogy (in which he starred Christopher Lloyd as the mad professor, remembered for his début as a film actor as one of Jack Nicholson's cohorts in *Cuckoo's Nest*), the innovative *Who Framed Roger Rabbit?* with Bob Hoskins and the 1992 horror

147

spoof *Death Becomes Her* with Goldie Hawn, Meryl Streep and Bruce Willis.

Douglas, who has always made a feature in his moviemaking of giving golden opportunities to unknown actors, directors and technicians, was frank enough to tell Zemeckis that he was offering him the job because he was personally averse to working with name directors, especially those with a tendency to autocracy. He wanted a young director with a viewpoint who wasn't scared of experimentation, within the limits of a strict budget, or of standing up for himself against an actor who was also producer.

Danny DeVito was also summoned at an early stage. Michael had long ago earmarked him for the part of the little Peter Lorre-style thug, complete with white suit, who would follow the two leading characters across South America. That was OK by Zemeckis, who enjoyed DeVito's performance in *Cuckoo's Nest*. Michael chose DeVito for his looks, not for his friendship: 'If you are my height and look the way I do and you don't have an abundance of ego and self-esteem, you become a basket case, one of life's prime losers, because height and looks and all those qualities are worshipped.'

The female lead was once again elusive. He wanted Debra Winger, who had just finished *Terms of Endearment* with Jack Nicholson, Shirley Maclaine and Danny DeVito, but she was unavailable. As in the past, several leading actresses of the day turned him down; it was Joe Wixan, production director of Fox, who suggested he should have a look at Kathleen Turner.

Douglas said, 'Kathleen who?' And then he remembered. She had co-starred with William Hurt in the steamy 1982 movie *Body Heat*. It was a well-praised screen début in a movie criticised for its overblown sex scenes, to which Turner herself was forced to contribute and did so with vigour. It was her one and only movie to date, and she was a virtual unknown.

Douglas had a private screening of *Body Heat*. At the end of it he had some reservations that she could portray the earnest innocence of the heroine in his new movie. He also had his mind set on someone more well known than Turner, someone who would be a draw.

However, he agreed to meet her for a talk. When they did so he discovered that she had something in common with his wife, coming as she did from a diplomatic family, and had also lived for some time in South America. Sally Grunwald, who set up the screen test at Fox, recalls: 'She was fabulous. She picked up Michael's vibes straight away, totally impressive. There is no doubt about it, he was knocked sideways by her!'

Kathleen Turner was signed, and she too was heading for stardom.

The movie tells the tale of a disorganised New York authoress who writes romantic thrillers, the kind where the lovers go into their clinches as the sun sets over the dead bodies of their enemies. Then she becomes embroiled in a real-life thriller, when she receives a telephone call from her sister in South America. Unless she flies to Cartagena with a treasure map giving the location of a priceless green jewel, her sister will be sliced up. The adventures that follow bring her into the arms of Jack Colton, a local hero in an area awash with desperadoes, bandits and killers.

The unfolding plot did indeed remind audiences of *Raiders of the Lost Ark*, filled as it is with images such as pits of alligators and last-minute escapes by the hero and heroine. But, as Zemeckis realised, the film might never have been made if Spielberg's movie had not come out first. The studio people needed to be shown that there was a market for this kind of comic adventure picture.

It is an adventure film *par excellence*, and one that extracted a fresh quality both from the actors and in the construction of the film itself. It looked a smooth and slick production, which totally belied the problems that Douglas encountered in getting it made. The weather almost washed them away. Though the screenplay was set in Colombia, Douglas and Zemeckis flew there in the late spring of 1983 and ruled out the territory on the grounds of accessibility, cost and, most of all, because of unpredictable weather. They settled on Mexico as the location, since the country is a mere plane hop from California and its weather would be more settled, or so they were told.

The weather forecast for the period of filming, which began in the early summer, was given as generally good with occasional showers. This was important, because virtually the whole of the picture is shot in the great outdoors, using natural landscapes for the backdrop.

The heavy rain that fell came as something of a shock to Douglas and his crew – it rained and rained, day after day, recording the wettest period for that time of year for more than forty years. Though rain was needed for some of the scenes, natural rain seldom works on film because it has a softer register and can barely be seen; invariably rain on film has to be artificially provided by hoses.

Zemeckis found himself in the ridiculous position of having his technicians hanging around for hours waiting for the rain to stop, and then ordering up the fake rain as soon as they could start shooting. He still dines out on stories of the making of *Romancing the Stone*: 'Douglas gave me a baptism of fire – corny cliché, but in this case true. We had everything thrown at us during those months in Mexico. I lost twenty pounds in weight and used to lie awake at night wondering if we'd ever get the goddam movie made.'

Douglas had double trouble. As leading man he was involved in major scenes throughout the picture, but his duties as producer also lay heavily as the weather went from bad to worse. 'We often arrived at predetermined locations to find that the road had been washed away,' said Kathleen Turner. 'Michael would stand us down, and the next morning there were thirty dump trucks full of gravel waiting to lay in that road. We were building new roads all over Mexico.'

Every day seemed to present a new problem as Douglas carved his picture out of a jungle and mountainous terrain. Several of the previously scouted landscapes had disappeared down the mountainside; lakes which weren't there suddenly appeared. There were also accidents in landslips and other mishaps: several members of the crew were injured, and the trainer of the alligators had his hand severed when one of them turned nasty.

The stunts and the action scenes were what helped make the

picture memorable. One particular scene, with Turner and Douglas sliding perilously down a mountain in a mudslide, was both hilarious and scary – and a natural for television when the promotion of the film began. The scene ended with Turner splashing, bruised and torn, into a pool of mud, with Douglas face-down between her legs. The clip was shown so often on television that *Variety* calculated that more people saw it than had seen the top ten grossing films of all time.

Behind that one scene, which lasted just a few seconds of screen time, lay another story of dangerous endeavour, involving life-threatening action shots and location filming which in fact took several hours. Jeannie Epper, who was Kathleen Turner's stunt double, reckoned it was the most dangerous action she had ever been involved in. She won the Academy Award for the Most Spectacular Movie Stunt of 1984. 'That clip – yes, it was terrific cinema,' she said. 'But I was knocked down by a thousand gallons of water, mud and all kinds of shit and ended up in a freezing mud pool. Still, they paid me well.'

They were in Mexico for most of the rest of 1983. Because of the circumstances of the shoot, tempers often frayed, and Michael Douglas finally lost his Mr Nice Guy tag. He blew his top and his cool, especially when gossip columnists began to rumour an off-set involvement with Kathleen Turner.

The couple were close, for sure, and Turner was clearly impressed by Douglas for the way he handled the production and performed in his acting role.

Those in the know reckoned the rumours were one of the reasons why Diandra made several visits to Mexico, flying down from California, bringing their son Cameron with her. She did not stay around too long, because of the conditions and the frenetic pace of the production, but the message was clear in a marriage going through the Hollywood mangle.

Romancing the Stone was completed on schedule and within the $10 million budget. Fox reckoned this was an achievement in itself, considering the weather and the logistics. Michael maintained his supervisory role throughout the post-production stage in the spring of 1984. Just before the launch, he had the Fox publicity people set up an exhausting round of interviews with press and television, giving full access to that mudslide clip, and with him talking his head off about the movie. He even appeared as guest host on *Saturday Night Live*, the American comedy show.

The result was as incredible as his two major successes of the past, considering that *Romancing the Stone* was no big story, not a movie of social consequence, just good entertainment. The reviewers were kind, giving Douglas and Turner some warm reviews and welcoming the arrival of a major new director in Zemeckis. Undoubtedly, the similarities to *Raiders of the Lost Ark* helped, and it was a favourable comparison that the reviewers made – that Douglas's film could stand alongside Spielberg's. Fox planned a nationwide opening in 800 theatres, which increased to 1100.

Within two weeks, *Romancing the Stone* had earned $20 million at the box office; it went on to exceed $100 million in gross takings. In anyone's language the film was a major hit. Kirk Douglas could be heard boasting: 'He's done it again.'

As the ticket sales mounted, Fox rapidly began to talk of a sequel. Douglas had barely stopped to draw breath, and Diandra must have despaired that there was no time for more than a couple of months at home before he was off again, in not one but two projects.

The personal effect of the movie was to make stars of Kathleen Turner and Douglas himself. At last, he had come of age as an actor. He might argue that he did nothing differently; it was the material that transformed him. He did exactly what Brodsky suggested might happen – showed the world a new image. The bland sheepishness of some of his more forgettable roles was put firmly behind him. 'I think he had to,' said Kathleen Turner, who had been as close as anyone to him during the transformation, 'and he comes closer to portraying the kind of rugged adventurer that was his father's stock-in-trade. Until *Romancing*, he had avoided for many years doing anything that resembled his father's style. But he came to a place where he felt very good about his output and who he was. His life came together in a lot of ways.'

There was a certain irony attached to it all, that, scared of being cast in his father's image for all these years, he takes the plunge and becomes successful – a major star at last after fifteen years of trying. And doing it like his dad!

13
Unsettling Decisions

The marriage-mending was an ongoing process after his return from filming *Romancing the Stone*, and Michael and Diandra decided to move to New York, maintaining their home in Santa Barbara as a holiday villa. It was a decision that astounded their friends, considering the time and money that they had spent in the past three years bringing their home in the hills to all its magnificent and opulent glory, capped as it was by the installation of a very large swimming-pool. And now they were going to leave it behind . . . a very serious move, said Anne Douglas, and one she could barely comprehend.

The decision was inspired mainly by Diandra's continued unhappiness in California. She gave Michael an ultimatum: she wanted to get away from what she termed 'the Hollywood quote unquote life'.

The move was seen among some of their friends as an emigration from the workplace atmosphere which Diandra believed was undermining their marriage and stifling her own development. She reckoned there was nothing for her to do there, nor could she be accepted as anything other than the wife of a Douglas.

She simply could not settle in that shadow of Michael's work or family and the intense public scrutiny. Like most families of celebrities, the Douglas sons had long ago learned that what is private is public and they were reared with the customary attention of the paparazzi. Diandra still had great difficulty in coming to terms with that.

The shift also represented final acknowledgement – if a

155

reluctant one – by Michael that a wife should have her own career. No matter how often he repeated, as Kirk had done before, that he could not cope with a wife who was involved with activities outside the family, Diandra showed particular signs of rebelling, not through any feminist-driven aspirations but as a qualified woman in search of greater fulfilment.

She had no interest in becoming a Hollywood wife – the bitchy lunches, the excruciating social order of the party circuit or the glitzy functions which neither of them enjoyed. And then there were the distractions to Michael . . . the women. His life, he will admit, had been led among women in the fast lanes of Hollywood. He had encountered them all, from the sharp, immaculately dressed young studio executives to the myriad of miniskirted, long-legged beauties who would adorn one of the fabled Swifty Lazar Oscar-night parties at Spago on Sunset Boulevard.

To the latter, Michael would be the catch of the century, and some would happily have replaced the young wife who was known to be none too fussy about movie people. Michael would also confess that to many – and perhaps to Diandra herself – he was seen to be darting around leading an exciting action-man life while she had no affinity with her surroundings and nothing to occupy her.

The move east had been discussed many times. It seemed a curious prospect to his friends. Michael, they said, initially balked at the idea: 'I have a living to make.' His argument was fairly sound. Directors could live anywhere, because they are hired on the strength of past work and seldom on the basis of dealmaking; actors are always represented by agents. Michael was a producer, first and foremost, and at the time was the most successful actor-producer in Hollywood since Warren Beatty. As such, he needed to be at the epicentre of the action, diving in and out of studios and available for power breakfasts.

At least he thought he did, until the experiences of the past few years slowly began to whittle away at his own commitment to this ideal. He became maddened and frustrated, then angry and even revengeful, about the people who had played games with him and rejected him first as an actor and then as a producer and then as an actor again. The wounds cut deep. Diandra's disaffection for Hollywood and its people forced him to look again at that aspect of his life and work.

Their marriage itself was a serious consideration. Hollywood has always been a very male-orientated town, and it is only in quite recent years that the situation has begun to change, with more women in top jobs in studios (though the actual number of films being produced or directed by women is still few). Women who were not in the business were not included in the conversation. Diandra would stand around at parties and be expected to talk to other wives about Hollywood topics, like who's hot in the therapy business or Zsa Zsa's latest facelift or who was having an affair with whom. Diandra hated the smallness of it all.

So he said: 'What the hell . . . we'll go.'

In fact, apart from the obvious necessity to commute to Los Angeles on a fairly regular basis, living in New York worked in his favour, as he was closer to the moneymen, whose decision now largely influenced the future of any major movie. There were other reasons why he accepted the move as necessary. Cameron was in pre-school and had come home once too often to ask if he could have a punk haircut like the rest of the kids in his class.

On the face of it all of the above sounded like excuses rather than reasons. New York sounded no better than LA as a place in which to bring up a family, although Michael could remember the strictness of his own schooldays there. At the heart of the matter was Diandra's overwhelming desire to extricate herself from 'those people' out west and do something else with her life, other than participate in the machinations of the close-knit clan Douglas and the Hollywood fraternity.

She made a point of doing things on her own account very soon after they moved to New York. First of all, she became something of a celebrity herself as an occasional fashion model. She also began a less public life as a behind-the-scenes organiser for several major charitable causes.

They had taken a rented apartment on the Upper East Side of Manhattan while they looked around for a more permanent home.

She had noticed that at the end of their street an old woman beggar lived in a cardboard box, a sight less prevalent in the parts of Los Angeles that she frequented in 1984 but becoming quite common in New York.

Not long afterwards she walked over to the American Red Cross headquarters and asked for an appointment with Robert Bender, its chief executive. She explained that she wanted to help, and suggested arranging a charity gala.

She seemed surprised that the Red Cross did not immediately fall on her with glee. There were certain procedures to be followed in organising charitable affairs and protocol to be adhered to – not least to avoid upsetting some of the more established socialite fundraisers. It took months of arguments, proposals and planning to get her scheme off the ground, and it would centre around a première for her husband's next picture, *The Jewel of the Nile*, a follow-up to *Romancing the Stone*, which would eventually raise $200,000 for the charity.

Diandra soon discovered in New York that her forte was organising such events. But she deliberately steered clear of the socialite set who are a permanent attachment to charitable causes; otherwise she would have been merely substituting the Hollywood crowd for the élite in New York. Socialising had never been a major part of their lives, partly because of Michael's work commitments and partly because when he was at home he enjoyed having no company at all except his family.

The wider family had always been around Los Angeles. Now, with Michael and Diandra out east, the Douglas clan had moved apart and came together at Kirk's house on fewer and fewer occasions.

Michael's re-emergence as a major producer-actor coincided with Kirk's own acting career dwindling out of sight. Kirk had remained moderately busy during the 1970s, making on average one film a year. Towards the end of the decade he was involved in few movies that would forge a lasting memory; most parts were, sadly, a caricature of his former self.

By the early 1980s he had slipped quietly into virtual retirement. He remained inactive for the rest of the decade apart from a reunion with Burt Lancaster for *Tough Guys* in 1986 – at the age of seventy.

Conversely, Michael was basking in the biggest financial glory of his career, and Kirk's other three sons had also met varying degrees of success 'in the business'. The advice Joe Kennedy had given him about giving his children their independence and 'watch them come back to you' had worked. Rather like the Kennedy brothers, they all also grew up seeking their father's approval by settling themselves in his world, in spite of his entreaties to them when they were young that they should avoid the movies and become lawyers or doctors.

When they meet, the boys talk about the days when their dad was at his peak, and the letters he would write cajoling them for their school grades or misbehaviour. Kirk still writes them letters, mainly on how to proceed and what to do about various projects they're involved in, urging them never to take any bullshit from anyone. He sent several letters to Michael while he was on location for *Romancing the Stone*, long gossipy letters which, he said, were the ones he liked to receive when he was on location.

Kirk would tell Michael about Cameron, and his joy at being with his grandson. He would tell him about the comings and goings in Hollywood, and, where necessary, offer some advice that may have been applicable at the time.

It was the same for all his sons, who, in spite of their father's sometimes distant involvement in their early life, are entwined by strong paternal and fraternal bonds. Joel, the second eldest, joined Michael's production company and was closely involved at every stage of Michael's recent productions. 'I am his mother, father, lawyer, doctor, accountant and shoulder to cry on.' Of the four boys, he was 'the teddy bear, the nicest member of the family', said his stepmother, Anne. She also noted that he fell in love almost every month and by the age of thirty-six was twice divorced.

Peter, the first of Kirk's sons with Anne, grew into a sombre young man and kept out of acting. He moved into producing and became an accomplished screenwriter. He cut his teeth on the 1980 movie *The Final Countdown*, which he produced for his

159

father's company Bryna; the film, which starred Kirk himself in the leading role, fared badly. Out on his own Peter enjoyed better success with *Fletch*, starring Chevy Chase, though compared to his brother he remained in the lesser zones of moviemaking.

Only Eric, the youngest and so named because he was born during Kirk's filming of *The Vikings,* went headlong into acting. He went to Europe, and trained at the Royal Academy of Dramatic Art. With the familiar Douglas square jaw which he sticks out ready for it to be socked if anyone dares, he is always ready to fight Hollywood convention. Directors thought him arrogant when he railed against what he termed 'the non-acting style of the brat pack'; consequently, he did not receive too many offers.

Michael, Diandra and Cameron had barely settled in New York when Michael had to fly back to Los Angeles for a series of meetings. Diandra was left alone to continue the apartment hunt. Michael hit the ground running and didn't stop for the next fourteen months; suddenly, he found himself involved in two major projects, much to Diandra's eventual dismay.

He had already been booked by Richard Attenborough to play Zach, the mean-hearted director-choreographer in the screen version of the smash-hit musical, *A Chorus Line*. He had agreed a small fee for the experience of the project. But then, in the wake of the runaway commercial success of *Romancing the Stone*, 20th Century-Fox summoned him to Hollywood to discuss its sequel, *The Jewel of the Nile*, to be produced in double-quick time while the public's memory was still fresh.

Sequels were in vogue. Though Michael always denied that it was his intention, the ending of *Romancing the Stone* looked like a deliberate anticipation of part two – Jack Colton pulled Joan Wilder aboard his trailered yacht in New York's West End Avenue and sailed off into the sunset for a world cruise, Danny DeVito's character promising to get even.

But it was a tall order. There was no script and no firm commitment from Fox until the early summer of 1984, when the box office returns showed the unexpected measure of the success of *Romancing the Stone*. Also, Spielberg was doing flat-out business with his spectacular sequel to *Raiders of the Lost Ark*, *Indiana Jones and the Temple of Doom*.

In fact, the figures for *Romancing the Stone* were sufficient to send Fox into orbit. In August 1984 the studio commissioned Douglas to produce the sequel, with exactly the same team. The budget was doubled, the settings were to be even more exotic, through Europe and the Middle East to Egypt – as exotic, incidentally, as the locations in Spielberg's *Indiana Jones*, which had just grossed $120 million.

Oh yes, and Fox wanted the film completed for release by Christmas of the following year.

Douglas pursed his lips and whistled. With $20 million in his back pocket, it was the biggest venture he had ever tackled, and there were to be none of the long preambles and rejections he had experienced in the past.

He had to get straight to it: script, production schedule, stars, locations, technicians, all to be set up within a matter of weeks rather than months. Plus . . . he would have to fit in the filming of *A Chorus Line*, which would be released around the same time.

Joel was already on board, and Michael needed more helpers and scouts to be sent abroad immediately to site possible locations.

The problems began almost from day one, and were mostly to do with the fact that Douglas had made his previous band of players and aides into major stars. Robert Zemeckis, who had directed *Romancing the Stone*, was already engaged on the first of the jumbo-hit *Back to the Future* movies which he had written and directed, and could not be prised away.

Also, there lingered some unexplained unpleasantness between Zemeckis and 20th Century-Fox, whose executives had apparently been deeply unsure about the potential success of *Romancing the Stone*. 'When I showed them the finished cut of that movie, they fired me from directing *Cocoon* [the aliens-with-a-difference movie for which its star, Don Ameche, won an Oscar]. It's the great mystery of my career why they did that.'

The replacement was Lewis Teague, best known for his direction of the politically funny minor-league *Jaws*-type monster movie, *Alligator*, made in 1980. Teague was signed up because Michael was impressed by his direction of the Stephen King thriller *Cujo*. Teague had no other major work to his credit and seemed to fit Douglas's usual penchant for entrusting his movies to comparatively new directors. It was debatable whether a director more experienced with a major-budget picture, with the huge logistical problems it entailed, might have been a wiser choice.

Kathleen Turner was also in great demand since *Romancing the Stone* and had signed for no fewer than three movies in the meantime – *The Man With Two Brains*, with Steve Martin, John Huston's *Prizzi's Honour*, with Jack Nicholson and Anjelica Huston, and Ken Russell's *Crimes of Passion,* with Anthony Perkins. She was also being sought by Spielberg for his next movie, and was already earmarked for Francis Ford Coppola's *Peggy Sue Got Married*.

However, she agreed to do the sequel, with the proviso that the script would be of a similar high quality to the first.

Therein lay one more problem which would explode into serious trouble later. Diane Thomas, whose original script for *Romancing the Stone* had been a foremost consideration for Douglas doing the movie – 'so fresh and virginal' – was also busy after her career had taken off (although it was short lived; she died tragically in a car crash in October 1985). The writing partnership of Mark Rosenthal and Lawrence Konner (*The Legend of Billie Jean* and *Real Genius*) was commissioned to write the script.

The two scriptwriters proceeded to Michael's own brief while he and Joel Douglas set about the mechanics of the production itself.

In between, Michael had to cope with his role in *A Chorus Line*, in itself no mean task. It was Richard Attenborough's problem, not Douglas's, that they had to try to bring a fresh approach to the film version of the longest-running show in Broadway's history, a show which had played with equal success in London's West End and by touring companies around the world.

The problem was singularly self-evident, and a succession

of writers and directors had anguished over it before walking away. The stage show had gathered pretty well all of the prizes and awards going. It had been running for almost a decade, had been seen in its original form by so many people and left so many audiences in awe of its strong stage performances that the movie would have to be spectacular in the extreme to beat the live show.

There would be many purists ready to pounce if anything went awry. In terms of Hollywood sagas, the film of *A Chorus Line* had an even longer history than some of Douglas's own production efforts.

It took nine years to bring to the screen after the rights were sold for $5.5 million in 1976. The delay was first caused by the original deal, which stipulated that the movie should not be released for five years and that a twenty per cent share of the profits should be paid to the owners after the film had grossed $30 million. The rights were sold several times; screenplay after screenplay came and went because, it was said, no one could discover 'how to open it up'. Finally, Attenborough was charged with the task. He chose Michael Douglas to portray the character around which the story is built.

Douglas always tended to be anxious about his acting. Though his role was by no means the most important in the show, it was he who had to draw out the bitterness and the heart-break of the dancers herded on to his stage for their audition. He had to be, as he himself described it 'closer to a prick than any role I have played, a guy totally insensitive to how others feel'.

In the film version, Zach had to be portrayed as more of 'a prick' than he was in the stage show. The atmosphere of the live theatre setting would be lost – another factor, perhaps, never able to be overcome successfully on the screen – and Zach had to be larger than life itself to achieve the desired effect.

As choreographer, Douglas's Zach mercilessly delves into the thoughts and fears of each one of the dancers he is auditioning, forcing each to pour out his or her heart and mind and troubles in front of the line. Douglas's actual appearances are brief. He is out there somewhere in the darkness of the theatre, where occasionally a cigarette lights up, and his voice bellows out instructions, relentlessly prodding and psychoanalysing his potential dancers. His mood is angry, though gradually we see it softening.

Meanwhile, a backstage drama unfolds – which is where the film differs from the stage show: Zach's former girlfriend and one-time Broadway star arrives for an audition, and slowly the story of his relationship with her unfolds. The tensions on stage, among the dancers desperate for the job, are matched by the build-up of whether or not Zach will give *her* a job.

Attenborough was his usual gushing self in the praise he gave Douglas. 'I found it refreshing that he should take on the role, without a huge salary or even star billing. I think it represented an actor looking for growth in his repertoire and his career. He played it exactly right, mean yet attractive. A miraculous performance. He brought enormous stature to the role, which doesn't work unless you believe there was a mind racing around somewhere out there in the darkness.'

Attenborough went further. He believed that in close-up shots Douglas was almost delicate, like a watercolour, but gave the impression that behind that façade lay an imminent explosion. 'Gary Cooper had it, and Spencer Tracy – that huge strength that lies behind gentleness.'

There were compensations of the sort Douglas enjoyed in the scenery. 'He never let a leotard go by,' said Attenborough. But the cast was so young that they kept referring to the forty-one-year-old as Mr Douglas.

14
Tears on the Nile

The filming of *A Chorus Line* fell behind schedule and overlapped with the preparations for the production of *The Jewel of the Nile*. Between meeting the demands of being Zach the terrible, Michael began to work on his own forthcoming movie. There was no time for niceties, or going home for lunch. He rented an office in the Mark Hellinger Theater, the location-base for Attenborough's movie.

It was there that he received the first draft of the screenplay by Mark Rosenthal and Lawrence Konner. He felt that there were a number of scenes which did not work and he began himself rewriting some of them between takes of *A Chorus Line;* every spare minute was devoted to his new production.

There would be accusations that he was spreading himself too thinly, but Attenborough never saw it that way. Douglas, he said, never once allowed his own matters to get in the way of *A Chorus Line*.

The only time he did was on the last day of filming. The shoot overran to such a degree that Douglas worked through the night to finish and ducked out of the customary end-of-filming party. By then, by his own admission, he was 'in deep shit' with *The Jewel of the Nile*.

Production on *The Jewel of the Nile* was disaster-prone from beginning to end – the most horrific filmmaking exercise of Douglas's life. It would, he said, have provided material for a classic film school lecture on how not to make a movie and how to survive when everything goes wrong, except that no one in class would have believed him.

His production managers had been dispatched to the Middle East to find locations, but they had been unable to settle on a suitable site. They all met up in London, as half-way house, to discuss the logistics of communications and landscape and politically sensitive areas. They ruled out Egypt and Israel and eventually settled for a main location in Morocco, with other scenes in the South of France. Douglas sent his people back to Morocco to find an actual site for production, and began smoothing away all the problems that accompany the setting up of a village of film people for a movie of this magnitude.

Douglas returned to New York, and moved on quickly to Los Angeles to finalise the pre-production schedule and to work on the script. He was also scheduled to attend the Oscar ceremonies on 25 March, where his old buddies from *Cuckoo's Nest*, Saul Zaentz and Milos Forman, were both in the nominations list for *Amadeus* (each won an Oscar, Zaentz for Best Film and Forman for Best Director).

A week before the Awards ceremonies, two disasters struck. First, Joel called to tell him that two senior crew members, the production designer and location manager, had been posted missing. They had gone up in a light plane to scout for location sites and had not returned. It was four days before the plane was found. It had crashed in the mountains; all on board were killed.

Michael was torn between staying in Los Angeles to complete his work or going out to Morocco. Joel assured him there was nothing he could do there. The bodies had been recovered and matters taken care of through official channels. It was a distressing time for all concerned, and there were rumblings among the crew, as happens at such times, that the movie was doomed. Three crew members resigned and went home. Joel and his staff then had to inform relatives, deal with the authorities and repatriate the bodies.

Going on, in parallel, were tedious negotiations with Moroccan customs officials over the importation of military equipment needed as props, and rows over accommodation, which was desperately short. As more of the film people began to arrive, it became apparent there would be trouble.

Then, the second disaster hit, back in Los Angeles. Kathleen Turner's agent told Douglas she was pulling out after having read the script. She reckoned it was full of sexist overtones and did not match the quality of *Romancing the Stone*; she had her reputation to think of.

The fact that others, like Spielberg and Coppola, were pressing for her services also had some bearing on the situation. It may have been a negotiating ploy, but if it was she took it very close to the edge.

Douglas's response was rather in the mould of the role he had just been performing for Attenborough. No more Mr Nice Guy. His schedule was such that there was no time for arguments. The sequel would work only if the two of them co-starred in a story that followed on from *Romancing*; it wouldn't work with a substitute actress. Turner knew that, too.

Despite their earlier closeness, Douglas had no hesitation in agreeing to Fox's command to sue her. They threatened a writ claiming $25 million in damages. Lawyers exchanged letters. 'Let's talk,' she said.

Douglas agreed to further rewrites to the script. They kissed and made up and prepared to move overseas.

Back in Morocco, Douglas was expecting to find arrangements well in hand to begin filming at the beginning of April. Even then, the three-month shoot would take them perilously close to the deadlines for completion and post-production work. What he found was mayhem.

Everything that could go wrong had, largely because of problems with the Moroccan government and customs officers, who insisted on checking every item of equipment, some of which had been standing in bonded warehouses for three weeks. There were also delays through the office of the king of Morocco himself, who had to sign everything once the lower echelons had approved it.

They were desperately behind schedule and the whole situation was chaotic. A row had blown up over the shortage of accommodation, too. Michael waded in angrily, expletives flying. He 'cleaned house' and fired half a dozen people, including the production manager. He instructed his crew to double up in available rooms, then stormed off to demand better co-operation from government agencies. Where verbal blasting did not suffice, he dug his hand in his back pocket and smoothed the way with fistfuls of dollars.

Douglas also had his usual problem with the weather, just as he had in Mexico. Morocco had had a drought for about seven years, but no sooner had his craftsmen finished building the palace that was the centrepiece of the story than it started raining and raining. Something in the Atlas Mountains gave way, and a wall of water eight feet high swept down through a dry river bed. In fifteen seconds everything they had built was washed away.

Once the rain had passed, the temperature soared to over 125 degrees; several members of the cast and crew became ill with heat-stroke and dehydration. In fact, sickness and disease became so bad that filming on many days was stopped. During their three-month stay, the unit doctor had to deal with forty cases of hepatitis, dysentery, sun-stroke or cholera, and a mild form of malaria hit pretty well everyone.

Other problems were discovered only as filming began – like the daily footage of film having to be sent to London for processing and occasionally getting lost between airports. But perhaps the most taxing problem was provided by the landscape. Unlike the location for *Romancing the Stone*, there was no framing backdrop of jungle and mountains – just miles of flat, uninteresting desert. 'We did not entirely account for that,' Douglas admitted. 'In *Romancing* we had the natural hazards of the terrain and fabulous mud and rocky chasms. Out there, it was just sand, so we had to fill it up with much more hardware and toys – hence the F-16 jet, a lot of horses and a cast of thousands.'

The film's storyline would pick up six months after the end of *Romancing*, with Jack and Joan not exactly seeing eye to eye in their life together aboard the yacht. She had grown tired of their nautical trek around the world and wants to settle down.

Jack, on the other hand, is happy with his nomadic life and
unwilling to make a commitment. 'I thought it was time to start
dealing with the real nuts and bolts of the relationship,' said
Douglas. 'I wanted it based upon two very different people living
together whose independence and vanity sometimes got it the
way of their relationship.'

There are no marks for guessing where he drew his inspiration
for that part of the plot, and he sought to paint a new scenario
where Colton and Wilder rekindle their love and discover that
they could not get along without each other.

The route to their discovery was much as before, only in a
different setting – an action-filled adventure across North Africa,
where Turner's character, unaware of the dangers that await
her, gets involved with a fabulously wealthy tycoon who is set
upon becoming the dictator of his homeland. Douglas becomes
an ally of a great spiritual leader known as The Jewel of the
Nile, who wants to put a stop to the tycoon's ambitions. Danny
DeVito, meanwhile, is left wandering aimlessly in the desert,
suffering various kinds of torture; perhaps he wondered exactly
what he was doing in the picture at all.

In spite of the many setbacks, Douglas met his deadline. But
there were problems with officialdom even to the last minute
which actually brought Michael to tears. Finally, he decided to
call it a day and pull out. He ordered two aircraft, a Boeing 737
and a transport plane, to come in immediately; the whole crew
moved to the airport with gear and trucks and cheered wildly as
the planes landed. They all went off to France for the final film
sequences, then Douglas and his aides flew to London for the
five-week edit and soundtracking, and delivered his movie on
time – much to Fox's surprise. He said he came away from Morocco
with the greatest feeling of accomplishment.

As a movie, *The Jewel of the Nile* worked fairly well. The script
was weak and pointless in parts; Kathleen Turner had been right
– it did lack the style and wit of *Romancing the Stone*. Douglas
should have taken longer on the script, but he was faced with
the insistence of the Fox people to have the film ready for release
by Christmas 1985, which he did.

Market research had targeted the picture towards family viewing in the cinemas, followed by the increasingly lucrative video market and then finally for television, the three elements of all successful Hollywood packages by the mid-1980s.

Douglas, as usual, became the film's promoter to ensure financial success in each area of marketing. He'd given a good deal of thought to attracting the younger audience that he felt stayed away from *Romancing* and came up with the idea of soundtracking the Billy Ocean song, 'When the Going Gets Tough, the Tough Get Going', played as the credits roll at the end of the movie. There was also a promotional video; in between clips of *Jewel*, Douglas, Turner and DeVito camped up an impression of The Temptations. It gave new life to Billy Ocean's song, and the video sold five million copies.

That Christmas of 1985, Douglas was appearing in movies running at 3000 cinemas across America. *A Chorus Line* opened around the same time as *The Jewel of the Nile*, to some lacklustre reviews. Attenborough had not achieved the mystical quality needed for the film to outperform the stage show; also, some script changes annoyed purist fans. It was a pallid outcome, though Douglas did not fare too badly. Over the years, as the memory of the stage show faded, the movie became more acceptable, particularly in its video form.

The reviews were also fairly harsh of *The Jewel of the Nile*, most repeating the view that the sequel was not as good as the original. Many rightly criticised its overbearing stunts and hardware. True enough, it was lightweight entertainment, but the critics ought not to have been surprised by that: such a setting, such a series of unlikely situations that these adventure-comedy-romance movies comprise can never really be taken seriously. The film exudes considerable energy and resourcefulness, and what comes over most was the partnership between Douglas and Turner. They clearly liked each other very much, and had a rapport and chemistry that carry very considerable appeal.

Above all, they seemed to be having fun – an achievement in itself, considering the circumstances of the shoot – and, with

DeVito intervening in the often silly contrivances of the story, the trio could be compared to Hope, Crosby and Lamour in the *Road* movies.

So now Michael Douglas put on his promotional hat and began his tour to sell his film to the public. First he travelled around America with Turner and DeVito, then he went abroad, to Europe and the Far East. He did not touch base again permanently until well into the New Year.

His effort was important. After the post-production costs, film print costs and promotion had been added in, Fox had invested almost $40 million. Douglas was rewarded by the audience response. *The Jewel of the Nile* took almost as much at the box office as its predecessor had.

Douglas headed back to New York shattered, vowing never again to undertake an epic production in so short a time or in a country whose facilities and difficulties merely exacerbated problems. He was richer financially and in experience, and he came back with the feeling, 'Now I can do anything'.

His father had long ago predicted that, one day, Michael Douglas's talent would explode on to the screen in a big way and that he would become a major star as an actor, not as a producer. He had not achieved it in the swashbuckling adventures of *Romancing* or *Jewel*. They were entertaining, were watched by millions and his face was known the world over, but the films were not classics by any means. Douglas knew that.

But something important had happened for Douglas on the two films: he had at last found his own inner strength. It would need another producer and another director, over whom he had no control, to bring it out on screen; the time for the explosion that Kirk had forecast was drawing near. *The Jewel of the Nile* had shown him to be one of the hardest-working artist-entrepreneurs in Hollywood.

The film had virtually brought him to his knees, given him a lot of grief, seriously damaged his marriage and made him another small fortune. But no one could deny the tenacity – a word that has to be used frequently in Douglas's case – of a man who had presided over two nightmare shoots, in Mexico and Morocco. He had also sold himself short in one way. As Kathleen Turner said: 'I don't think he had time to give himself the indulgence he should have as an actor. When he does, he's going to be very powerful. Very, very powerful.'

15
Fatal Attraction

Promoting *The Jewel of the Nile* kept Douglas busy until the beginning of May 1986. He had barely been home for a year, and when he came back to New York his physical and mental exhaustion showed in his face. His marriage was in deep difficulties, and the enforced separation from Diandra through his work looked at one stage as if it would become more permanent.

She repeatedly told her friends: 'I don't know how much longer I can go on living like this. When he's working, I'm never sure where he is, or when he's coming home. He eats, drinks and sleeps movies. He has a telephone growing out of his ear.'

Nor was that situation helped by the innuendo surrounding an interview Kathleen Turner gave for *GQ* magazine during the shoot in Morocco, in which she described vividly her feelings for Douglas the man, the actor and the producer: 'He takes my breath away, like in a scene where he turns to me and says, "God, I love you, lady." He turns on that switch. Michael really is a man who likes women.'

Diandra had lived with publicity-oriented statements like that, and, for that matter, with claims by dozens of unknown women in the past who gained some pleasure, perhaps benefit, in alleging that they had slept with Michael Douglas (though more often than not he had never even met them). This is not to say that Diandra supposed for one moment that Michael was monk-like out of her sight; she knew then, as she knows now, that there were plenty of women around who would gladly fight to take her place, given the opportunity.

Diandra tried hard not to let the allegations of her husband's

173

wayward sexuality threaten her marriage. 'I was admittedly quite shocked, taken aback by it when I first went to Hollywood,' she said, adding curiously, 'though crazy people know no geographical bounds, do they?' It was always present: some gossip or inference hanging over them like a cloud. That, together with Michael's work schedules of the preceding three years, might well have driven a less determined woman into the arms of another, or to a divorce lawyer, long before. She would admit the thought had not escaped her.

Diandra had made her own life in New York, which she had been unable to do in Los Angeles, and extended her interests across a broad spectrum. In addition to her efforts on behalf of the Red Cross and her occasional modelling, which had put her on the cover of several international magazines, she had also become associated with the Metropolitan Museum, where eventually she went to work full time in the Office of Film and Television. She was planning to produce a fundraising film for a forthcoming Goya exhibition, work that would take her to Europe.

Michael sounded a touch patronising once again when he told *Cosmopolitan* that 'she has blossomed into this extraordinary lady. She's become what my sixth sense always told me was there, beyond her beauty and aura.' Undoubtedly she had, and enjoyed the New York lifestyle conducted from their recently acquired gracious four-bedroomed apartment in one of the more venerable older buildings on Manhattan's West Side. Visitors are met by a white-coated butler and shown into a high-ceiling drawing-room, where the polished wood floors gleamed like mirrors and the tall windows overlooked Central Park. The décor was not entirely to Diandra's liking, but there had been no time to call in the designers with Michael being away.

Now he was back, and he scooped her up and whisked her off to their home in Santa Barbara. The venue was significant. Their hearts and souls were in that house, which possessed the atmosphere needed to repair their relationship and for him to recuperate from the arduous months he had just come through. Just as a reminder he had had their wedding vows framed and hung on his den wall.

They lounged around in their hilltop eyrie for as long as they were able. But an hour and forty minutes away down the fast lane to Los Angeles, in a production office somewhere in Hollywood, a secretary's nimble fingers were already clattering over a word processor keyboard to produce a draft script of a new and sensational project.

Fatal Attraction had been around for a long time – more than six years, in fact. The film didn't have that title yet. Douglas had bought the rights to Gloria Nagy's book, *Virgin Kisses*, in the first of his abortive three years with Columbia. The project had been dormant ever since; he had simply been unable to get anyone interested.

He knew the theme off by heart and could trot it out at the drop of a hat – on a plane, in a car, at a party: 'a bored psychiatrist, who cheated his way through medical school, got the right wife, a good practice. Gets involved with a woman, pleasant looking, and there's something about her turns him to adultery. Lust. It's about lust, about male obsession, about the ethics of a professional, and how his life and his practice fall apart.'

One day in 1983 he struck up a conversation with Stanley Jaffe. Ironically, Jaffe was the son of Leo Jaffe, head of Columbia at the time Michael was *in situ* when the idea was first rejected. They met on a plane from New York to the West Coast. Jaffe was then an independent producer looking for projects with his partner, Sherry Lansing.

The Jaffe and Lansing team had surprised Hollywood when they left lucrative studio jobs to form their partnership. Both had strong production track records. Jaffe, four years older than Michael Douglas, had become one of the youngest-ever studio bosses when he was appointed head of Paramount production at the age of twenty-nine.

Lansing, born in the same year as Douglas, had the distinction of becoming the first woman president of a major studio when she was appointed president of 20th Century-Fox in 1980. She had worked with Michael Douglas on three previous occasions, and had been one of his earliest supporters at a time when others were rejecting him. They first met when she was executive story editor at MGM twelve years earlier, when he was working on *Coma*. She was also involved with *The Star Chamber* when she moved to 20th Century-Fox. They had an excellent working rapport and understanding.

Both she and her partner were seeking more personal creative freedom when they joined forces in 1983. They were to prove themselves in the next decade by producing some of Hollywood's most successful movies, including *Fatal Attraction, The Accused, Black Rain* and *Indecent Proposal*.

At the time they had completed only one movie together, *Firstborn*, and were looking for other suitable scripts for development. Jaffe and Michael talked about *Virgin Kisses*; eventually, the Jaffe–Lansing team acquired the rights. They put together a package and proceeded to hawk it around Hollywood. Although they were under no obligation to do so, Jaffe and Lansing offered Douglas the lead. 'He was a dear friend,' said Lansing, adding quickly, 'though our relationship had been purely on a professional basis. It was Stanley who suggested we give it [the leading role] to Michael. I said it was a fabulous idea, because we would not only be getting a vulnerable, funny, hang-loose guy but also someone who was a producer and could give us a great deal of creative input.'

Like Douglas in the past, Jaffe and Lansing came to know the pain of rejection. Studio after studio, director after director, turned them down, largely on the basis that no one could have sympathy with a story like that. It was Douglas himself who inspired them to keep trying. Lansing remembers: 'He told me, "Don't worry, Sherry. It took me years to get *Romancing* made and I finally got old enough to play the part myself." He was right. We had to keep trying.'

Eventually, they found a sympathetic ear at Jaffe's old studio, Paramount. By then, the time was exactly right. The vociferous background to the feminist movement was fermenting, and the whole social scene was in turmoil through the arrival of AIDS. Women the world over, it would seem, lived in the dread of being infected with HIV by a promiscuous partner. The horror stories

176

were already beginning to appear at a time when media attention to the disease was at its peak.

The era had caught up with the book, which would be viewed as a modern morality tale. The screen interpretation became one of the most discussed movies of the 1980s, highlighting matters, it was said, of considerable sociological importance.

For Douglas, it was a pleasant experience that someone else was doing the worrying and the lobbying. All he had to do was act. The drama for him came not in the build-up to getting the movie made, as had been the case with every one of his own productions, but in the aftermath, the worldwide reaction to the film. Of course, the film also represented a completely new departure for himself. As he said, the movie was about lust and sex, the ingredients that would send his career into orbit.

That summer, he relaxed. He had promised Diandra that he would stay home and become a father again. They returned to New York after the holiday on the West Coast and Douglas did nothing except spend time with his wife and son. But the phone still rang, incessantly, and future projects were discussed.

Oliver Stone, the controversial director of the recent hit *Platoon*, for which he won an Oscar, was courting Douglas for his new movie, called *Wall Street*. By late August the script for *Fatal Attraction* was nearing its final draft. There had been many rewrites because of the implications of the book, which was strongly attuned to the feminist cause, and nine different endings were under discussion. Lansing said they still wanted to maintain the feminist theme, but Jaffe, an eye on the commercial aspects, erred on the side of trying to inject a sympathetic balance. The extent of their anguish became a subject of Hollywood myth and legend. Finally, two alternative endings were written to James Dearden's screenplay to make the film most commercially appealing.

By the late summer, all was falling into place. Douglas was to be joined by Anne Archer, who would play the wife; Glenn Close, fresh from the thriller *Jagged Edge* would be the one-night stand, the psychotic who refuses to be ignored.

They all moved to a suburban location an hour's drive north of New York to begin filming. Michael and Diandra rented a large lake-front colonial house at Pound Ridge. The rustic building was so ordinary as to be unnoticed, but they liked it so much they kept on the lease for some years to come and used it as a weekend home.

The film was set in horsy territory. Very soon, the Douglases were equipped with suitable steeds, which they housed in nearby stables. Cameron, then eight years old, loved riding as much as his mother. Diandra was a skilled horsewoman and rode a spirited dapple-grey stallion which galloped at speed at the touch of her heel. She was clearly at home in company that rode with the hounds. Michael was not. He had to learn to ride, and the stables provided him with a docile chestnut gelding. It was the first time in years that he had been able to relax while making a movie, and some days he even got home in time to have dinner with Cameron.

So the cameras started rolling. The final storyline differed quite substantially from the book. The characteristics of this enthralling psychological thriller were maintained, but the producers felt it necessary to inject some Hollywood gloss that compromised plausibility in the last third of the picture. However, the strength of the performances and the sheer terror of the ending overcame the areas where disbelief was not entirely suspended.

Michael Douglas is a young and successful lawyer, Dan Gallagher, who has been happily married and entirely faithful to his wife Beth (Anne Archer) for nine years. They live in Westchester with their six-year-old daughter, and life is apparently idyllic – until one evening he meets a beguiling blonde, Alex Forrest (Glenn Close), at a business party. She makes the running and they strike up a conversation. Before long, he has invited her out to dinner, while his wife is away for the weekend, and she makes it plain that she is quite amenable to seduction. Dan, by now lusting, embarks on mad and passionate intercourse, with sexual acrobatics occurring in various unlikely places.

Dan has, throughout, insisted that this is a brief encounter, 'just two adults who saw an opportunity and took it'. Alex, however, cannot let it rest. She begins to make demands on Dan, who rejects her in no uncertain terms. Gradually, we see her becoming obsessed by the need to continue the relationship, visiting him at his office, phoning him at night. She throws acid on the car, calls to see his wife on the excuse of wanting to buy their house and generally gets in the way of his life.

Dan responds first with reason, then with anger and threats. It is from here that the movie compromises plausibility in a series of sequences where Alex kidnaps the daughter, Beth drives so frantically that she has a car crash and breaks her arm and, in the end, Alex is killed in gruesome style.

The movie became a massive talking-point, inspiring miles of newspaper and magazine print and hours of television debate around the world. Audience identification was aroused on an unprecedented scale.

In America cinemagoers are likely to participate in the action on screen with screams and catcalls. Audiences were gripped immediately by the suspense and tension in *Fatal Attraction*, which they released by incredibly vocal reaction, even hysteria, so much so that Douglas and his fellow-actors were amazed.

Fatal Attraction struck a nerve at a particular time in modern history. Arguments raged in bars, homes and television chatshows. Several influential American critics, while generally praising the film and the performances, took exception to some of the more bizarre scenes and the film's ending. 'I walked out feeling cheated and betrayed,' wrote critic Roger Ebert.

He was particularly critical of the gradual narrowing of Glenn Close's Alex so that in the end she was portrayed as a raving monster. The feminist lobby in virtually every country where the movie was shown took up exactly that point. When the dust had settled, Glenn Close herself said she agreed with the feminist point of view.

At the time, she said, everyone on the movie was surprised at how it terrified people. Her character was every unfaithful man's nightmare, and it was a telling fact that many women dragged their spouses and boyfriends to see the picture as a warning.

While the film tapped into anger, fear and frustration, it was also guilty of an exaggeration, changing the emphasis heavily in Dan's favour to give the audience some sort of catharsis.

'I saw Alex as a very tragic figure,' said Close. 'But they did a lot of work on the script to make Michael Douglas's character look more sympathetic. They made a greater effort to make him look nice than to make her truly tragic. So she got the shaft, and I resented that deeply. She wasn't a psychopath, but they changed the ending to make her into one. But Alex didn't let somebody fuck her over. And that was what women responded to . . .'

Sherry Lansing, as the only woman among the production team, was forced heavily on the defensive. She maintained that *Fatal Attraction* was conceived as a feminist movie; she said she herself was a strong feminist and was 'shocked and hurt' when the picture was criticised as being anti-feminist.

Michael Douglas sat back in amazement as he became the number one bastard to the female population. He called his father and told him: 'They're going nuts in the theatres. People are screaming and getting hysterical.' But his personal assessment of the situation was sanguinely professional: 'This is what making movies is all about.' And it was – it made people talk, brought them out in droves and made lots of money.

Whatever the rights and wrongs of the producers' fiddling with the emphasis to make their product more commercially appealing, few movies in history have created such an outburst of public reaction and discussion. It also goes without saying that everyone involved made a large fortune, as box office records began to shatter from the first weekend of opening. *Fatal Attraction* became the fifth highest-grossing film of that year.

The side-effect of all this for Douglas was equally important. The restrained sexuality of his own two movies, *Romancing the Stone* and *The Jewel of the Nile*, had turned him into a reasonably bankable Hollywood star, praised and respected for his achievements both in front of and behind the camera. It would have been an overstatement, however, to say that he had yet matched the wicked zest of his father – and the comparisons were still unavoidable.

Had he gone along in the same vein, a few more pictures would have probably been his lot before he assigned himself completely to producing films for the rest of his life. Indeed, he was already making plans at the time to form a major new company with the publicly stated ambition of producing two or three pictures a year.

Fatal Attraction changed that. Douglas zoomed instantly and unexpectedly to join Hollywood's top five sex symbols. The explicit sex scenes shocked everyone, and his name became synonymous with the most talked about movie of the decade. Both he and Glenn Close became 'hot' in Hollywood.

Every major news magazine wanted to interview them, and producers and directors began flinging scripts at their doors. Nor did he try to play down the image, and the media, ever anxious to find a new angle, began looking to his own life for comparisons to what had happened in *Fatal Attraction*.

Douglas, ever the co-operative one when it came to jacking up a good story, kindly obliged in the mass of publicity interviews that followed: 'Oh, yeah . . . I sympathise with Dan Gallagher. His character is the closest to who I am. I remember first looking at the story and saying, "Wait a minute, that could be me!" I had to strip away at myself for that!'

While the role of Dan Gallagher introduced a massive change in Douglas's life, it was almost by accident. It came about, in Sherry Lansing's view, because Douglas himself was ready for it and the part offered him the opportunity, though even he did not anticipate the repercussions. He played Dan Gallagher to seek sympathy for the character: he had cheated on his wife, but he reacted with wounded vulnerability in the face of mounting terror.

He had at last been faced with a part that had depth and darkness, and that is what brought Michael Douglas out of himself, aided and abetted by director Adrian Lyne, whose boss he wasn't. As one close observer succinctly put it: 'As soon as Michael dispensed with the wholesome image that generated the theatrical impact of a glass of warm milk, his career curve shot off the graph.'

Fatal Attraction was important in that respect; it was the movie that made him a star. But it was Oliver Stone, waiting for Douglas on the set of *Wall Street*, who would make him a star actor and bring about the explosion of talent that Kirk Douglas had long ago predicted would happen.

16
No More Mr Nice Guy

In a way, Michael Douglas was the film world's equivalent to a thrusting Wall Street operator of the kind that became famous in the 1980s, and that is what Oliver Stone saw in him. He was light on the killer instinct; too much of a nice guy still. But gradually the cutting edge was beginning to show. He lived in a world of high finance, which was in many ways similar to Wall Street, where money is power. In Hollywood power is having choices, and choices are possible only with money and success. There are other parallels. No one has a long memory in either place. In Wall Street you are as good only as your last deal, and the same applies in Hollywood. And no one is happy about someone else's success.

Michael was a bit of a poseur and the power game provided the inspiration for his energy. The next big deal was always just around the corner. The Armani suit, the style, the looks, the glare or the stare that could melt any woman and scare any man: he was confident, sure enough, and peppered his sentences with manly expletives. The smart offices on Fifth Avenue and a personal assistant who was never quite sure which continent he had just come from ... A wife so young and beautiful that everyone in the business marvelled that he had been able to hang on to her, given his own behaviour, and a break-up imminent – if the gossips were to be believed – virtually since the day they were married ...

Michael Douglas was, in the common parlance of Sunset Boulevard, one cool dude, one smart babe. He could give the answer to a question before you'd even asked it. He could quote statistics like grosses and viewing figures and audience trends as if he had just swallowed *Variety*'s database. Symbols of his power were gathered around him: the houses, the cars, the travel.

But where was the malice, the anger, the flaring nostrils? Where was the knife ready to carve his initials on someone's back or, these days, front? Did all this even exist, either as a man or as an actor? Jack Lemmon once said that when Douglas gave you his best shot, it was like being hit with a thousand powder puffs.

Douglas had learned a lot since those days, hardened by a thousand smacks in the mouth by people he would remember when he got to the top. But basically, when it came to selling his image – even for *Fatal Attraction* – the publicity people, in consultation with his managers and producers on that picture, had gone for the soft option and promoted his most winsomely appealing 'vulnerability'.

Oliver Stone saw something else.

He saw Kirk Douglas and he saw what Kirk himself knew was present in his son's make-up and genes, but which needed drawing out. Stone, the controversial filmmaker of considerable commercial judgement and perception (*Platoon, Salvador, Born on the Fourth of July, JFK,* etc.), saw him as the slick-haired Gordon Gekko, the Wall Street wizard of the trading-floor who was the key figure in a story of 1980s greed and avarice which was about to explode on screen, entitled simply *Wall Street*. As Stone looked around for an actor to play that role, he drew up the usual list of potential stars and put Michael Douglas at the top.

Why?

Douglas had shown not the slightest hint of a mean streak in any of the characters he had played on screen. At the time Stone offered him the part, Stone had not even seen his performance in *Fatal Attraction* because the film had not yet been completed. He did not, when he chose Douglas, have the knowledge that *Fatal Attraction* would become one of the most successful movies of all time.

Stone based his judgement on a career that had at the time

reached the level of *The Jewel of the Nile*. As one of Douglas's aides pointed out with some frankness: 'That wasn't Oscar-winning, kick-'em-in-the-ass stuff, now was it?' No, it certainly wasn't. But Stone looked deeper, not so much at Douglas the actor as at Douglas the dealmaker: the ambitious man who flew by the seat of his pants; the wheeler-dealer who had single-handedly pulled off some of the most remarkable business coups in Hollywood history; the gambler who had taken chances with unknown actors, unknown directors and some very dodgy merchandise and bet his own judgement against failure . . . But not one of his own productions *had* failed, and that's what mattered.

Stone could run the career of his fictional character Gekko against Douglas's own as a producer and come up with something very similar – except for the mean streak. The trader Gekko is a millionaire; Douglas is too, many times over. The trader spends his days making as much money as he possibly can and will stop at nothing to achieve his ambitions; Douglas does the same, although he stays on the right side of the law and his goals are tempered by the addition of 'art' – the art of being an actor and filmmaker.

Money? Gamblers like Gekko and Douglas are actually not that interested in money once a sufficient amount of it has been acquired. They get their kicks and excitement from making it, going for the big deal and seeing it through to the end. The bottom line, cash at the bank, is just a way of keeping score.

They have the stunning wife, the luxury homes, the swimming-pools, the Ferraris and Porsches, the antiques and the art collections. Like Gekko, Douglas could smoke a pack of Marlboro in a morning, lighting up and blowing the smoke furiously into the air, pacing around the desk with his phone lodged between an arched shoulder and his ear, or sitting back in his chair and talking into the speaker-phone, gesticulating wildly as if the person on the other end could see him.

He'd stab out the cigarettes with eight or nine jabs at the ashtray and make a pattern in the ash, sometimes of a cross. They would both have several balls in the air at any one time, and would not stop until their goals had been achieved. They both had persistence.

And Gekko was ruthless which Douglas was not – yet.

So in several respects Michael Douglas was very similar to Gordon Gekko, the corporate sting-ray. But Douglas remained, above all, Mr Nice Guy, and that was the difference. He was so decent that even when he played the adulterer in *Fatal Attraction* he was still respected by his audience in the morning.

Oliver Stone saw in Douglas the capability that he could *become* Gekko. That was important, because the whole picture rested upon a performance of naturalistic realism. Stone selected Douglas not as the actor he was but as the businessman he was and the actor he could become: bitter, predatory, sharp as a razor, one very cool and nasty dude.

This was, as it all panned out, the real turning-point in Michael Douglas's career, the final breakthrough that put him into the multimillion dollar bracket as an actor.

A gecko is a 'small, terrestrial lizard that preys on insects and never blinks its eyes'. Gordon Gekko was thus aptly named as the arch-predator invented by Oliver Stone and his co-writer Stanley Weiser in their modern morality tale of Wall Street, a tale almost documentary in its conception and its detail of close-to-home financial skulduggery.

Stone's story was packed with dealmaking, insider-trading and life on the fastest track in New York, where it was all happening in real life, where people were making millions and collecting all the flash symbols of power in the go-for-it era of the 1980s. Though the story centres on the rise and fall of a young rookie in the broking business named Bud Fox, played by Charlie Sheen, Gekko is the movie's driving force.

Stone was gambling by choosing Douglas. 'It would not be truthful of me if I did not admit to having some reservations about casting him,' Stone recalls. 'Everyone I spoke to in Hollywood warned me against Michael. They said he couldn't act, that he was a producer more than an actor and would spend

After the previous years of hyper-activity, his lesser role in *Shining Through*, which starred Melanie Griffith, should have been a less demanding task. But troubled location work and mixed reviews left him wondering why he had bothered

Enter Sharon Stone and Michael Douglas's greatest hit, *Basic Instinct* which smashed box office records around the world (*Yardley Collection*)

Alone and proud, Michael Douglas accepts the awards and honours that
have been heaped upon him with a modesty that is topped only by his
reputation as Hollywood's Mr Nice Guy—on this occasion an award of
merit from the Italian film fraternity in Milan in 1993 (*Hulton Deutsch*)

all his time in his trailer on the phone doing deals.'

Stone arrived at his decision by studying Douglas's past performances, especially in *Romancing the Stone*, which he watched several times before he made up his mind. 'What I saw was a competent acting job, but I wasn't looking at that. Beneath the veneer, I saw a distinct edge that I thought could be developed,' Stone recalls.

Stone had met Douglas only twice, at social occasions, and he was swayed by his presence as a person more than as an actor: 'I actually thought his acting was soft and formulaic. We had to change that and he had to adapt to our style of moviemaking. I was planning a good deal of hand-held camera work, just a few inches from his face, and there were long monologues. I don't think he had ever worked with anyone like me before.'

Michael's dormant qualities were in the Douglas genes – fiery, eye-blazing reactions and a mischievous, edgy sexuality, like a man who would require his partner to indulge in adventurous sex (though in *Wall Street* this would not be explored). Oliver Stone had never seen these qualities displayed in any previous performance by Douglas, but he was sure they existed.

It was just as Kirk Douglas had once predicted to his son: 'One of these days somebody is going to show you what a prick you really are.' It had happened just like that for Kirk. His own career languished in nice-guy parts until 1947, when he portrayed a ruthless lovesick gambler in *Build My Gallows High*.

Another aspect of all this tends to be overlooked: Michael had never had the kind of training where he could draw up these emotions from within himself. Most of his contemporaries had gone through the acting mill, as had his father, training at various establishments, mostly in New York.

The most naturalistic actors came from the same background as Brando, Karl Malden, Robert De Niro and Paul Newman, all having been weaned on the Stanislavsky Method, which is all about using one's inner self, drawing inspiration from within. James Dean, for example, used to go into a foetal position before starting a major scene. The director always knew when he was ready, because he would let out a great moaning wail as he prepared to stand up and go into his lines. Many actors of the 1970s and 1980s – though fewer now – attended classes and lectures long after they had become established actors. Paul Newman remained in contact with the Actors' Studio for most of his career, and Robert De Niro was, and still is, constantly returning to his acting roots.

Michael Douglas was, paradoxically, a superstar in terms of Hollywood values. He had made huge money for himself and the studios as a producer. He had launched several major actors, actresses and directors. Yet he languished personally in a limited repertoire of acting techniques which showed as blandness. Whatever emotions and edge he possessed had never been exploited because he had been playing largely in his own movies as an 'accompaniment' to the likes of Jane Fonda and Kathleen Turner. He was very good as the sidekick and as a foil for others to bounce off. But his style had barely changed since his days in *The Streets of San Francisco*, when he was Karl Malden's gofer.

Fatal Attraction changed that, and gave him the challenge at last to tap into human emotions, such as love, fear, hate and loathing. But at the time this performance had not been viewed and could not be considered.

Douglas read the script of *Wall Street* and was thrilled. *Fatal Attraction* apart, it was the first major dramatic role he had ever been offered in his twenty-three-year career. The dialogue was exceptional, and some of his monologues were long and challenging. The whole characterisation appealed to him, but it also worried him. Though normally confident, he had never seemed a hundred per cent certain about his ability as an actor. He was no Brando or De Niro in that regard; he was more like a high school dropout fighting for a position among university graduates with a clutch of honours degrees.

His training, as we have seen, was of a very cursory nature compared to that of other major actors of his day. For Douglas, the *Wall Street* script presented the ultimate challenge. He could see it was the one film that would make him or perhaps break him. The day of reckoning had arrived: he could either put his finger up to the many detractors of his acting talents or prove them right once and for all.

He also went into *Wall Street* without realising the kind of mentality he would be battling against in Oliver Stone – and an eyeball-to-eyeball battle would develop, as Stone cajoled and goaded him towards the right performance, the visually correct portrayal of the character he had himself created in his mind's eye.

The two men, strong in character in different ways, were actually like two gladiators circling each other. Stone had the upper hand because he was the boss and giving the orders. Douglas did not react well to the director's methods. There were disagreements from the beginning. 'I thought he was a lazy actor, and I told him so' said Stone. 'He came to the picture with that Hollywood attitude of "Well, if it's not right, we can shoot it again". I don't work that way. I shoot fast, and do not leave much margin for error. He did not cotton on to that for some time, and we had some problems. Yes, and I did get tough with him.'

Stone taunted Douglas: 'Where the hell's your father? I want the kid of Kirk Douglas in this movie. You're a wimp.' In response, Douglas would remind Stone of Stone's career before he became controversial with *Salvador*, mischievously mentioning the director's 1981 horror *The Hand*, an appalling remake of *The Beast with Five Fingers*.

To all on the set, Stone seemed to deliberately antagonise Douglas. There were several explosions of temperament. Some days Douglas was afraid that the part would overpower him, that he might not get on top of it. Then came the realisation that Stone was goading him and pushing him to what might well be the performance of his life.

Until then he had thought Stone was just a 'bastard' in his directorial style. But he began to appreciate Stone's technique one day when he was confronted by a particularly difficult monologue that he thought he had spoken well. In the run-through, Stone appeared not to be happy and made his displeasure quite clear to Douglas.

Douglas retorted testily: 'Christ, if you're unhappy, let's reshoot it.'

Stone looked at him coldly, straight in the eye, and said: 'John Ford never reshot.' Then he turned on his heel and walked away.

Worried by this confrontation, Douglas broke the rule of a lifetime as an actor and went to view the daily rushes, the unedited film of the day's shoot. He would normally never go to see them unless there was a problem, and Stone seemed to be saying that there was.

He could see nothing wrong with his performance, and went back to Stone and told him so: 'I think it is pretty good,' said Douglas.

'It is, isn't it?' Stone replied.

'You fucker,' Douglas stormed.

Later, in his trailer, Douglas reflected on the situation and decided it was Stone's way of saying: 'Let me see whether you can cut it.' He was brutally honest, a director some actors might not like initially, though would end up having a lot of respect for. Douglas reckoned he had to keep reminding himself: 'Hey, this guy *offered* you the part – you didn't apply for it.'

Gradually, Douglas saw the Gekko mystique developing in himself, which was Stone's aim, and he as good as said to the director, as Gekko would have done in a similar situation, 'OK, if you want to go eyeball-to-eyeball, that's fine by me!'

The toughening-up process that Stone initiated to bring out Douglas's dormant streak worked. Douglas also drew upon his experience of producing movies to realise that 'revenge is wonderful . . . Gekko thrived on the energy of anybody who's ever crossed him. He cherishes and holds grudges; it gives him the fuel to keep going. I know that feeling, too, getting turned down and rejected. I'd always try to be as congenial about it as possible, but at the same time I used this in a positive way. It gave me stamina, endurance.'

Underneath, he was still Mr Nice Guy – 'totally charming, so don't waste your time trying to find out he's not,' said the movie's young star, Charlie Sheen. That was something for Sheen to admit, because Douglas stole the picture from him.

Sheen's role was the ambitious young Bud Fox looking for a fast lane to the top in the Wall Street trading-house that employs him. He's on the telephone, calling clients, dealing in second-hand advice and dreaming of making it big. Gordon Gekko, the successful older man, becomes Fox's hero because he apparently has it all and the kid wants to get into his dealing circle.

Michael Douglas's Gekko is slick, sinister and scary. He is threatening and at times ready to tear out someone's throat while keeping an air of appealing charm. There were plenty of real-life models around at the time. Gekko agrees to give Bud an audience, seeing in him a younger version of himself, someone he can use. Fox is so hungry for a killing that he will do anything, and so becomes drawn into one of Gekko's shark-like schemes. Anxious to impress, Bud passes on some confidential information gleaned from his father, a blue-collar aircraft mechanic and union leader – played by Charlie's real-life father, Martin Sheen – who becomes pitted against Gekko for his son's soul.

Ultimately, when he has enjoyed success and a taste of the high life, Bud becomes disillusioned and inquires 'How many powerboats can you ski behind? How much is enough?'

He had missed the point, which is not about money or materialistic pleasures. Doing the deal, screwing the next man is the point of the system. Stone's triumph in the movie was to delve into the financial details of Gekko's world and still make them understandable to the average cinema audience.

The real target of Stone's film was not the financial wheeler-dealers who broke the law, and whose day of reckoning the movie prophetically forecast, but the system that allowed them to prosper. There were a number of identifiable similarities with reality. Douglas's nine-minute monologue on 'greed is good', which he made to shareholders of a company he was planning to take over, echoed an infamous speech by the discredited billionaire investor, Ivan Boesky, who was arrested in November 1986 for illegal insider-trading.

Boesky himself had declared: 'Greed is good . . . greed works . . . greed is right.' It *was* for him, until the authorities caught up with him, stripped him of large sums of his wealth, gave him a prison sentence and barred him for life from trading in US securities. He was one of many.

Deep down, Stone's movie was about modern values, a critique of the financial community, using a traditional and simplistic Hollywood plot about good versus evil, the good guys and the love interests.

It was a seductive if over-the-top portrait of Wall Street extroverts and the pace of their city life, a scenario that could be witnessed at virtually every financial centre around the world at the time. Gekko was the typical asset-stripping manipulator, swooping around the corporate scene carving up the spoils of big market killings. Sheen himself was not grasping enough in a script that used him as the pawn of first evil then good, and his character became lost *en route*.

Douglas, on the other hand, was faced with no such diversion; nor, oddly enough, was he to be personified as the 'evil' element. His was a role that allowed the utmost development of the most ruthless of men, and in that Oliver Stone and Douglas himself scored brilliantly in their drawing of the character. Douglas's portrayal was so good that Gekko actually became a hero of some sections of Wall Street: the term 'Gekko' fell into popular use and the character became a fashion leader too, his familiar braces suddenly appearing on the backs of young men all over the trading-floors.

Douglas had done his homework, physically and mentally. He had lost ten pounds in weight to fit the sleek image. He had studied the clippings files on some of the men like Gekko who abounded at the time. His Gekko had charm, wit and style as well as a killer instinct, and that is what Oliver Stone had sought.

In hindsight, Stone saw casting Douglas as an interesting exercise in locating an actor who was ripe for change and to bring that actor to the point where he sees the change as not only possible but desirable. One of the more exciting aspects of directing good actors, he said, was to find something new in them and 'bringing them to the boil'.

When the film was made, Douglas was frank enough to admit that for too long he had been playing himself in movies, even, to a degree, in *Fatal Attraction*. He explained that it was one of the reasons why he was successful in that movie – because he envisaged himself in exactly the same position as the fictional character. In *Wall Street* it was different, and as different as it had ever been: he had had to create the character – to be an actor – though in a way the character already existed within him.

The movie itself was a major commercial hit which received considerable critical dissection in view of what was happening in the financial world. Stone's overall concept would be heavily attacked by the establishment and by Wall Street itself, which saw it basically as a story resting on the Ivan Boesky case – 'and we are not all like him'.

Fate and the Douglas luck made a remarkable combination just as they had done when Douglas released *The China Syndrome* and when *Fatal Attraction* caught the attention of the public in the mounting fear of AIDS.

Not long before *Wall Street* was released, the 1980s, as personified by the financial world, ended early – on Black Monday, to be precise, 19 October 1987, when the Stock Market crashed and billions of dollars were lost all around the world. On that day, as thousands of small investors lost their shirts and bigger ones their yachts and mansions, Michael Douglas's career went further off the graph and interest in his character creation in *Wall Street* was absolutely assured.

And so 1987 was Douglas's year of coming out. Douglas had starred in the year's two most successful films. Within the space of a few months he became, temporarily, Hollywood's most acclaimed actor.

Fatal Attraction had relaunched him, but it was the brilliance of his performance as Gekko that brought the recognition of a latent talent that many thought, at one stage, was beyond him. And it was this role that figured when the time for the Academy nominations came around.

Fatal Attraction had picked up five nominations, but Douglas did not figure in the list. Glenn Close was nominated for Best Actress, Anne Archer for Best Supporting Actress, and the film picked up nominations for Best Picture, Best Screenplay and Best Editing. In a year of intense competition, none of the *Fatal Attraction* nominees won the coveted Oscar.

Wall Street, on the other hand, was credited with only one nomination – Douglas himself for Best Actor. He was lined up against four other strong contenders: his old pal Jack Nicholson (for *Ironweed*), William Hurt (*Broadcast News*), Robin Williams (*Good Morning, Vietnam*) and Marcello Mastroianni (*Dark Eyes*).

The winner is . . . Michael Douglas for *Wall Street*.

Twelve years after he had picked up his Oscar for producing the best film of 1975, *One Flew Over the Cuckoo's Nest*, Douglas was back to receive acclaim from his peers as an actor.

The media, in its coverage of the clan Douglas, assumed that because Michael Douglas had survived his father's fame he was not touched by it. This was never really true. The assumption lay in the belief that the whole family had a history of relative normality in Hollywood terms, i.e. not many marital break-ups and none of the familiar tales of tragedy, suicides, hard-line drug abuse, alcoholism or general bitterness which have afflicted many of the 'star' families down the years.

Michael Douglas represents something of a total departure to norm in that respect. Friends put this down to the genes of his mother and the early influence of his stepfather, Bill Darrid, a kind but firm man whose life was uncomplicated and slow compared with the frenetic activity of Kirk's. But Michael Douglas was also a man of contradictions which seemed to encompass elements drawn from all sides of his upbringing. His public image was of a soft, gentle and polished manner with the elegance of his mother, well preened and polite.

The private Michael Douglas had the language of a naval rating and a burning fire of revenge for early hurts and rejections, revenge which he stored up in his brain but never had the ability to administer. Oliver Stone had had to draw upon that rough and dangerous edge he inherited from his father; the elegance was his mother's gift.

That Kirk's influence touched Michael more than the pundits

realised was shown in his Oscar acceptance speech. Such speeches are notoriously emotional, but Michael Douglas's was made more poignant by references to his father. Kirk had starred in more than seventy films, including several major, unrepeatable movie classics, and was one of the few Hollywood 'greats' never to win an Oscar.

Now his son had been awarded two. Michael spoke with a touch of revenge about winning his Oscar in a role that not many people thought he could play. He went on to dedicate the award to his family, who had always been so supportive, 'particularly my father, who I don't think ever missed one of my college productions . . . and for helping his son step out of his shadow. I'll be eternally grateful to you, dad.'

That night, after watching the award ceremonies at home on television, Kirk hosted a huge celebration party for the clan Douglas. The emotions can barely be described of a family so completely bound up in the movie business and to whom these prizes really matter. Suffice to say that, when Michael walked in, Kirk rushed forward and hugged him, kissed him on the lips and held aloft the golden statue that had eluded himself for forty years.

The shadow in which Michael had walked was finally cast aside. Michael had achieved something rare, virtually unheard of in Hollywood, of matching – if not surpassing – his father's fame.

Having followed Kirk to the profession, he always seemed intent on leaving a different set of footprints. In the end he made his own name through expanding upon two characteristics that were the trademarks of his father – rage and intensity.

There was an eerily familiar pattern between the lives of father and son, the only difference being that Michael's acclaim came much later in his life. Kirk himself spotted the similarities one day soon after the awards ceremonies. They were talking about fatherhood, and Kirk asked Michael what kind of father he had been. He had asked the question many times before, but seemed to want to check up on the answer every now and again.

Michael said Kirk was 'a loony ... and so uptight, you were always jumping from one picture to another'.

Kirk laughed. 'You mean, just like you ... right now.'

17

Long Days, Lonely Nights

Kirk Douglas had picked up on a very good point. Though Michael regularly said he would not make the mistakes of his father in doing so many pictures and spending half his life away on location, he had done exactly that for years. He could certainly afford to slow up, and that was the promise he made to Diandra when he finished *Wall Street*. She had been patient for long enough over many things. She needed a commitment from him. The question was, would she get one? And if she did, could he possibly honour it?

He had made an enormous amount of money in recent times. His salary from and equity interest in *Fatal Attraction* had earned him millions, as indeed would his fee for *Wall Street*. One estimate of his fortune at the time was put at in excess of $60 million, based on his profits slice of the movies he had been involved in to date. The success story was an incredible one, considering that until recent years not many people were interested in hiring him as an actor.

In the aftermath of his 1987 career explosion, he was the hottest actor around. He let it be known openly that anyone wanting his services for a film would be talking of $10 million-plus. He had already been approached by big business conglomerates owning Hollywood studios with job offers to head his own studio. Three times this had happened. He rejected all of them. It was a tempting thought – to become a modern mogul – but modern moguls tend not to stay in their jobs too long. They are far too vulnerable to the failings of others and too stifled by the economics of the parent company.

Hollywood's turmoil of the 1980s, when the executive shuffle went on by the week, offered little attraction to Douglas. He could now earn with one picture what it would take a mogul five years to amass in salary, ending up with a bunch of stock and a pay-off.

He would also lose his freedom, his friends and the ability to make choices – and the latter was the mark of real power in Hollywood. There were other, more personal reasons why he had to refuse. It would have meant moving back to Los Angeles, which he and Diandra did not want to do – at least, not then. Anyway, he had made a deal with his wife that after finishing *Wall Street* he would take a year off.

He had also pledged that, where possible, he would complete two pictures back to back and then take a long break. And this time he needed a break and some quality time, as the new saying went, with his wife and son. The darkened strips under his eyes, the lines around his face and the taut jaw were the signs of exhaustion and pressure from virtually two years' non-stop work. He would talk about being the consummate homebody, to whom heaven was relaxing with a cold beer, with his two dogs, a Russian wolfhound and an Irish terrier, at his feet, and his family around him, but the reality was quite different.

His schedule for 1987 into 1988 shows that though his oft-spoken intentions to relax were undoubtedly well meant, the demands of his professional life were such that the pressures were on-going. His involvement with the Jaffe–Lansing partnership was already giving birth to a new project, which he would co-produce, called *Black Rain*, and off in the distance Danny DeVito was preparing to bring himself, Douglas and Kathleen Turner together again in his black comedy, *War of the Roses*.

The publicity demands of *Fatal Attraction* and *Wall Street* had consumed literally dozens of hours of his time, because he makes a point of being accessible to the media around the launch of each movie; the advantages for an actor with a profit-share deal are obvious. He had snatched some time off during the autumn of 1987, prior to the launch of *Wall Street*, but by December he was heavily into the promotion of *Wall Street*. On a more personal note, he allowed a writer and photographer from *Life* magazine to prepare an 'at home with the Douglases' in January.

Ahead of him was a series of meetings with the Jaffe–Lansing team and later with Columbia, now under the presidency of his old friend Dawn Steel. Steel was another of the new breed of all-powerful Hollywood women. She had begun her career marketing designer toilet-paper and *Penthouse* magazine tie-ins. She moved into the film world in the 1970s as director of merchandising at Paramount, rising to become president of production.

In 1987, Steel became the first woman in Hollywood to oversee production and marketing when she was invited to become president of Columbia in the wake of a reshuffle which had led to the departure of Britian's David Puttnam. Among the people on her list of friends and associates to invite for breakfast was Michael Douglas.

Steel wanted to re-establish a Columbia contact with Douglas, who, it will be recalled, had left the studio in 1983 after a bitter three-year relationship during which he had not produced a single picture. The problems at Columbia, hit by a run of flops inherited by Puttnam, had barely improved. Even as Steel took over, there were rumours that the company was being sold off by its parent, Coca Cola. 'So let me tell you how difficult it was to bring in new talent,' said Steel. 'It was virtually impossible with all the talk around. It's very hard to say to a creative community, "Come and work with me. I will nurture you and support you and provide you with an environment where you can make movies." '

By the spring of 1988 talks were under way which would eventually lead to a new alliance. For the time being, Douglas had other fish to fry.

A screenplay for the tough cop movie, *Black Rain*, was already being finalised, and Stanley Jaffe and Sherry Lansing were in the final stages of negotiating backing for the film. They hoped to start filming by the late summer. Douglas was put on stand-by for a long stint in Japan, where most of the movie was set.

Meanwhile, he was wanted in Europe for the publicity of both *Fatal Attraction* and *Wall Street*, and was booked to attend the Cannes Film Festival in May followed by a round of meetings in

Paris and London. It was while he was in Cannes that he met a twenty-four-year-old Italian B-movie starlet named Loredana Romito, a thick-lipped and pouting brunette who was discovered by Federico Fellini and appeared in his movie, *The Interview*.

At the time Romito was promoting her appearance in an Italian film called *Fatal Temptation*, which was screened at Cannes; as everyone could see, the film was a rather obvious rip-off of *Fatal Attraction*. When Romito and Douglas both attended one of the lavish promotional parties for which Cannes is renowned, Romito secured an introduction.

A photographer just happened to be on hand to capture a shot of the two of them together, Michael in elegant tuxedo and Loredana, attired in a low-cut black dress nestling close, with her arms around his shoulder. Such a photograph, of course, soon made its way into the American press. Loredana says that their encounter at Cannes was brief, only two days, but claims it was 'wonderful' and that Douglas kept in touch. During the next six months they met again, first in Paris and, towards the end of the summer, in Rome and later in Japan.

Only Douglas himself, as the other party, can confirm whether or not they had an 'affair', as Loredana claimed. To the trained eye of any Hollywood watcher, such a claim would bring rather blatant publicity advantages to herself. Nothing leaked out at the time, apart from the photograph, which could be dismissed as taken at a purely innocent meeting. However, it was no secret among his closest friends at the time that Douglas's marriage was once again passing through stormy waters. He and Diandra separated for three months in 1988 and he had recently gone alone for a holiday in Hawaii.

The focus upon Michael and Diandra, particularly in the wake of *Fatal Attraction*, had been intense, more so than at any time during their marriage. Douglas, now a major star, was an obvious target for the sexy innuendoes of life matching art, the 'other woman' syndrome that Glenn Close had so dramatically portrayed to his Dan Gallagher. The American tabloids kept him under fairly close observation.

When the headline-hitting publicity for *Wall Street* followed, along with the emerging picture of Michael's schedule of work, meetings and travel for the coming months, Diandra found the whole situation intolerable. 'She had been fairly patient with Michael,' relates one of their friends, 'during the years when he was fighting to get his various projects off the ground, but then he began making very serious money and just became busier and busier. She had to develop her own interests or she would have gone crazy. She found enjoyment in her social activities and work for charities in New York which embraced the upper echelons of society – she was the youngest-ever hostess for a New York City Ballet annual benefit. Michael went to these soirées pretty much under protest, but the whole scene had developed where he was doing his thing, and she was doing hers and never the twain shall meet. They had also just come through a fairly emotional period when Diandra suffered a miscarriage. She became quite depressed about their marriage, and was especially fed up with seeing constant references to herself and Cameron in media interviews he did in which he spoke about "family values" and how important family life was to him, and to society at large. Honestly, that was a bit of a joke simply because he could not stop working, or flirting. He kept promising quality time, but it never happened, not really.'

Their time apart in the early months of 1988 jolted him. Even so, there was nothing he could do about the immediate future, which involved a further long, enforced separation through his work. In September he was scheduled to begin five months' filming in Japan, and then, immediately on his return, he would go straight into Danny DeVito's movie, which was scheduled for filming over five months in Los Angeles.

After that, there would be at least two months of post-production work on *Black Rain*, publicity interviews and then whatever was required in the post-production of *War of the Roses*. The days, weeks and months could be ticked off on the calendar as an absolute commitment, unavoidable, unbreakable. As his brother Joel observed: 'How can any relationship survive being parted for ten months?'

That, as Diandra acerbically observed, meant another year of their life given over to sixteen-hour days, with no foreseeable gap in between. Was there any point in staying together? Douglas himself was occasionally questioned on the subject and admitted that the problems in their marriage, the separations and the comings together, were largely the result of the imbalance between his work and private life. 'I know it must be horrible being married to me,' he said, 'because I work, work, work and my family takes second place. It's an all-consuming, obsessive business. I also get a lot of attention from women, and that can't be easy for Diandra. Generally, she copes with that pretty well, but there are occasions when time apart can be constructive.'

He did not, however, appear to accept all the blame. But his accessibility and openness to the journalists who came to call to discover the inner workings of Michael Douglas, superstar, during the early months of 1988 could only have fuelled the delicacy of the situation.

A fairly typical example was an interview he gave for the respected American monthly, *Ladies' Home Journal*, in June 1988. He spoke firmly about realising that the only thread left in society was the family, and he tried his best to provide a strong base of love and security. That was fine, but a touch eyebrow-raising in view of the circumstances.

He also made comments which seemed pointedly directed to the view that a woman's place was in the home waiting for the husband to come home. He told writer Barbara Paskin: 'It is a very difficult time for women right now. It's a struggle to be superwoman, successful career woman, superwife and supermom. If you don't succeed at all of them, you're considered a failure. The women's movement has been effected in terms of equal rights, but it puts undue pressure on women's personal lives and takes away the art of homemaking as a valid alternative.'

Was he talking from personal experience? We would never discover, because the question wasn't asked. But for Diandra it was one more piece of misplaced verbal diarrhoea from the talkative Michael and she was furious.

The preparation for *Black Rain* took longer than normal. By midsummer 1988 he was already deeply involved in the characterisation, and had spent time researching with the homicide detectives with the New York City police. He also committed himself to a hefty muscle-building training programme. Whereas he was required to be slim and sleek in his last picture, this one required a tough, strong physical presence, and he had to build up his body with weight training.

The role represented another massive change in Michael Douglas's screen persona. *Fatal Attraction* had brought him attention in the arena of a middle-class environment with ample sexual exploration. *Wall Street* uncovered his darker capabilities. *Black Rain* was different again. It was a tough, violent, all-action movie in which Douglas would portray a mean, maverick, racist homicide detective named Nick Conklin.

The role, however, could not be categorised as simply that of a gritty policeman; his cop had no qualms about pocketing drug money. So it was surprising that the New York police were ready to co-operate. Were they told of the slant? Douglas said they were, taking the view that the police had to deal with reality more than anyone else. Many homicides were drug-related, and the money involved, often found at the scene of the murders, was so large that the temptation always existed for a cop to put a few thousand dollars in his pocket.

In doing his research for the film, Douglas worked with a detective aged fifty and nearing retirement. The detective was divorced and had two children in college, yet he had no home of his own and often slept in the locker-room at the police station. Douglas took account of this in his portrayal of the New York cop and in his attitude to the film as a whole. There was an underlying social comment beneath the violence and the spectacle.

The script was filled with searing emotions and very physical scenes which would provide Douglas with the opportunity to expand again his acting dimensions. From his point of view, *Black Rain* brought a sharp contrast to anything that he had done before, and was a role that at the end of the day might well have sent confusing messages to his fans.

The film opens in New York, where Michael Douglas and his

partner, played by Andy Garcia, witness a murder in a restaurant and arrest the killer, a Japanese mob leader named Sato. When they are asked to escort him to Japan, the story explodes into an odyssey of contemporary conflicts set against a Japanese background.

In theory, *Black Rain* was a cops-and-robbers thriller whose difference to the many others of that decade would be its location and its exploration of the social and cultural gulf between east and west. But such an exploration turned out to be one of the lesser of the film's achievements, and basically the film came down to Douglas ranting and raging and delivering such lines to his partner as 'Until you sign off on this, dickhead, his ass is mine'. It was the kind of dialogue that was not entirely unfamiliar in late-night movies on television.

Michael Douglas seemed to know it, and his facial expressions at times appeared to have a rather wincing appearance. But he gave a spirited performance that overcame the shortcomings of the script. His character is the ultimate protagonist of the Dirty Harry-type cop devoid of feelings, except anger and paranoia when he is confronted by the intricacies of the alien Japanese culture.

Conklin's problems begin when the three characters arrive in Osaka, where Sato escapes immediately, leaving Douglas and Garcia facing a morass of local bureaucracy. Against all odds, Douglas insists on getting his man, regardless of the ethnic barriers. The clash of cultures is ever present as Douglas becomes closely tied to a Japanese detective played by Ken Takakura.

There were numerous sub-plots to *Black Rain* which came neither from the script nor from the actors. The movie's particularly unique feel derived from the influence of its director, Ridley Scott. Though by no means a mainstream director, Scott has become one of the most controversial – and imitated – stylists of visual effects in modern cinema. From his British beginnings at the Royal College of Art, Scott was one of the few to throw off the shackles and the cottage-industry constraints imposed by British film, ranging through commercials to television and into filmmaking.

In movies like *The Duellists, Alien, Blade Runner* and *Someone to Watch Over Me*, Scott established his credentials in directorial experiments. He created strong, forceful characters and generally pursued a theme of examining social divides. Douglas found him difficult to follow at times, frustratingly ambiguous about his intentions and yet intriguing in his overall approach, particularly in his camerawork. Douglas was filmed in some superb action shots and hand-held camera close-ups which made sure no member of the audience was allowed to be distracted for a second.

Douglas's involvement in the production side was more in consultation, with Lansing and Jaffe seeking his observations at the end of a day's filming. His input came in post-production and promotion, by which time Lansing was ebullient and confident: 'I've got a movie with substance, hot and sexy, and Michael Douglas is a huge star.'

Hollywood never misses an opportunity to sell a film, and as it turned out this one would need some selling. The moody, urban landscapes of modern Japan created a startling pictorial kaleidoscope of dark, arty backdrops illuminated with flashing neon lights amid a shroud of swirling steam and mist. But at times they were all too far removed from the introspective vision of modern American audiences, which are renowned for their general lack of interest in the mysteries of far-off lands.

Discomfort about the mounting Japanese influence on American commercial and business life (not least in Hollywood) was also gnawing away at contemporary American society.

It did not necessarily inspire empathy among the all-important home audience to see a racist New York cop darting through a murky labyrinth of Japanese psychoanalysis and observing, at the movie's most basic level, the bonding of the American detective with his Japanese counterpart.

Black Rain was only moderately successful in America, in spite of a massive publicity campaign featuring spectacular, high-action promotional clips which were given a good airing. It fared far better in the rest of the world and, ironically, in Japan. For Douglas, it represented another successful extension to his repertoire.

Homeward bound, he slumped exhausted into the comfort of a

first-class seat on the jumbo jet. He had been in Japan for almost five months, with only a few brief excursions and a thousand long-distance phone calls home. Filming *Black Rain* had overrun by almost six weeks. Now he had just five days to make peace with Diandra and renew his acquaintance with his son before going to Hollywood to team up again with Kathleen Turner and Danny DeVito for their next appearance together in *War of the Roses*.

Other pressing matters required his attention, too. He had finally agreed to commit his production arm to Dawn Steel's Columbia at a time, coincidentally, when the Japanese electronics giant Sony was stalking the studio. Sony would eventually make its bid, and Columbia became part of its empire later that year.

Douglas was one of the talents Dawn Steel had long wanted aboard, though ironically her own position looked rather more tenuous than it had eighteen months before when she had first approached him. True, a new air of optimism fluttered through the debt-laden studio, and the talk was of new money and unlimited development potential when Sony took control. But who would be at the helm? There were still some question marks.

Douglas formed a new company called Stonebridge Entertainment specifically to 'get back into bed with Columbia'. His old company, Bigstick, established years earlier for the production of *One Flew Over the Cuckoo's Nest*, had since diversified into property and real estate.

He appointed a new partner for Stonebridge, Rick Bieber, the thrustingly successful young head of production at Home Box Office Pictures, noted for his television biography of Nelson Mandela. Bieber is a fast, smooth talker, a modern operator in Hollywood. Film production was just the start, he said, and once under way the company would move into other areas of entertainment, notably video production, music publishing and recording, and would give a chance to new talent. He hired a staff of eight, plus four contracted retainers, and they all moved into some smart smoked-glass offices in Hollywood.

Overnight, Stonebridge took on the air of a mini-conglomerate. Businesses like that need close attention and a regular supply of capital. The company certainly had the wherewithal and, between them, the expertise.

Columbia would contribute up to $1 million a year to the company's 'housekeeping' and would fund the development costs of the projects submitted by Douglas and approved by the studio's executives. But that would cover only part of Stonebridge's operating costs; Michael would have to finance the rest personally.

Apart from Bieber's plans for non-movie activities, Stonebridge's declared intention was to produce two movies a year in the medium-budget range of between $15–20 million, which would need a return of around $60 million to make a profit. Columbia, for its part, was guaranteed right of first refusal.

A number of projects were proposed for development, the first announced immediately. It would be *Flatliners*, a horror movie starring Julia Roberts and Kiefer Sutherland, with a budget at the top end of their range and Douglas committing himself as co-producer. The picture would be ready for release in 1990, which meant that he would go straight into the film after completing *War of the Roses*.

Actor, producer, superstar – and now plans to become a major player in the back yard of Columbia. Diandra received the news with mixed emotions, but was really dismayed. His friends wondered why he was bothering. And even his father told him: 'You are a big star now – an actor, not a producer.'

Whenever was he going to slow down? How much is enough?

18
In Danny's War

The summer of 1989 was long and hot and the smog hung low over Los Angeles. Michael Douglas spent a lot of it in a shabby, claustrophobic caravan which served as his dressing-room, smoking pack after pack of Marlboro, near the Beverly Hills studios of 20th Century-Fox waiting for his turn in front of Danny DeVito's cameras.

He was restless and edgy because the work on the movie was intense and psychologically disturbing. *War of the Roses*, though a black comedy, was heavy on the emotions, and the team would have to convince everyone in the pre-publicity that it was not *Romancing the Stone* part three. There was no connection at all.

Michael was doing the picture for Danny on Danny's second directorial effort for the big screen (the first was *Throw Momma from the Train* with Billy Crystal). The fee was nowhere near the money he could now command, but, even so, he and Kathleen Turner do not come cheap even for friends. The three stars will each be paid a fee and will also take a cut of the gross profits – so the film has to do well.

One of the peculiarities of Hollywood filmmaking where the costometer ticks away in millions, is that the comforts for the stars are not always what they might be. And the Fox studios themselves are tucked away on a small corner of their former huge site, where, in the past, some of the classic movies of all time were made.

The Fox downfall began with the first $1 million fee ever paid to a movie star – Elizabeth Taylor, in *Cleopatra*. The film marked the beginning of the end for Fox of the so-called Golden Age. To keep the production alive for what was then the most expensive film ever, and to stave off imminent bankruptcy, Fox began selling off its back lot for development. Eventually, the studio ended up with less than a twentieth of its original landholding.

Fox was now in the hands of Rupert Murdoch, and had since been shunted into the last piece of ground on its once-magnificent estate, on Pico Boulevard, in the shadow of the few skyscrapers built in the earthquake zone of Los Angeles. Inside the plush office suites are the hundreds of ancillary people who feed off Hollywood – the dealmakers, the lawyers, the movie packagers, the agents, the brokers . . .

There are a dozen other classifications hidden away behind the smoked-glass windows, swivelling in their chairs and bellowing into speaker-phones and watching their miniskirted secretaries walk up and down.

In the shadow of this activity Michael Douglas drew hard on another Marlboro in the smoky caravan and waited to be called. His part was the husband in the fictional marital traumas of Barbara and Oliver Rose, a charming, middle-class couple whose separation after seventeen years of marriage develops into such a terrifying and painful affair that both he and Kathleen Turner were nervous of the emotional blackness of the comedy. It was funny and tragic and would strike a raw nerve with too many people, not least Douglas himself, and demanded the kind of intensity that was difficult to shake off after a day's work.

In fact, Turner had been worried about the script from the beginning; although she had promised Danny she would do it, she backed off after her first reading. She thought her character was so unbelievably malicious that she could not play it. Even Douglas scratched his chin for a while before agreeing. If Turner had rejected the part, it is unlikely that he would have taken the film, either.

He recognised immediately what eventually became evident in the film itself – that the existing relationship between the main actors is what made the film possible. 'It was one of those chemical things,' said Douglas, 'that neither of us can explain. We have a mutual understanding of the way we each operate and it just seems to work without too much effort.'

He reckoned, as did Danny DeVito when he first read the script, that their comic rapport was established among audiences and would be appreciated in the new film. Even so, Turner took some convincing. Twice she turned DeVito down, and there were long discussions between them. In the end she agreed to do the film if the ages of the Roses' children were increased. She could not agree to submitting any young child to the scenes of marital mayhem called for in the script.

Danny DeVito co-stars in and narrates the movie, as well as directing it with considerable style and confidence. He appears as the lawyer for Oliver Rose; as such, he provides the Hitchcockian-style narration of the story, taking the 'war' between the two Roses through its violent, screaming exchanges until it reaches its deadly climax. It was one of those deeply demanding scripts where the two leading characters had to psych themselves into an emotional state each day before filming began.

Turner recalled that she and Douglas made a pact. At the beginning of each day, after they had put on their make-up, they would give each other a hug and then go out and fight their fight with each other. At the end of each day they would give themselves another hug and try to calm their emotions over a drink and a pasta at Danny's and Michael's favourite Italian restaurant on Pico Boulevard. They enjoyed the place so much that Michael and Danny actually put on weight during the making of the picture.

The movie itself is an over-the-top, blacker-than-black comedy which should have carried a health warning for all animal-lovers and couples of a nervous disposition or whose marriage or relationship was in a fragile state. The lives of the well-heeled Washington couple are torn apart as their separation develops into the most acrimonious of divorce proceedings, a messy catastrophe in comparison to their seemingly perfect, well-ordered existence. The Douglas character refuses to move out of the house and abandon his children, and the couple attempts to share the property while pursuing their legal parting.

They make life hell for each other. He accidentally runs over her cat while making an angry dash from the house; she attacks his beloved Morgan sports car and wrecks it; he urinates all over the fish dish she has spent days preparing for her socially important dinner-party; she serves him dog pâté in a scene reminiscent of *Whatever Happened to Baby Jane?* . . . and so on.

Each sequence started out as a scene of domestic upheaval that most could identify with. But it was the extreme and exaggerated proportions that provided the horror; a kind of shouting match between politicians that turns into an unstoppable nuclear war.

For the final scene, DeVito had Douglas and Turner rehearsing for three days suspended on a chandelier forty-five feet above a hard marble floor. It was a joke among them that DeVito was getting his own back for the physical exertion Douglas had put him through in *Romancing the Stone* and *The Jewel of the Nile*. At the end of the film there is a hint that the couple were on the brink of calling a truce and making up. Then Douglas tries to rescue Turner from the chandelier from which she was swinging precariously above the marble hall, and the movie reaches its terrible conclusion.

For Douglas, *War of the Roses* remained in the category of roles that gave him the opportunity to explore the darker side of human nature. He did not, however, appear to be completely comfortable with the comedy, as dark as it was – nor, indeed, were the reviewers when the movie was released in the spring of 1990, three months after *Black Rain*. Both films were given a mild reception in America, although, as usual, Douglas's army of fans in the foreign markets boosted what would otherwise have been disappointing box office returns.

In the context of Douglas's overall body of work, *War of the Roses* was interesting but did little to advance him in the superstar league. As an actor he might still be viewed more as a prince than a king of Hollywood.

That is not to say that, in the sycophantic world in which he had re-immersed himself on the West Coast, he was not held in some awe. The demands of work, the two pictures back to back, the formation of his new production company, and the events that attend such a high-powered life – all had virtually enforced his removal back to Los Angeles. Michael Douglas's presence at any function now counted.

His pressurised world left little room for any extended family life, which worried him when he finished *War of the Roses*. 'Yes, I admit, I could align what happened to the Roses to my own situation. I could see first hand how marital situations can just slide out of control for a succession of reasons.'

He had promised Diandra that he would take time off as soon as he had finished *War of the Roses*. The likelihood of her seeing much more of him, however, was remote. As the production of *War of the Roses* wound down, in September 1989 he was involved in late post-production matters on *Black Rain* and deep into negotiations with Rick Bieber for the first of the Stonebridge productions. His schedule was mapped out for weeks ahead, taking him well into the new year.

At the end of the month, Sherry Lansing and Stanley Jaffe had arranged a special screening party on the Paramount lot prior to the general release of *Black Rain*. It was the kind of party for which Hollywood is renowned, and more akin to the good old days when the moguls would lord it among their hirelings. The carefully arranged lighting in the room would do justice to any film set, gentle enough to give the young a certain glowing splendour and so as not to be unkind to the older generation. A fake mist swirled around the hall where they met to pick finger-delicacies from the Japanese-style buffet designed to match the setting of the movie.

Michael Douglas arrived alone soon after ten, chauffeured to the Paramount building in a black limousine. There is a ripple of applause as he enters, and all around him are faces he knows and recognises, some from when he was just a boy coming to visit his father.

He is calm, relaxed and utterly charming, showing no agitation at being stopped at every pace by people who want to shake his hand and tell him he is marvellous. He heads towards his father and kisses him, then slowly mingles, moving around the room, shaking hands and getting lipstick on both cheeks. This is why

213

he is there. He is the star of the show and there are many who are grateful for that.

For all the charm, however, the man who has for so long been dubbed one of the nicer types in Hollywood has a definite edge to him which is not just a reflection of his change of style in the movies he makes. He has the air of a man whom a rival would upset at his peril, as if work and the surroundings are beginning to give him stress.

Among these people who are his associates, he is known to have a fairly wide spread of financial and business interests. There was a film servicing company run by his brother, Joel, at the Victorine Studios in Nice. He is talking of miniseries, he has a record label, a part-interest in a magazine, property and real estate . . . But his main preoccupation is the deal with Columbia. Such deals are precisely what David Puttnam attempted to get rid of when he was *in situ* at Columbia. They had become a built-in part of Hollywood since the demise of the old studio 'system' and remain so to this day, aimed at securing the most talented and creative people around.

Douglas says that, unlike Warren Beatty and Dustin Hoffman, he respected Puttnam but could not understand what his agenda was or by whose authority he tried to buck the Hollywood system. It was only when Puttnam began to achieve some success in that direction – stepping on some powerful Hollywood toes in the process – that Coca Cola shuffled the pack, and Puttnam left. 'It wasn't as if the American film industry was in a terrible state at the time,' said Douglas. 'The money that is available to me at the moment is absurd.'

Douglas had come to Columbia when Dawn Steel took over as head, and now there were disturbing rumours that she was about to depart following the takeover by Sony. At that moment, his new company had three pictures in production; the situation was worrying and the fast pace of Stonebridge's development time-consuming.

Indeed, there was something in Douglas's manner at the time that suggested a personal crisis, one that covered several areas of his activity, from work to his private life. His father could see in his son's green eyes that all was not well. There was too much going on; Kirk knew better than anyone what effects this could have on Michael's life and marriage. 'So he's a big producer, big offices and all that smart stuff,' said Kirk, with his usual frankness. 'Why is he putting himself through all of this? He's a big star, and he should take advantage of that. I told him: "Michael, look at your life. Your strength is Michael Douglas, actor. That's what you are, now. The rest is crap." He hadn't reacted to that yet.'

All around him at the Jaffe–Lansing launch party were the people who would love his success for themselves. The film was shown, the applause was substantial and the well-wishers departed saying nice things about the new movie, whether they meant them or not.

Douglas had no time to relax. Day by day, the tiredness resulting from two movies and his other business ventures became more apparent. But there would be no let-up. Some late dubbing work was still to be done on *War of the Roses*, and his partner Rick Bieber was frantically involving him in the Stonebridge projects.

Douglas had chosen personally to produce the first, *Flatliners*, and had already selected its director and stars. Filming would begin immediately; any chance of a long holiday was impossible.

Douglas's friends had little doubt that his activities these past months back in Los Angeles had once again put his marriage under renewed strain, while his private life remained in constant media focus. Douglas, according to the gossips, had been severely reprimanded by his wife over his association with other women and had warned him that she would leave him if it continued. On his part, Douglas dismissed the rumours as 'tabloid stuff'. But the reports were becoming far too frequent for comfort and were an embarrassment to Diandra.

However, it was a fact that he had sought marriage counselling that year, although he was still avoiding any kind of therapy. The counselling targeted his schedule, and he kept admitting that he 'owed Diandra a lot of time'. For the time being there was no opportunity to repay it.

While filming in Hollywood, he kept a suite at the Beverly Wilshire Hotel, going to their home at Santa Barbara at weekends. Diandra commuted from New York when she was able, but she was also heavily committed to her own work.

Since she went to work there, the film and television unit of the Metropolitan Museum had grown considerably, making promotional films and documentaries which were in great demand throughout America and Europe by television stations and by universities.

The sheer logistics of their work meant that their marriage was going through another trough of clashing schedules, with rumoured infidelities on his part and jealousies on hers. She had no particular problem with the women he worked with, but his work also meant that he was thrown constantly into the arms of some of the world's most desirable women. 'I think jealousy is quite common among Hollywood couples,' she admits, 'and I would not say I've never felt a pang of it. But you have to look at the situation objectively and not dwell on it, otherwise you could not survive. If I am troubled by something like that, believe me I am the first to say so.'

Diandra admitted to longing for the family to get away from the business of making movies; that was possible, she believed, only out of the country. Whether they were in New York, Los Angeles, Santa Barbara or at the $2 million ski lodge Douglas had bought them in Aspen, Colorado, it was never far enough to discourage either the incessant demands on their time or Michael's obsession with his work.

They had holidayed in Spain and Majorca on several occasions, and it was to the island where she was born and spent her early years that she was drawn in the search for solace. Michael, not without some measure of guilt over the lack of time he had spent with his wife and son in the previous twelve months, agreed to buy Diandra the holiday home she had wanted, back in the territory of her childhood.

In the autumn of 1989 they finalised the purchase of a small estate called Passesio de S'Estaca, between Valldemosa and Deia – where her mother lived – in one of the most rugged and secluded parts of the Majorcan coastline, not far from the area that is a favourite holiday spot for members of both the British and Spanish royal families.

The square, castle-like villa is perched precariously on the side of a cliff surrounded by lush vegetation and has spectacular views over the Mediterranean. Once owned by the Archduke Louis Salvador or Austria, the estate had been unoccupied for many years when Diandra found it. The price was $3.5 million; the cost of renovation and furnishings, and developing the overgrown grounds into formal, workmanlike gardens, added another $1.5 million to the bill. Michael, who made a flying visit to Majorca to finalise matters, commented to the agent: 'Well, my wife was looking for a place that would give us peace and quiet, and now it looks as if we'll be able to have just that.'

Not yet awhile.

Back in Hollywood, the Stonebridge production of *Flatliners* was well under way. Julia Roberts and Kiefer Sutherland were introduced by director Joel Schumacher; they hit it off straight away, and became the obsession of the tabloids for the next two years on the question of whether or not they would get married.

At the time she was selected for *Flatliners*, Roberts had made only two movies of any substance. *Steel Magnolias*, which did well in 1989, was her first major role and won her an Academy Award nomination for Best Supporting Actress. The second, *Pretty Woman*, would be the smash hit of 1990 but was unreleased at the time she was working on *Flatliners*.

The Douglas movie was a horror story about a group of medical students who experiment with death in an attempt to resolve the question of an afterlife. Douglas kept the budget to well under $20 million. At the time of its release, some Columbia executives were dubious about its place in the highly competitive markets as the 1990s dawned.

In fact, *Flatliners* was the surprise success of the year, grossing more than $150 million worldwide. Its success was aided to some degree by the on-off saga of the Roberts–Sutherland marriage, which ran in the newspapers for a year or more until Julia –

then a big star through *Pretty Woman* and *Flatliners* – called it off.

Douglas's company Stonebridge and its sister company the Stone Group, however, did not enjoy the success he had hoped for. The three movies which followed, *Double Impact, Stone Cold* and *Hard Promises*, were disappointments, bumpy productions which had problems with directors and stars and made little impact on the market. Douglas was not personally involved in any of them, except in his capacity as joint owner of the production company.

The company also produced one other picture from its initial list of projects on which Douglas himself was involved, this time only as executive producer. It was titled *Radio Flyer*, a delicate picture which addressed the topic of child abuse. Released in February 1992, it also failed at the box office.

By then it had become apparent to Douglas that he could do without these headaches. Out of the five movies produced by his company at the beginning of 1990, only his own production, *Flatliners*, had been a success. In the meantime, also, Dawn Steel had left Columbia to set up her own independent production company. In 1991, after much heart-searching, Michael Douglas did exactly as his father had suggested eighteen months earlier – he cut back on the business side to concentrate on acting.

By then he was already deep in discussion with the producers of a new film called *Basic Instinct,* which would reportedly pay him a fee of $14 million. Thus, he could afford to reassess his life and get some perspective back into his workload and his personal life. He was disappointed, anyhow, with Stonebridge's development; the following year he split with Rick Bieber, announced he was drastically curbing Stonebridge's operations and cut the staff back to a level which was in line with that of his old, smaller production company, Bigstick.

He ditched the production-line philosophy of two or three movies a year announced by Bieber in 1989. Douglas could now see that 'the quality is so variable and the pressure to find a new project is constant'. Instead, he would produce only when he fell deeply in love with a particular story. That in itself was a milestone in his life, and the benefits would eventually filter through to his family, though not for some time yet.

His workaholism was relentless that year: promotion for *Black Rain* in overseas markets at the beginning of the year; production of *Flatliners*; meetings and power breakfasts with Bieber on other Stonebridge matters; *War of the Roses* released in America and then in the rest of the world; film festivals in Europe plus media interviews; discussions on two new movies, *Shining Through* and *Basic Instinct*; back in France for the Deauville Film Festival in September; *Flatliners* is released, and he is involved right to the last . . . In December he flies back to Europe again to begin filming *Shining Through*, after which he will go straight into *Basic Instinct*.

The whole period of 1990–91 was one of selection and choices by Douglas which actually revamped his professional life in many ways. His career graph suffered a blip during that time, and he realised, as Kirk said he would, that he had spread himself too thinly across too broad a spectrum of activity.

His choice of films in which he would appear – and again they were choices he controlled personally – had to date not followed any stylistic pattern, unlike other top male box office stars of the day.

In a way, because of his age and to some degree because of his lack of a more extensive track record of movies, Hollywood had never really categorised him in particular characterisations that were familiar to some of his contemporaries. He was positioned somewhere between the old school of movie stars, like the eternal romantic hero Robert Redford or the craggy-faced violence of Clint Eastwood, and the sexual appeal of modernists, like Bruce Willis, Mel Gibson and Tom Cruise.

To retain his commercial appeal, and that is the bottom line for any actor, he had to select his roles with care. The blandness of his early career had been well and truly banished. The pace and impetus he had established since needed to be maintained.

Black Rain and, to a lesser degree, *War of the Roses* had followed the pattern of exploration in darker psychologies of human behaviour. He made two further choices in 1990. One, *Basic Instinct,* would prove to be truly boundary-breaking in terms of promoting his notoriety, in every respect, while the other, *Shining Through*, starring Melanie Griffith, was a more gentle movie altogether and sat rather discordantly in his career pattern. In both he was approached purely as an actor, which had the advantage of relieving some pressure on him.

He began what would become protracted and difficult negotiations for his appearance in *Basic Instinct* in the early summer of that year (that project is dealt with more fully in the next chapter). He had committed himself to *Shining Through* long before *Basic Instinct* became a definite runner; in view of his intention to go for roles strong on character and content, it was a decidedly odd choice to make.

Shining Through was a rather soapy story of the wartime exploits of an American secretary who becomes a spy in Nazi Germany, based upon Susan Issac's bestselling novel. It had the feel and appearance of a script more suited to a television miniseries than to a feature movie, and that's the way it turned out in spite of the presence of Douglas and a superb contribution from Sir John Gielgud. Griffith herself was competent, though the producers had blatantly cashed in on her starmaking performance in the 1988 movie *Working Girl*, for which she received an Oscar nomination and a Golden Globe award.

It was really Griffith's picture. Douglas's role is very much a supporting one, as Melanie's boss with whom she falls in love; he eventually gives way to her pleadings and sends her behind enemy lines to spy on a senior officer in Hitler's Third Reich.

For Douglas, accepting the part seemed to be a monetary decision, a picture he could slip into his schedule, not a part that would advance himself in any way. There were no particular heroics in his role until the end, when he gets shot and badly wounded, and no real scope for dramatic interpretation. His performance, by nature of the script, harked back to the callowness of his past roles.

The film also tied him for three valuable months at a time when Rick Bieber was still busy on Stonebridge productions.

Shining Through was shot extensively in Europe, and Douglas had to suffer the discomforts of location work in parts of East Germany where the telephones – vital to his business connections in Los Angeles – were still not in good working order and where neo-Nazis demonstrated in front of them. Critics gave the movie a low-key reaction and it fared disappointingly.

For Michael Douglas the trip to Europe was marked by the rekindling of his friendship with the British heiress Sabrina Guinness, a former girlfriend of Prince Charles and latterly seen in such company as Jack Nicholson, Mick Jagger and Rod Stewart. The paparazzi spotted them leaving a London nightclub and pursued the couple as they dashed to a waiting car.

Douglas, always a target for photographers, came under further scrutiny after the appearance in America of an article in *Celebrity Sleuth* devoting four pages to him and his supposed mistresses.

The price of fame continued to take its toll, but what came next was sensational – and put Douglas on the cover of every glossy magazine around the world.

19
Hot and Sexy

After the modesty of *Shining Through*, Douglas said he was looking for something sexy, and he'd found it. Let us recall the scene, rolling forward in time to the release of *Basic Instinct*. It is March 1992, the night of the première of his new movie, and Michael Douglas is wondering how he can possibly accompany his wife to see it without very considerable embarrassment to her, not to mention to himself. She knows the score, all right. It is a very sexually explicit picture. But no verbal description can do justice to the actuality.

Inside, the theatre is packed with friends, colleagues, associates and critics. They are all there to see his character *en route* to possible sexual suicide and to observe above all the scene about which there has been so much talk: when his forty-seven-year-old bottom, as bare and as pink as the day he was born, is in full view and the long legs of Sharon Stone are locked around it. He is steamily engaged in apparent intercourse with the said Ms Stone in the most daring scene of copulation ever filmed for a mainstream movie.

She reaches a loudly appreciative orgasm, which sends her lover, Douglas, into the sexual equivalent of an atomic explosion. Nothing like it has ever been seen before outside the restricted-entry doors of porno picture houses. Everybody is asking the same question: did they or didn't they? And he loves that question because it proves he's a good actor, whatever the circumstances.

Outside, at the front of the theatre, the street is filled with pickets from gay protest groups waving placards bearing Douglas's portrait and daubed with the words MISOGYNIST and

223

HOMOPHOBIC. One proclaims: MICHAEL DOUGLAS – FUCK YOU – RACIST – SEXIST – ANTI-GAY. The furore that has dogged the making of the film reaches the kind of hysteria that the publicity people would have willingly lost an arm to achieve.

Basic Instinct is the film of the moment, of its time, of its era, of its decade and, perhaps, curiously enough in the long term, the sex film to end all sex films. Michael Douglas, by a measure of luck and a lot of judgement, is in the thick of it; even he was surprised by the impact it made and by the strength of the protests.

Whatever doubts may have lingered about his future career after his heroic but somewhat genteel adventures with Melanie Griffith, he was on top, in every sense, as Hollywood's number one – the hottest, sexiest actor around. There is no doubt that Douglas had reinvented himself yet again, this time on his approach to fifty, courting scandal with kinky sex in a sensationally erotic psycho-thriller and in a manner that few male superstars of the day would have been either willing to do or capable of doing. The film sent shock waves through the movie industry and put him and/or Sharon Stone on every glossy magazine cover around the world.

We have witnessed the amazing feats of cinematographic shock tactics he has pulled off in the past: getting audiences laughing with mental patients in *Cuckoo's Nest,* scaring them half to death with a nuclear accident in *The China Syndrome*, giving every wife, girlfriend and unfaithful lover apoplexy in *Fatal Attraction*, providing new meaning to the word loathsome in *Wall Street* . . . But *Basic Instinct*, overrated and overhyped though it may have been, none the less put the others in the shade. What had gone before, each and every movie in Michael Douglas's varied and often callow career, was a mere Sunday School outing by comparison. Douglas burst into the 1990s with a confidence and audacious stridency that will assure his presence as a major screen actor, in the top league, for much of the decade.

Let us go back to the beginning of the *Basic Instinct* story, because, as always with these big-impact movies in which he becomes involved, there is a background saga waiting to unfold.

The movie began as an outline and then an original screenplay from the sharp, modern pen (or word processor) of Joe Eszterhas. He already had a name and a reputation. The Hungarian-born former journalist had become well known in Hollywood in the 1980s for writing screenplays that reflected current social trends – notably in *Flashdance* (1983), an elongated pop video which was an enormous success, and the far more substantial 1985 courtroom drama *Jagged Edge*.

In 1990 he sold his latest script, *Basic Instinct*, to an independent company called Carolco Pictures, which was looking for another major picture to drag itself out of a burdensome debt of $180 million. It had been spending heavily on the expensive futuristic Martian epic *Total Recall*, starring Arnold Schwarzenegger. The movie had set them back more than $60 million, and at the time the results were unknown.

Hollywood was laughing at Carolco's plight: to Hollywood's despair, the company had single-handedly raised the stakes of the film industry's inflated values by giving Big Arnie $10 million plus fifteen per cent of the gross for his starring role. (In the event the investment would be handsomely recouped, the film eventually making $290 million worldwide.)

Carolco shelled out $3 million for the rights to *Basic Instinct*, and in June 1990 Joe Eszterhas became the latest beneficiary of Hollywood excess.

A lesser-known fact was that Eszterhas had a clause built into his contract whereby he could choose the producer of the movie, for which another $1 million was put on ice. The writer insisted upon hiring the much-respected veteran Irwin Winkler, producer of such movies as *They Shoot Horses, Don't They,* the Sylvester Stallone *Rocky* series and several Martin Scorsese/Robert De Niro pictures including *New York, New York, Raging Bull* and *Goodfellas,* along with another of Eszterhas's screenplays, *Betrayed*, in 1988.

Carolco's boss, Mario Kassar, accepted Joe's terms with the proviso that he himself would choose the movie's star and director. He had only two names: he wanted Michael Douglas as the all-important male lead and the controversial Dutch director Paul Verhoeven. Verhoeven had just finished *Total Recall* and had several interesting Dutch films to his credit, including *Spetters* and *The Fourth Man*, a movie which explored various sexual themes, and more recently, in America, the spectacularly violent *Robocop*.

Douglas was approached towards the end of June. He liked the sound of the project but was nervous about the content. True, he had been looking for a sexy thriller to take his career on again from the recent peaks of *Fatal Attraction, Wall Street* and *Black Rain*. He was prepared to shock the world and, on one level, he wanted to do exactly that; the post-AIDS theme of celibacy and self-denial was simply not up his street. But *Basic Instinct* was right over the top in terms of sexual explicitness.

As far as Kassar was concerned, Douglas was the *only* man in Hollywood who could make the picture work. He was probably right. As Kassar pointed out, Douglas had recently played a succession of slimy, weak, flawed, guilty-as-hell characters but by and large still managed to keep the audience on his side. In short, he was the man who could be dropped into the mire of moral sleaziness and come up smelling of roses. That was Douglas's unique ability, one that few other stars of his calibre possessed and, even if they did, dared not risk putting it to the test in such a blatant, controversial way.

Money was discussed. His agent, so the story goes, had a target figure of $15 million and settled for not much less plus the usual shareout if the film made a profit. If Douglas was going to put his career on the line, he needed adequate compensation.

Kassar and Verhoeven had preliminary talks. The director grasped the mood of the project as perceived by Carolco: sensational sex intertwined with a riveting thriller of a story. This in turn meant that the original script would have to be 'sexed up' and various other sub-currents, such as no-holds-barred lesbianism – merely hinted at by Eszterhas – injected. Verhoeven settled for a $5 million fee after showing what he could do in *Total Recall*, which he had directed for a lot, lot less.

All the principals met for the first time in late July at a meeting called by Kassar. The talks rapidly descended into disharmony. Verhoeven, a mischievous shaggy-haired mid-European whose accent was not unlike Schwarzenegger's, came to the meeting scruffily dressed in jeans and a woollen shirt, with a clear notion of what he wanted for the movie.

Winkler found Verhoeven too domineering by half and did not like the plan to add a more explicit lesbian love scene; nor did he like Verhoeven's flamboyant intent with the heterosexual love scenes, holding nothing back, showing the naked bodies of the characters writhing in various stages of excitement; Verhoeven talked of 'maybe' being the first mainstream movie to show an erect penis.

Eszterhas objected with similar displeasure that his script should be interfered with in this way. He was a notorious battler for his corner; they all knew he could stand his ground in no uncertain manner.

Douglas, for his part, was more concerned about aspects of the script that involved himself, clearly protecting his own position. As he saw it, his character was much too passive, merely a device and a pawn for the leading character, the woman who is a murder suspect. 'She leads, I follow,' Douglas protested. 'It needs adjustment.' Kassar said he did not think that would be a problem.

The meeting ended with a good deal of acrimony. They adjourned for a month or so to give Winkler and Eszterhas a chance to consider their positions. At the end of that time the whole project, as Douglas described it, 'imploded'. Winkler and Eszterhas had a second meeting with Verhoeven and they ended up at each other's throats. Winkler said he had been 'mugged' and Eszterhas reckoned they were taking intolerable liberties with his script.

Soon, both Winkler and Eszterhas called Kassar and said they were both pulling out unless Verhoeven was fired. He wasn't. Author and producer exited, wheeling away their $4 million but leaving the screenplay to be written as the others wished.

At this point in time, Carolco was already committed to a $20 million-plus cost – Winkler's $1 million, Eszterhas's $3 million,

Douglas's $14 million and Verhoeven's $5 million – but all the company had to show for it was 220 pages of double-spaced typing. The row made its way into the newspapers, and the backbiting community smiled widely at the misfortune of Mr Kassar and co.

Come September, Douglas departed for England and Europe to attend the Deauville Film Festival and then to begin filming *Shining Through*, as we have seen in the previous chapter, leaving Verhoeven determinedly revamping the screenplay before passing it over to Gary Goldman, his author on *Total Recall*, for a final treatment.

When he returned to Los Angeles, however, Douglas found the situation no further forward. Verhoeven had rejected Goldman's new version and, after two unsuccessful rewrite attempts, had decided to go back to the Eszterhas original, with the exception of a couple of adjustments and a strengthened Douglas role, as Michael had requested.

With new traumas in his personal life and fresh from the London press hounding of his liaison with Sabrina Guinness, Douglas was tetchy. He screamed blue murder. There had been a great deal of anguish over *Basic Instinct*, conducted publicly and with every episode reported in the trade papers – all for nothing.

They held a long and frank discussion: 'Fuck this; fuck that; fuck you; fuck you, too.' The exchanges were strictly of the four-letter variety. When they calmed down, Verhoeven took Douglas through the script line by line, explaining as he went the emphasis and the beats.

Verhoeven was forced to admit that the extended lesbian scene – the one over and above that written by Eszterhas – did not work. 'So we left it the way it was, made up in the papers and I sent the new draft over to Joe, who said he loved it. I acknowledged that my proposals were stupid, and I said so to reporters. I have no problem repeating that,' said Verhoeven.

There might well have been a touch of distance-putting by Verhoeven by then. Even as they began to kiss and make up, there were already rumours of protests by gay activists, alerted to the movie by the rows and the publicity.

Douglas, still nervous that the movie might backfire on him, made a point of calling Eszterhas and said, 'Trouble is brewing on the gay front. Do you have a problem with that?'

'None at all,' Joe replied. 'I am reporting what is truth, that in every group there's deviant behaviour.'

There it rested. But Douglas's fears over the extent of the gay protests would prove to be well founded, and the matter would explode in their faces very soon.

Douglas was concerned on another major point. During all this toing and froing, Verhoeven had been unable to attract the interest of a major actress for the central role of Catherine Tramell, the bisexual crime novelist. From the beginning, Verhoeven had pushed the name of Sharon Stone, whom he had directed in a supporting role in *Total Recall*. But she was unknown.

A string of minor roles since *Stardust Memories* in 1980 had failed to give Stone either challenge or fame. She had meandered through mediocrity delivering all that she was asked, which to date had seemed to be mere pouting lips and blousiness.

Verhoeven had changed that in *Total Recall*, casting her opposite the muscular Arnie in a role that did not rely solely on her sexiness. The director drew from her an excellent performance as the killer bimbo with, it was reported from the set, some reluctance on her part. Thus, it was a surprise to many that he wanted to renew their working partnership. Even so, the future remained uncertain, and Stone was seriously considering giving up acting to study law when they approached her for *Basic Instinct*.

Douglas still did not think she was a big enough name to join him on the credit above the title. He insisted: 'I need someone to share the risks of this movie. I want somebody of equal stature. I don't want to be up there all by myself on this one. There's going to be a lot of shit flying around.'

He suggested Julia Roberts, who was currently on view in his own production, *Flatliners*. The names of Michelle Pfeiffer, Geena Davis and Ellen Barkin were also on the list. More than fifty actresses in all were considered for the key role of Catherine Tramell.

To Michael's dismay, there were no takers among the bigger names. The nudity scared them all away. Eventually, the process of elimination brought Sharon Stone back to the top of the list. Douglas had to admit that her screen test was strong. Verhoeven suggested he took another look at *Total Recall*. Finally, Douglas agreed to her. Stone, desperate for a major part, did not flinch at the requirements of the movie. As far as she was concerned, this was it – if she failed now, she would definitely plump for a career change. It would prove unnecessary.

Basic Instinct is a many-layered movie, running through stratas of sexual activity which evolve around a winding, intricate storyline. There is a dramatic opening scene – severely edited in the US, on the instructions of the censors, but not in Europe – where a nude blonde, her face hidden, stabs her lover, an ageing rock-and-roll star, to death with an ice-pick at the moment of climax in a scene that has shades of both Polanski and Kubrick, with a hint of Hitchcock. Verhoeven keeps his camera held as the lover stabs her victim repeatedly.

Next, we have the Michael Douglas character, the San Francisco detective Nick Curran, who is sent to investigate and witnesses what is apparently a lesbian kiss between Catherine Tramell and her lover Roxy, played by Leilani Sarello.

Douglas himself carries a bundle of troubles of his own, ranging through a drink problem and coke snorting to the possibility that he may have deliberately shot and killed a suspect. He is under orders to receive therapy from the police department therapist, Beth Gardner, played by newcomer Jeanne Tripplehorn.

For her part Jeanne has to stock up on stunt undies, twelve pairs of cutaway briefs fastened with Velcro so that they could be easily ripped off, and some make-up to cover the real bruises and a real love-bite obtained during tough rehearsals with Douglas. There big scene took eight hours in total to film. That was where Douglas unzips his trousers and forces himself on her to her cries of, 'No . . . no . . . please, n-o-o-o'.

Verhoeven pushes them to the very brink of a date rape scenario which would also give the censors palpitations.

The central sex scenes are played out with Douglas and Stone.

Douglas's character, detective Curran, begins to suspect that Catherine Tramell gets plots for her books by acting them out. But it was the sexual asides which caused the furore among the gay activists.

In a nutshell, Stone's character has a lesbian lover, Roxy, sketched out by the scene in which the pair are seen kissing passionately. It is that relationship that Verhoeven wanted to extend, until he thought better of it. Catherine is also seen to have a relationship with an older woman who has served a prison sentence for mass murder; the third key female character, the therapist Beth Gardner, is also revealed to have a lesbian past. What caused ire among the gays was that all three women were involved in deviant sex, and put into situations where each was a possible suspect in the murder Douglas had been assigned to investigate.

Cut down to a sentence: detective Nick Curran, investigating the murder, has heavy sex with his therapist, who is a closet lesbian with a mysterious death in her past, and even heavier sex with his murder suspect, who has a current lesbian relationship, if not two.

The suspension of disbelief would clearly be considerable.

By the spring of 1991 the cast were all circling one another ready for filming, the whole set filled with tension. The scene of confrontation between Douglas and Stone, when Douglas enters his apartment to find Stone's Catherine Tramell waiting for him, was one they had to get past before filming could proceed.

Douglas remained unbowed on his views that his character was still too passive, and was obviously intent on rectifying the situation as they went along. The cameras were running and Verhoeven asked Douglas to take a step towards Stone.

Douglas would not budge. He said Stone should come to him. Stone kept out of it. 'I was in the middle of these two stags,' she said. 'So I kept it buttoned.' The argument went on for hours, literally, until a compromise was reached. Douglas agreed to take a half-step towards Stone and she would take a step towards him.

The scene was set up. Verhoeven called: 'Action!' Douglas made his half-step and Stone turned away. The tension of the moment brought her to a halt. Verhoeven could not understand it. 'What the hell is going on?' he cried. He later perceived it to be a combination of the tension of the role combined with the tension of the real-life characters, and that he, as director, was caught in the middle.

Stone felt she was the one who was trapped. 'I was locked between two very territorial, very intelligent, very sexual men. Each was demanding something different from me. I had to do a lot of tap-dancing.'

Douglas had a different perspective. He reckoned there was 'some kind of soap opera going on' between Verhoeven and Stone which he did not know about or understand. 'It was a love–hate relationship,' he said.

'Yeah,' Stone chipped in. 'He loved me and I hated him.'

It was at around this stage of filming that trouble was brewing on the streets of San Francisco, where the movie was being filmed on location. By then, Verhoeven and author Joe Eszterhas had rowed again, and the whole thing had spilled over into the newspapers, with accusations about exploitative gay sex.

Before long, the activists were picketing. Verhoeven and Douglas made no secret of the fact that they blamed Joe for his 'treachery' in going over to the other side. Douglas talked in terms of a double-cross; Verhoeven said it was playing havoc with his movie. The whole business erupted into a media circus.

The set remained closed. No one was going to get any previews. And the action was hotting up.

First, there was Douglas's near-rape scene with Tripplehorn. Verhoeven has visualised it in his mind, as he does every scene down to the last detail. He takes Douglas and Tripplehorn into a choreography of the scene which Douglas speaks out loud to Tripplehorn as they go through the motions in clinical fashion.

OK, I throw you up against the wall . . .
Kiss kiss kiss.

Leg up, and around.
Kiss kiss kiss.
Movement . . . back, back, up against the next wall.
Your hands on the back of my neck.
Kiss kiss kiss.
Your hands moving up on top of my head.
I scoop you up.
Into next room.
Over back of chair.
You are shouting.
Face in pillow.

They ran through it time and again and there were several retakes. Tripplehorn described it as being in a rodeo, yet always she had to be seen to be on the emotional brink. 'Eventually it panned out right,' she said, 'because we had scripted our own signposts and, as we moved through each one, the intensity and the emotion increased, higher and higher, so much so that Michael bit me for real and I did not even feel it. It was only later I saw the redness on my neck. Then, in the take we eventually went with, my bra popped open when it shouldn't have done. That was a surprise, but it heightened the moment. Verhoeven kept it going, pushing harder and harder. The adrenalin was flowing. I was scared, and I couldn't feel anything. We just kept going until it was right. I had so many bruises the next day that the make-up people virtually had to perform cosmetic surgery. But Michael was terrific. He is just the absolute professional; absolutely cool.'

The movie moves on. Sharon Stone unwittingly shows her pubic hair. The scene is in the police station and she sits opposite Douglas and his partner for interrogation. 'Have you ever fucked on cocaine?' she asks Douglas, uncrossing and recrossing her legs. As she does so, the camera is pointed directly at her and picks up the visual confirmation that she has on no underwear. Douglas, and the audience, is given the brief glimpse of her pubic hair.

The next episode of lust and desire takes us into the scene in which the Douglas character describes 'the fuck of the century'. The hottest scene since *Last Tango in Paris* is just short of five

233

minutes in overall length and took five days to shoot.

The sex was choreographed almost to the last gasp, and Douglas swears 'on the Bible and my son's life' that he and Sharon Stone have never been intimate. He makes that statement because a number of people did not believe they could have faked the lovemaking; a number of people also said they must have been having a relationship off screen to get to that position in the first place. He denies both charges.

First, they spent three days rehearsing with their clothes on, three exhausting ten-hour days until they had it right. Then they stripped down to fewer clothes, Douglas in a robe and Stone wearing a flimsy kimono with a crotch-pad and G-string, to begin to feel their bodies touching.

The controversial oral sex was a crucial element. Verhoeven, sometimes chuckling mischievously, pushed them further and further. Eventually, Stone's fear of the nude scenes and the racy sex was overcome by sheer bravado. When the time came, she stood up, threw off her kimono, ripped off her crotch-pad and said: 'OK, let's stop pretending. I'm nude. You're nude. We all know it. Now let's go . . .'

So they went. Douglas said later the kid had got guts. He slung his robe on the floor and walked naked into the lights and on to the bed where the scene would be filmed. Verhoeven was chuckling an evil chuckle. The scene was shot over the next two days, not in a complete take but in sections, with several parts of the action done over and over for contrasting camera angles, which would be edited together, particularly when Douglas goes down for the oral simulation.

Though Douglas refused to be shown full-frontal, his bare bottom is copiously displayed in various stages of movement. He wanders through scenes with nothing on, and he is not especially overtaken by modesty. Sharon Stone said he was an 'absolute gentleman', and after each scene he would get her robe before she got up.

Several sections of the scene needed a number of takes to get right. Verhoeven called out instructions: 'Lick her now . . . ja! ja! Stick your tongue out . . . ja! Bite his nipple now, quick . . . ja!

Very goot! Move your leg . . . no, no . . . to the left, I can see more of you than I want.'

When, finally, the scene was filmed to Verhoeven's satisfaction, including the explicitness of the oral activity, they all went to look at the rushes. Michael laughed out loud when he saw them.

Verhoeven was mystified. 'Why are you laughing?' he asked.

'We will never get away with that,' said Douglas. 'You might in Holland or France – but this is America.'

'You don't have to tell me,' said Verhoeven, who had had earlier run-ins with the censors over the violence in both *Robocop* and *Total Recall*.

Far from being dismayed over the abundance of flesh, including pubic hair, shown on screen, Sharon Stone was enthusiastic: 'The sex scenes are unusual – they let the truth of how some women feel about sex privately and with a partner really be seen.'

However, they did cause some friction between Douglas and Verhoeven. The star complained that the director was too interventionist in the takes, to the point that it interrupted Douglas's line of concentration and rhythm on what were, after all, heavily rehearsed scenes. On the other hand, for the rest of the picture Douglas felt he was being neglected by Verhoeven, who paid great attention to the women members of the cast and pretty well left Douglas to his own devices to the point where he felt ignored.

There was no regular contact between the two men and very limited discussion. Douglas was heard to complain more than once: 'What the fuck's going on here?' Verhoeven's incessant demands for multiangled camera shots, which meant filming the scene over and over, also upset Douglas. 'It is like Chinese torture, or worse – a fucking Kafka nightmare,' he was heard muttering in his chair.

With hindsight, Douglas recognised that some of the director's behaviour was probably deliberate, to increase the tension, just as Oliver Stone had done on *Wall Street*. But at the time Douglas was annoyed and constantly nervous about Verhoeven's approach.

Douglas described him as a 'talented but whacko Dutchman' and was heard to complain loud and often that it was he, Douglas, who was taking the risk on this picture, not Verhoeven. 'A director can fuck it up and walk away,' he said, 'but an actor can be made to look a complete asshole. I have my career to think of – and on this one I am on my own.'

The latter point shows that the making of *Basic Instinct* represented something of a hallmark in Douglas's career: he took a close interest in every part of the film, not from a producer's or director's viewpoint, but as an experienced actor concerned with quality and his reputation. Sharon Stone agreed that, in many ways, Douglas carried the movie along on his own back, both as an actor and in his professionalism towards others.

He had only one major confrontation with the director. His disquiet over a number of things blew up into a row in his trailer. He called Verhoeven inside, slammed the door and began what was described as 'a very animated discussion', during which Verhoeven suffered a severe nosebleed for which he was taken to hospital. Rumours abounded that Douglas had landed one on the director, but Verhoeven said afterwards that he was susceptible to nosebleeds.

Production of the movie was shut down for a few days. Several of the actors, Douglas included, were glad of the time off. It had been an exhausting and emotionally draining shoot, and the pain was beginning to show. Filming *Basic Instinct* had been scheduled to take sixty-five days but took eighty-nine days; it was only slightly ahead of its budget at $43 million. To that, of course, would be added the post-production costs of an additional $25 million.

When it was all over, and in the afterglow, Douglas sang Verhoeven's praises and reckoned he would work with him again in a second. For both, the battle of *Basic Instinct* was won in regard to getting it on film – the next hurdle was getting it past the censors.

In America both censors and cinema-owners had returned to a level of caution in the amount of sex shown on screen. The push for fewer controls in the 1960s and 1970s and the arrival of overt sex and choreographed violence – as in everything from Beatty's

Bonnie and Clyde to Polanski's *Macbeth* – had turned full circle by the late 1980s. Moral majorities had gained more control in America, far more than they had in Britain and the rest of Europe.

Verhoeven's first version of the movie, which contained the full works, without a doubt fell into the NC-17 rating, a rating created two years earlier and specifically an adults-only classification. But that would guarantee a box office disaster.

Many newspapers and television stations would not accept advertisements for NC-17-rated films, or even review them, and Blockbuster Video, which at the time controlled close on 15 percent of the video market, would not accept NC-17 movies. And so Carolco and Verhoeven were under strict orders from the distributors, Tri-star, to deliver a movie that would have an R-rating, which would overcome all the above problems.

The only way to achieve an R-rating, in America at least, was to accept the censors' demands for cuts. Having conducted similar battles on *Robocop* and *Total Recall*, Verhoeven ensured he shot the sex scenes in several ways, some less provocative than others; this is one of the reasons why the main sex scene took five days to get on film. He submitted the cut version several times before finally achieving his R-rating for viewing by over-thirteens. European censors were less strict.

Meanwhile, the various activist groups were ready to do battle at the time of the launch. Douglas rightly suspected that feminist groups would object to the large amounts of female nudity. He reckoned that he could argue that the movie was not sexist in that respect because he had bared just about every part of his body other than his genitalia.

He did not get away with matters that easily, and the protest movement gradually developed into a spectacular drama. Major groups, such as the Queer Nation and the Gay and Lesbian Alliance Against Discrimination (GL), teamed up and announced that representatives would be outside every cinema in the country where *Basic Instinct* was showing and would shout out the ending to the crowds going in.

They were joined by four separate women's organisations of varying kinds, but all protesting at the same thing – Douglas's violent act of intercourse with Jeanne Tripplehorn, which they claimed was no less than glorified rape. Douglas angrily rejected their claim, classing the scene as aggressive sex between consenting adults. 'To me,' said Douglas in an interview at the time, 'this is a sign of how lost this country is – how it has no direction and everyone is floundering, hanging on to their own special interests. Am I supposed to make a movie with representatives from gay/lesbian organisations, from women's organisations, from Arabs, from Jews, from everyone else going through the script telling me what I can and cannot do? That's not what life's about.'

The protests turned out to be self-defeating. The publicity was huge, and the old adage that all publicity is good publicity still hangs true as far as the movies are concerned. Everyone flocked to the cinemas to see what all the fuss was about. In the first weekend *Basic Instinct* took $5 million at the box office and zoomed instantly to number one in the American charts, taking more than $70 million in the first four weeks. Globally, the situation was repeated. *Basic Instinct* was on target for another $250 million blockbuster for Carolco.

Douglas himself remained steadfastly unrepentant. He invited the world's press in to talk to him, to explain his position and to defend the movie. He refused to get impatient with hostile interviewers. His eyes sparkled mischievously, and, with his familiar, friendly intensity, put forward a persuasive case: 'We make a movie and do you know what the ultimate thing is for protest? If you don't want to – don't buy a ticket, don't go and see it! But don't tell someone else that he can't see it, that he can't read a book or see a painting just because you don't like it. I guess I just believe in our constitutional right to make our own choices.'

He agreed that protesters had a legitimate reason for stating that there were not enough positive gay or lesbian characters in films today. But he believed the activists also saw the opportunity to get publicity for their causes by attaching themselves to an international movie. 'I abhor any violence against any minority group. So I am out of touch with this crowd objecting to *Basic*

Instinct. I made the film because I thought it would be fun with all the repression that exists right now. If – in this area of safe sex and no sex – the cinema is the only place where people are really going to get off, then so be it. I thought it was exciting, titillating even – but nowhere near pornographic.'

Douglas was at his best in every respect, from acting to public speaking. The critics roundly trashed *Basic Instinct* as an unimportant piece of eroticism that had no social or moral back-up. The performances of the main protagonists were lost in the discussion about the rights and wrongs of the movie itself. But there was no questioning the power of Douglas's performance, matched by the ice-coolness of Sharon Stone.

The critics knew as they wrote their reviews that their words would go unheeded by an intrigued public anxious to see the hugely hyped 'fuck of the century', Michael Douglas's forty-seven-year-old 'very flat' bum and Sharon Stone's everything, including pubic hair, which she claimed Verhoeven had tricked her into showing.

After the America furore, the stars trooped off abroad for a repeat performance. They all chatted away merrily to the media, and the cinema tills jingled loudly. As had happened in the past with Douglas's co-stars, Sharon Stone became a major attraction overnight, and the people whom she had hoped and prayed might take one of her calls during the last ten years were now leaving messages for her to call them.

Her fee rocketed from a few thousand to $2.5 million. At the 1992 Cannes Film Festival, where in the past she could have strolled pretty well unnoticed through the lobby of the hotel, she now required ten bodyguards to hold back the crowds clawing and grabbing at her. Achieving overnight fame after ten years in the business may turn one's head and loosen one's tongue. Stone's reaction to her success was as over the top as her movie. She talked frankly, acknowledging that down the years all the movie people ever wanted her to be was a blousy, beautiful blonde and they tried to get her to succumb to the casting-couch routine. She wouldn't.

She had been the typical Hollywood beauty hoping for a

breakthrough. She wasn't dumb; just cynical of all that had gone before. She was basking in it: 'I just realised,' she boasted, 'that now any man in Hollywood will meet me if I want that. Correction: make that any man anywhere. That's the up side of fame.'

Douglas, cool about Stone from the beginning and never entirely comfortable with her stridency while filming, would not begrudge her anything. Like everyone else who worked with him, Stone praised his professionalism, saying he had been 'kind and generous' to her throughout, which seemed to have come as a refreshing change. A number of people said that. Diandra had another view on the matter.

20
Inner Demons

There was a kind of irony in the fact that Michael and Diandra Douglas celebrated their fifteenth wedding anniversary on the day that *Basic Instinct* opened for general release in America. The movie unleashed a microscopic examination of Douglas the man, and it was almost inevitable that his and his wife's attitudes to the most sexually sensational film of its age should be probed.

Quite apart from the prurience of tabloid exploitation of the same sexual explicitness that the movie itself was exploiting with the minimum of excuse, there was a serious undercurrent to the whole business.

For one thing, life in Hollywood has a nasty habit of imitating art, examples of which are to be found virtually everywhere. For another, the clichéd images of mid-life crisis for Douglas, which have cropped up intermittently in the past, would also arise, and a picture emerges of a man disturbed both personally and professionally.

The difference was noticeable in his face and general demeanour. The bouncy personality and generally relaxed features had taken on a greyer tone, the mouth and lips were more pursed and certainly much harder than the jovial expressions of the past. He had taken on the appearance of a man suddenly plagued, even overtaken, by the emotions of the characters he had been portraying of late, similar to a psychiatrist becoming too involved with the problems of a client. It is not an uncommon situation among actors.

Looking again at *Basic Instinct* – because it is the type of film that needs a second or third viewing to see beyond the shock

241

tactics – there is a certain shallowness to the story, one too many coincidences for the sake of keeping the plot turning. It was a thrilling, enthralling movie, high on entertainment value. But what emerged from the detail of how the film came into being at all, as explained in the previous chapter, was an undeniable feeling that the sexual content was artificial and contrived for the purposes of controversialism and titillation – hotly denied, of course, by all concerned.

The reality was that *Basic Instinct* had nothing to do with art. Instead, the film went straight for the audience's jugular. As a result, ultimately Douglas's own motives are brought into question.

What made one of Hollywood's most respected inhabitants, a husband and father, expose himself in such a manner? His art? The money? Change of image or time-of-life pressure that demanded he make a new impact? And did he ever stop to consider the quite basic premise of family values – in his own family?

What was the reaction of Diandra, the very model of exemplary social correctness, to (a) his decision to make the film at all and (b) seeing her husband's body on public display in such erotic circumstances? Anger verging on rage ... disappointment ... embarrassment? A mixture of all three?

Douglas's loudly professed attempt to try to separate his professional activities from his personal life was under constant attack. As the year developed, Michael seemed to be having greater difficulty than at any time during his career in keeping the two apart.

The demands of being Hollywood's new Mr Sex became a heavy burden, particularly as he was already cast by gossips as a philandering husband – without, it must be said, a great deal of tangible evidence except his silence and lack of denial. On the probability of actors being drawn increasingly to acting out their most famous roles in real life, the Douglas marriage looked set for a more trouble.

It is possible to chart several points on the compass of matrimony where Michael's and Diandra's interests and activities were poles apart. The previous June, while the gay/lesbian lobby was mounting its vociferous attacks against her husband and the movie, Diandra was named Philanthropist of the Year by the American Red Cross for her work to benefit the homeless.

Then, as Michael became the focus of the most virulent and exploitative worldwide publicity seen for the launch of any picture in recent times, she was beginning her own major project. His and her work were the unlikeliest of bedfellows. Diandra was producing a film documentary about one of the earliest and most avant-garde artists of New York, Beatrice Wood, then ninety-two years old, entitled *The Mama of Dada,* to be released early in 1993.

With public recognition of her own acclaimed work for charitable causes and her new film aimed at the most élitist section of American artistic society, Diandra had reached a certain career pinnacle herself. Even in the most harmonious of marriages, her contrasting world would have lain uncomfortably next to her husband's explorations of overt sex and violence.

The flush on their faces when that very contrast was asked about by friends showed that the subject had been the cause of debate at home. That popular phrase from marital discussions – 'How could you . . . ?' – springs to mind.

Diandra was told about the sex scenes only after Michael had accepted the role. She knew the money was sensational, and that that kind of money does not come without strings. She was heard to comment dismissively, as if it hurt, that there was no prior discussion except for him telling her he had 'decided he wanted to play a leading man with a sexy image or something'.

The 'or something' came out waspishly, as if it was meant to sting but at the same time register her disinterest in whatever he chose. The extent of the sex content was unknown to her until the movie was under way, and she did not know of its explicitness until she sat with some discomfort watching it on the screen. And she would add, 'Oh yes, it did hurt . . .'

Basic Instinct was a counterpoint to what many saw as their essentially separate lives. With their son away at school, the family anchorage was less focused than it otherwise might have been. The underlying explanation for their 'separate' lives was the same now as it always had been: when he was working in Hollywood or on location, he would stay in a hotel, and ninety per cent of the time Diandra would be in New York or wherever her own work took her.

She used those periods of separation to do the things she wanted, except that the time he spent away working had become more prolonged over the years. Similarly, her attitude was the same as it always had been: 'I'm not going to wait around in some anonymous hotel room all day while you are out filming.'

Diandra had repeated her position to Douglas often enough, and she told her friends that the realisation had dawned on her in the early 1980s during the despair and anger of their ten-month separation: 'Everyone has to have their own identity. My own position, with Michael being away so often, was that I either had to tag along behind – which, believe me, I never intended to do – or go out and do something on my own. I really did have no one to count on except myself, and that's basically why I finished my education, so that I could get a job. I did it without help from anyone, and it was important for me to do that. I did not want to fall into the ambiguity of becoming one of the so-called Hollywood wives.'

Only in 1992, as Douglas disengaged himself from some business interests to commit himself more wholeheartedly to being an actor, were more blank spaces appearing in his future schedule. He predicted that by the end of 1992, after filming his next movie, *Falling Down*, he would take that much-promised but never accomplished year or more off work and spend his time with Diandra – just the two of them. Diandra has heard it all before, and commented acerbically: 'I'll believe it when I see it.'

Basic Instinct also inflamed that other constant in the Douglas's marriage, which was the publicity, the merging of fact with fiction, art with real life. Statements such as 'Douglas's steamy sex with Sharon', used in headlines the world over, never take account of the fictional element, that it's all make-believe; in terms of mass public belief, the actors are temporarily the characters they are playing but recognisable only by their real names.

That is the difference between movies and television. In long-running television series or soaps, the name of the actor invariably takes second place to the name of the character: the actor whose name is William becomes universally known by the name of the character he portrays, which might be Ken. And so it is 'Ken in sexy romp' whether the romp is on television or in real life. In the movies the headlines deal with the name of the star because the star, not the character, enjoys the fame and/or notoriety.

Yet, behind that media image of an actor is a man with a wife, and usually children. They attempt to keep their lives together on some kind of even keel, in which camera lenses poking through their keyholes eventually becomes part of normality. The novels of Jackie Collins and Jacqueline Susann have created a particular picture of Hollywood wives, though that picture is out of date and less accurate than it was.

The modern term of Hollywood wives is an anachronism. As Diandra Douglas fought to prove, the female half of movieland partnerships does not necessarily have to be assigned to minor social activities, adorning the mansions in their gowns and jewels, spending their lives entertaining the people in power, and disguising their sadness and insecurity in pills, drink and an affair with the tennis pro.

They either settle for that life – and many still do – or confront it head-on. Even so, the history of the movies is littered with lives shattered by the pressures imposed by the work of the spouse, a fact that does not change.

The Hollywood studio 'system' used to be blamed for the woeful events in the lives of its stars, and to a degree it was true. The feeding of uppers and downers to a youthful Judy Garland is one of many such horror stories. Dozens of off-screen 'romances' created by the publicity people – as with Rock Hudson and Marilyn Maxwell – were ludicrous in the extreme, but all part of the misty glamour being projected to the ticket-buying public.

More often, however, Hollywood's personal traumas, tragedies, addictions, broken marriages and self-destruction were the result of temptations placed before mere mortals who had achieved wealth and fame beyond their wildest dreams. Excess in its various forms was and is abundant and available to all who could pay for it, in cash or favour.

The line of vodkas, soft drugs or cocaine, the stream of voluptuous, ambitious young men or women, sexual deviance in all its forms for everyone who wanted to play, the temptations of on-screen romances spilling over into real life, all have become part of both the reality and the mythology: everything is available in plentiful supply to those who want it.

Even the reasons themselves are many layered and often psychologically based. Lust, loneliness, the need for excitement, the need for attention, the sheer inability to ward off temptation, and any one might mask a far deeper fault-line among what is basically the most insecure, complex-ridden and maladjusted group of people anywhere on this earth. Excess mixed with insecurity equals addictiveness, as Elizabeth Taylor, Elvis Presley, Montgomery Clift, Elton John and 1001 other celebrities of the last half century have shown.

Fame itself is the first addiction, usually followed by the chemical and physical antidotes to the effects of that fame.

When life is lived in the fast lane, something has to give. That is what led to the troubles that Douglas and his wife have struggled through at various times of their marriage. More recently, the concerns that had driven Diandra to occasional despair have as much to do with their son Cameron as herself.

The situation they found themselves in was the one that Michael knew existed and knew how it could affect a young boy, because it had happened to him. He had walked in on that heavy love scene between Kirk Douglas and Lana Turner, so heavy that Kirk had told him to shove off and had made a point of explaining it all later. It was a difficult situation, one that Kirk likened to cowboys and Indians or cops and robbers where everyone in the movies had blanks in their guns.

Michael might not have had the courage to challenge his own father. His own son did, and mentioned that guns might have blanks but kissing was kissing, etc. The age of innocence is long past. Cameron, his formative years spent in New York, was certainly not ignorant of real life. It was through him too that

Michael and Diandra shared another bone of contention, a matter on which Diandra was prepared to argue even if her case indirectly attacked her husband's career.

Her view, quite simply, was that films and television had contributed enormously to the upsurge in crimes involving sex and violence, making the most horrific scenes so commonplace that people generally, and young people in particular, had been desensitised. Local television in American cities, in Diandra's view, was worse than the cinema because it always zoomed in on the bloodstains of the most violent stories.

If they were ever on a discussion panel together, Michael Douglas would argue that he felt it was a 'cop-out' to blame the movies and television. The causes were much more deeply rooted, multilayered and complex. At the same time he would have difficulty in defending *Basic Instinct* in that respect, and openly admitted that he did not think it was a picture that should be seen by anybody under the age of seventeen.

Having said that, he then discovered that Cameron had already been to see the movie with four of his friends – at the age of thirteen, proving that the R-rating system was not rigidly policed at the cinema box office. It was not the first time Cameron had deliberately gone against his mother's wishes to watch his father engaged in screen sex. Douglas learned that he had watched *Fatal Attraction* at the house of a friend a couple of years earlier. It was clearly a sore point with Diandra that filmmakers – of whom her husband was one – 'keep turning out this kind of product'.

Diandra made no secret of her dislike and disdain for such material and its negative effect on social values. She believed, too, that the effect was demonstrated in other areas of American and western life. The whole question of family values clearly weighed heavily on Diandra, as was demonstrated by a discussion she and Michael had on the topic with writer and broadcaster Deborah Norville for *McCall's* magazine.

As a woman who was brought up with politics and whose interest in political life had extended through her own education and personal interests, Diandra was critical of the 1992 election campaign. She felt this had developed into a 'superficial character assassination' involving seedy sex and the alleged corruption of the participants instead of focusing on the issues of the day. She had been disappointed at the way the Republicans had targeted Bill Clinton's private life.

Her husband agreed with her. He spoke of that election year being 'so destructive' for so many people. He scorned the fact that the Republicans had made so much of declining 'family values' when the Reagan and Bush administrations had been largely responsible 'for dismantling a lot of the social structure that existed to help families'.

Beneath that aura of political and social concern, however, lay a much deeper and personal worry that was central to their own problems. Diandra bemoaned their fate of being a high-profile family in a culture that was 'star crazy'. In what seemed to be almost a direct attack on her husband's position, she complained: 'It makes me sad to observe what is happening in America, and I see the idolisation of television and movie stars and people looking to them for morals and direction. We should be focusing on positive aspects of life.'

Once again, she appeared to be absorbed by a feeling of bitterness which at times verged on hatred of the 'star' syndrome in which her husband and his father had been pivotal figures for the entire second half of the twentieth century. Hollywood, as far as Diandra was concerned, was as phoney as a three-dollar bill, its values inflated, its people self-obsessed; even her own father-in-law – on Michael's own admission – could not take his eyes off himself, even in his seventies.

The whole cultural influence of films and television worried her to the degree that she felt almost taunted, if not tainted, by her husband's work when he engaged himself in such projects as *Fatal Attraction* and *Basic Instinct*. The money he earned financed a superb lifestyle, but she had said privately many times that she would and could settle for much less if their married life could assume a measure of normality.

Therein lay a particular plea from the heart which concerned not so much the public side of filmmaking and its debatable social side-effects but the personal aspects. Michael Douglas's own *raison d'être* had altered significantly in the last few years, and it had led to a further exaggeration of all the things she did not like about the business and his involvement in it.

Furthermore, he had failed dismally in his attempts to spare more of his time for the family. One further thing aggravated their situation: media scrutiny. *Basic Instinct* tipped the balance from what had been a fairly controlled level of publicity focusing on his work to a more prurient exposé of his private life.

Michael always made himself accessible to the media. Doing so meant that by and large he could control the level of media coverage and, by being the interviewer's friend, maintain a generally acceptable press.

The tabloid coverage after *Basic Instinct* was engendered by the sexual connotations, as it was to a lesser degree after *Fatal Attraction*. Diandra's new woes, curiously enough, coincided with the 1992 election campaign, when Bill Clinton's social arrangements and the business involvements of himself and Hillary were under close scrutiny. A strikingly similar parallel could be drawn in the Douglas household, but in their case – as opposed to the Clintons – the media was all but invited in.

At the very time of her openness on family values, Diandra faced what she told friends was the most disconcerting and destabilising period of her life, one that came very close to finally ending her marriage. Though the underlying problems, as we have seen, had existed for years, the current troubles, culminating in an explosion of upsetting differences in autumn 1992, actually began earlier in the year.

At the time Michael had just come through his massive international publicity campaign for *Basic Instinct*. First he had been confronted by a barrage of American media attention – hard on the heels of the gay lobby protests – and then went on to London, Berlin and, in May, the Cannes Film Festival, where he was met by a veritable stream of interviewers and writers.

While discussing the sexual and violent content of *Basic Instinct*, Douglas was prodded about his own preferences. The publicity was sought, and he gave his responses of his own free will. To be fair, most of the coverage was restrained, but it was none the less explicit – it had to be, because they were dealing with an explicit movie.

Fairly typical was the coverage of the London *Evening Standard*. 'Lust, human nature and basic instinct, by Douglas . . . Michael Douglas says he can be a real animal when it comes to passion and it is an instinct which lurks deep in everyone. He said, "I've always been interested in lust and everybody has lusted for someone at some time or other. The fact is that whether they've acted it out or not, there's a carnal, chemical reaction that's fascinating, especially if someone acted on it and then lost control of their life after the animal side took over." '

With such quotes Douglas played into the hands of extrovert coverage of his life – and it followed, month after month. Even Cameron was brought into it – by Douglas himself, incidentally – when he revealed to a writer that his son had come home from school distraught and with a black eye: a playground punch-up had followed taunts by other boys that Cameron's father slept with a lesbian. Diandra herself had to put up with a succession of telephone calls from women making pretty awful remarks about her husband's body.

Not long afterwards Douglas gave another interview, not an off-the-cuff encounter but a relaxed, tape-recorded one in which he had time to consider his replies. Out of it came a sentence that would be highlighted: 'I *love* women. I love women in general and I love any woman with intelligence and a sense of humour. Those are the most important things – and a couple of other things as well. But I think it's demeaning for a woman to make the first move, to become the hunter. Maybe it's old-fashioned, but I was brought up to believe that a man chases a woman, until she catches him!'

It was probably an innocent enough observation, but taken out of context, as these remarks often are, such statements become, in the end, relentless for the partner.

Media interest reached such a pitch that even Douglas himself felt overexposed. He took a family party, including Diandra, Cameron, Jack Nicholson and Rebecca Broussard, to Spain in June for the 1992 Olympics, and carried on their holiday at their hillside retreat in Majorca. They remained for as long as he could, then he had to return for work on the movie *Falling Down*. Thus, he was bound to Hollywood for another period.

The bombshell of events that almost drove a permanent wedge between them came while he was there. The now-legendary confrontation between Diandra and Douglas was reputed to have occurred in the Beverly Regent Wilshire Hotel where *Pretty Woman* was filmed (and where Warren Beatty kept a suite for years before he married Annette Bening, as indeed did Howard Hughes). Michael booked suite 719 whenever he was filming in Los Angeles.

On the night of 3 September, so the story went, Diandra arrived to discover him in bed with one of her best friends. They had a furious row and Diandra stormed out of the hotel. Later, she telephoned Michael and gave him her ultimatum: 'Get help or get out!'

That was when he agreed to undergo therapy. He checked himself into the Sierra Tucson Clinic, Arizona, on 17 September, under the name Mike Morrell. Wearing a blue shirt, jeans and sandals, he looked depressed and morose. He signed in for treatment under the clinic's $19,500, thirty-day programme for curative guidance of sexual addiction and alcohol abuse.

The Sierra Tucson Clinic is a secretive place, dealing as it does with famous clients suffering from the most private of demons. It is located at the foot of the Catalina Mountains, and can be reached only by a special security pass. It was described for the author by one of its counsellors as 'a medical oasis', where bodies torn asunder by addictions and excess may be restored to good health.

It deals with a variety of afflictions, including alcohol and drug abuse, but is known particularly for its therapy for the sexually maladjusted. Clients are required to sign an admission statement which defines their problems; they then follow a course of treatment consisting of private counselling and group therapy.

The clinic defines a sexually addicted person as 'someone who has an uncontrollable urge to indulge in sexual practices without emotion'. Patients are expected to take part in two-hour group discussions in which they must be completely honest in admitting to everything relevant to their afflictions, past and present.

Michael Douglas, encouraged by his counsellor, began his programme of self-discovery when he stood up, head bowed, and gave a lengthy commentary about his inner demons and the problems that had turned him into something of a Jekyll and Hyde character. He confessed to the group of eight fellow sufferers: 'Sex is just a wave that sweeps over me, an impulse that is overpowering. I'm helpless. Every time.'

In keeping with the programme of therapy, each group member was asked to define their sexual preferences, ticking off the headings of pornography, homosexuality, obscenity of any kind, voyeurism . . .

Douglas dismissed all except one specific problem: as he saw it, this was an overactive libido towards women which had made him take some stupid risks. He also admitted a tendency to excessive use of alcohol and occasional use of drugs, usually in a social setting, although he did not class himself as addicted to either. He said he had lost the trust and respect of his wife, which was why he had sought help. She had 'kicked me out' of the marital bedroom and was repulsed by his actions. 'I love my wife and my son very much,' he told his group, 'and I am here because I am destroying myself and destroying them.'

He reiterated that he had decided to take a year off work when the promotion of his current movie was completed. He intended to move on, sustained by the therapy and support he had received at the clinic which had made him look inside himself. He was determined, he said, to discipline himself to a more settled, less pressurised life, where his family would come first and his work second.

Michael Douglas, world-famous movie star, had humbled himself to an acceptance of what is already evident: that he had driven himself fast and furiously along the Hollywood boulevard to fame and great fortune, just as his father had done before him, and in the process risked losing those he cared for most. He had now seemingly come to an abrupt halt just in time.

The irony of what happened that autumn was that he was on

the brink of another massive publicity round, to talk up his new movie, an explosive story about an ordinary American white-collar worker who, faced with the pressures of modern life, finally snaps.

Life and art had mixed and matched. Michael Douglas brushed himself off and strode away from the Sierra Tucson Clinic towards his private jet to carry him back to the world of make-believe. Reality is too heady by far.

21
Some Kind of Hero

Regardless of the Tucson experience, a credibility gap was about to become a problem for Michael Douglas. In recent years the movies in which he chose to appear were, by and large, a reflection of current social issues; they were always controversial and invariably pushed the subject-matter to permissible extremes. That's what made him a superstar.

The underlying theme lately, however, could be seen as an exploitation of those issues rather than an explanation of them, recalling perhaps that famous saying of the mogul Jack Warner to one of his directors: 'If you want to send a message, use Western Union, not my movies.'

Douglas did not send messages, just bald facts, and he let his audience react to them as they pleased. In many ways he gambled with critical and audience reaction. When he spoke, as he often did, of wishing to maintain some kind of integrity in his work, it was not difficult to challenge this intention when the roles he had played in his last few pictures were examined.

He had chosen the dark path, the heroes who turned bad. They were characters no other major star would touch with a barge-pole for fear of damaging his image. He had courage in that respect, but, as he has said, he had no image to sustain. He wasn't a romantic idol or even a tough guy who always redeemed himself in the final scene. He shows us the flaws of his characters, regardless of putting himself in a bad light.

That had been obvious in every role he had played since *Fatal Attraction*. Of all the current male stars in Hollywood, virtually none would take the risks he took – with the exception of Jack

Nicholson and Robert De Niro, Hollywood's two supreme princes of darkness.

The integrity of those two actors came from their ability, the sheer power of their performance. Douglas was on the brink of joining them, and, although he could not have done so without his innate talent, he had come to the major league by his careful selection of roles that were aligned to issues of current social consequence.

His portrayals and plots threw up masses of debate which usually resulted in one thing: the total projection of Michael Douglas and the movie he was promoting at the time. This was no accident. It was skilful manipulation achieved through his sound judgement of current affairs and an open-door policy which drew in the media hordes to listen to him.

If he cared about personal integrity, and he said he did, it had to be maintained through himself, from his explanations and his attitudes. So far, he had managed to operate on two distinct levels – as Douglas the actor, who gave us these flawed characters that struck the rawest nerve of his nation, and as Douglas the man, who was able to stand above his work and provide reasoned arguments as to why he had pushed himself and whatever current topic engaged him to such extremes. He always followed one with the other, always ready to explain and defend.

In that way he has managed to retain the integrity and the respect he had built up in his profession over the past decade. But, very suddenly, the question was being asked: has Michael Douglas gone too far?

His new movie, *Falling Down*, showed every sign of landing him, as one close associate put it, 'in the deepest of shit!' The groundwork for attack had already been laid by himself. The tabloids had given him a severe thrashing over the alleged infidelities and his reputed obsession with sex and lust. The Mr Nice Guy who had shown us a ruthless streak in his pictures really did possess some basic flaws of his own. Was it possible that the darker side of human nature, deliberately injected into his career by his selection of roles, was rubbing off on the man himself?

Of course, rumour-mongering had for years put him into bed with every attractive female he met, although the evidence was rather less specific. But, now, dark corners of his life began to be exposed.

Falling Down was already completed and ready for release by then. The publicity surrounding his personal problems would become part of the huge campaign that Warners were about to set rolling to launch the movie. It didn't matter to the PR people, really: publicity would be achieved with a spiciness that was like a rekindling of the last days of the Golden Age, approaching the Taylor–Burton scandals.

Only a supreme PR cynic would suggest that even Douglas himself would benefit from leaks from the Tucson clinic, by the effect that the stories would have on the public and the box office, in which he had a percentage. The ingredients were all in place for a rip-roaring few months in which all the above elements would figure.

It all began the previous spring. He was still involved in *Basic Instinct* when he accepted the assignment for *Falling Down*. The much-promised time out with his wife and family was put off again because the new project became almost an obsession with him. It had all the hallmarks of a Douglas classic – if for no other reason than it had been turned down by virtually every major studio in Hollywood.

By coincidence, Douglas had already had a meeting with his agents to discuss his next film; he had made it clear that this time, he wanted to be the initiator in the movie. 'I'm fed up with being the fall guy for women,' he told them. '*Fatal Attraction* and *Basic Instinct* both put me in a corner – I was the reactive character to female dominance.'

Such roles were getting to be too much of a habit. They had already been seen in *Shining Through*, *War of the Roses*, *The Jewel of the Nile* and *Romancing the Stone*, where he was the other half of a double act with a major female role. Whereas he had sought something 'sexy and bad' for *Basic Instinct*, he wanted its follow-up to give him a solo outing with no reliance on the female input. *Falling Down* was just such a vehicle. By chance, it arrived virtually in the next post. The screenplay, by Ebbe Roe Smith, had been touted around by producer Arnold Kopelson for months; it scared the mainstream people, and Kopelson was on the verge of selling it, watered down and cheaply, to a cable television outfit when Douglas read it.

He got in touch immediately and enthusiastically announced that it was without doubt one of the best scripts he had ever read. His judgement on such matters had proved pretty well infallible to date, so no one was going to argue – least of all his pal Joel Schumacher, the director whom Douglas had employed for *Flatliners*. Once again Douglas had stumbled across a script that would take him on to the front pages; a movie exactly of its time.

His relationship with Schumacher went back far longer than their last encounter. As with so many friends of the past, Douglas was indebted to him for his loyalty and support. They had been friends for twenty years. They used to attend the same Hollywood parties when no one wanted to know them, so they talked to each other. Schumacher's arrival as a contender for major work had been a long and tortuous process. Softly spoken Schumacher, two years older than Douglas, is a reformed drug addict who describes himself as a bleeding-heart, ponytailed, ex-hippie, liberal moviemaker. He was carefully chosen by Douglas, who insisted on his directing the movie if the project were to proceed.

Schumacher was born in a poor neighbourhood of New York. His family was so poverty-stricken that they could not even afford a television set. As a young man he worked nights to put himself through a design school. After graduating, he went into window-dressing then fashion designing for Revlon. In the 1970s he moved into television and film, struggling to stay afloat as a $200-a-week costume designer on such films as *Sleeper* and *Interiors* for Woody Allen.

Inspired by Allen's humour, he began writing screenplays of his own, including *Car Wash,* starring Richard Pryor, and then *The Wiz*. His first outing as a director was *The Incredible Shrinking Woman* in 1981. He followed this with *St Elmo's Fire*, which he wrote and directed and which launched several names which would endure, such as Rob Lowe, Demi Moore, Emilio Estevez and Judd Nelson.

But it was Michael Douglas's *Flatliners* that gave him his mainstream chance. After that, he was reunited with Julia Roberts for the emotionally upsetting *Dying Young*, about a terminally ill young woman. It was sensitively made, but a box office clinker.

He had done nothing since until Douglas contacted him and asked him to stand by. 'When I read *Falling Down*,' Schumacher recalls, 'I could not understand why no one had made this movie. Then I realised that Ebbe had struck a nerve right at the heart of American culture. It had political, social and economic ramifications. There was an everyday insanity about it. Darkly funny, but containing a monstrous anger that actually reflected the views of a wide cross-section of American society. It was a script that dealt with racist, bigoted people who were angry that all they had worked for was disappearing.'

There were already examples of what happened in the film: the McDonald's hamburger massacre, for example, when a man returns to the place he once worked at and lets loose with an automatic rifle to vent his anger, killing several people; then, even as filming began, the Los Angeles riots broke out in April, and for a time it looked as if the movie might be halted.

Schumacher would deny that he had envisaged the impact *Falling Down* would have or the controversy it would cause. He suspected that Michael Douglas had a good idea all along that they would be stirring up a hornets' nest, a whole hotbed of simmering emotions, but they never discussed it.

They just got on with the job and made the picture. Schumacher admits he was 'shocked rigid' by the furore that followed. Even Douglas himself would say that anyone who reckoned they foresaw *Falling Down* becoming the blockbuster it turned out to be was 'talking shit'.

As Douglas saw it, the concept was remarkably simple. He plays an 'ordinary, invisible Joe' whose personal tensions and frustrations have reached the point of explosion. In Douglas's

259

vision, this man represented millions of people who were angry but did not know what they were angry at. His character was an anonymous everyman. He was white, patriotic and had worked all his life in the defence industry, which meant so much to him that he had a personalised number-plate on his car: D-FENS.

He wore his hair in a crew-cut, had half-rimmed spectacles and a short-sleeved white shirt with pens in the pocket. Then, this once-valued worker is made redundant. He has money and marriage problems and is getting angrier by the second. He finally cracks under the pressures of modern life when his car becomes gridlocked on the hottest day of the summer in the crazy circus that is the Los Angeles freeway system.

He gets out, locks the door and walks away, intent on forcing himself on his estranged wife and child. This man, in Douglas's interpretation, is supposed to be the embodiment of all the pent-up anguish of middle-class America at the time: a white, suburban male laid low by the recession, seeing all that he has worked for decline in value, his home and family under threat, and, above all, upset by the invasion of what he perceives as foreign cultures into American life.

The paranoia explodes into terrible vengeance when he stops at a store run by a Korean grocer and asks for change. The unhelpful grocer forces him to buy a Coke to split a dollar bill; he blows his top and proceeds to smash the place up. As his adventure proceeds, he wades into an attack on the many layers of Los Angeles communities: the Latinos, when he is attacked by a couple of muggers whom he beats off with a baseball bat; the blacks, in a burger bar where he is refused breakfast because it is almost lunchtime; the white upper classes, by his confrontation with a couple of Republicans playing golf.

The process was intriguingly paced, so that for the time being the audience was on his side, with Douglas cautiously portraying his character as a victim of injustice. That was Schumacher's major contribution to the movie. Originally, the script had D-FENS going wild very quickly; but the director slowed the action, to let the tension build to achieve audience identification, so the audience could see there was some justification in everything that D-FENS did.

Then, the parallel character is introduced, the retiring policeman played by Robert Duvall. He too has his problems; he is angry for very similar reasons, but contains himself with compassion and restraint. Duvall is the classic foil to the turmoil and mayhem unleashed by Douglas, who eventually shows us that D-FENS is a psychotic.

Or is he? Douglas stands upright, asking: 'Am I the bad guy?' It was a moment in the movie at which those who saw him as a hero could stand and cheer, which is what they did. But he wasn't supposed to be a hero.

A number of explanations, if not excuses, would be made about this picture. 'As I saw it,' says Schumacher, 'this movie was reflecting existing attitudes in society. Usually, the movies that reflect anger in the street do so from the standpoint of Afro-Americans, a race thing. The fact is, they are not the only angry people in America. This is a multiracial, multicultural city, and the story could have been on any six o'clock news. I tried to give it a face and a soul.'

Schumacher called a wrap in the late summer and retired with his editors to the post-production suite at Warners. Douglas popped in every now and again to watch the progress. But by then he had his own problems and had checked into the clinic at Tucson.

Few knew of his intentions until they burst into the public arena from a tabloid exposé. He certainly gave no indication that his troubles were anything other than those related to self-indulgence. Perhaps his therapist might well have argued – as others have done in the past with similarly troubled members of his profession – that it is impossible to totally cleanse the actor's soul of a particularly intense character.

In Douglas's case there had been a string of such parts, a veritable theatre of psychological imperfections. Well, yes, it was only play-acting, only a movie, but remnants from the imperfect and flawed people he had created for the screen may well have lingered.

There was an apparent weakness – indeed several – in his

psychological make-up, but also very considerable strengths. As an actor he proved once again his ability to absorb a character created in the mind of a writer and to expand that creation into extreme but entertaining proportions.

That Warners had a remarkable piece of cinematography on their hands was borne out at a test run in Santa Monica a few weeks before the film's release. The location was carefully selected, a little pocket of middle-class WASPness in Greater Los Angeles, overlooking the Pacific Ocean, virtually devoid of multiracial tensions, and no guns or gangs. The screening was staged to judge audience reaction, and to give the promotional effort a direction.

Schumacher, who attended, had been warned that past marketing exercises of this sort showed that up to a third of the audience of five hundred, randomly invited off the streets, would leave before the end. Warners realised they had a winner on their hands when not one member of the audience walked out before the final gasp of the picture. That did not mean they liked what they saw. As they filed out of the theatre, many said they hated what the film stood for, but were enthralled by it just the same.

Douglas looked at the test-screening reports and gave his own assessment: 'It scared them. It scares me. The audience is brought face to face with their denials of what exists in America today.' The blue touchpaper had been lit. Now he stood back to await the explosion, which came when the movie opened across the country at the end of February 1993.

The advance publicity had brought out the pickets in force. Dozens of cinemas were besieged by lines of anguished minorities and ethnic groups, not least the Latinos, American Koreans and defence workers, whose industry in California had been decimated by the end of the Cold War and who thought Douglas was slighting them.

Once again, the movie became much more than just a well-hyped, well-made vehicle of entertainment. It started a national debate. Newspapers and magazines devoted front pages to it, talkshows brought out all kinds of pundits and experts for discussions as a kind of exercise in self-examination by the American people. Douglas himself, as the focus and inspiration of this outpouring, was in the greatest demand, first in America and then in Europe, where the film opened in June.

He was heavily criticised in America by a broad range of commentators, who branded his film violent, irresponsible and racist, just as the nuclear power lobby had tried to discredit him fifteen years earlier. He surely knew it would happen. Other Hollywood stars would have played the sympathy card, softened up the character or got the writer to change the emphasis to fit the image of the actor. Douglas didn't. Sex was the thing in *Basic Instinct*; playing an action man who was also a bad guy was what drew him to *Falling Down*.

The fact that the 'action' was largely at the expense of ethnic groups aroused particular ill-feeling, on the grounds that in their encounters with D-FENS the ethnic groups came off worst. Charges of racism were laid against Michael, and even Kirk was brought out to fight a rearguard action for his son. 'People don't seem to realise or accept that Michael is playing the villain,' said Kirk, 'and as such the rest are his victims. That's not racism, that's honesty.'

The lines of interviewers who waited to see Michael at each stop on the promotional tour were still not convinced, but he gave them the same unapologetic reply: 'Certainly, racism is part of the man I play. I don't defend it, nor do I intend to be identified with it, but I do have the right to demonstrate that it exists. You cannot make a movie today if you have to worry whether you're politically correct.'

That was the point, in a nutshell. Douglas had dared to challenge that new fad that came sailing in with the 1990s: political correctness. He spits out his objection to the notion that movies today should in some way provide a formula for the conduct of society.

No, he wasn't sending messages. There was no hidden agenda in *Falling Down* and nor was one ever intended, according to Douglas. The film was a presentation of facts, an accumulation of disturbing incidents that could happen, were happening, with no sub-text and no last-reel solution. The problems were thrown at the audience for them to take home and ponder.

He chose to get involved in this head-on confrontation with politics because Hollywood is no longer making movies that tackle social and moral issues. The studios have for a long time now concentrated on escapism and nostalgia. Even Oliver Stone and Kevin Costner delved way back into the past for their most controversial efforts.

Modern message pictures do not sell. The only way to tackle social issues commercially is Douglas's way: make them sexy or violent or both and show the world that problems exist. In that regard he has cornered the market and is an exceptional moviemaker.

The fact also remains that, in the absence of social-probing movies, productions like *Falling Down* and *Basic Instinct* become the target of attention by indignant minority groups. What Douglas found startling was that audience reactions varied almost from seat to seat, depending on the kind of person it was, what class or ethnic group.

The Koreans, it was said, were ready to put the finger on him for insulting them. He refused to apologise and said he felt anyway that the Koreans had an image problem in America. It was no different from the prevailing sensitivities about the Japanese, which was so obvious in the way he dealt with the issue in *Black Rain*. If there was a problem – and it existed in both cases – then political correctness should not deter a filmmaker from addressing it. Nor did he think the film would encourage people to go around beating up Koreans, or any other group. That was the point of the movie, examining the context of American society. What *Falling Down* managed to be was entertainment with political, social, economic and even romantic layers.

Both he and Schumacher avoided making a political statement because they are agreed that it is a misuse of power. 'Even so, I felt there was a deep, dark, growing cancer in the streets of our cities,' said Douglas, 'and more and more people are going to disintegrate. This film, in a darkly humorous way and hopefully in an entertaining way, was giving those problems a voice.'

* * *

This is Michael Douglas, back on form and in full flight again, explaining his mission, telling the world why he makes this kind of movie and why he makes up his own mind about his work. That's called choice. And choice is power, power is money. And the only thing that more than slightly undermines a case for the defence of Michael Douglas is the certain knowledge that he was getting $10 million plus a slice of the gross to make the film.

That's Hollywood.

It's a job. It's art. It's the movies. But, above all, it's entertainment. It is also Douglas's life. His peers recognised it as such when they presented him with a Lifetime Achievement Award in October 1993, applauding his contribution to cinema over the past twenty-five years. Jack Lemmon, who handed over the plaque, remembered the old days when Douglas was just getting started and was driven by a need to prove himself.

Today he is a star of modern stories, but the mixture remains much the same. The actors, the producers, the directors and the moneymen do what they have to with the aim of filling cinemas and pleasing the customers, and Diandra Douglas still worries about the 'star' culture.

To see film people gathered in all their glory at the swank, ritzy Hollywood glamour parties, one sometimes wonders why anyone ever takes them seriously, with all their troubles and woes and hang-ups. The gloss has faded over the years and the glamour has gone tacky. Money does all the talking. There is some integrity left; some faces among them are motivated by things beyond the next big pay cheque and are not attracted by power. There is some kind of humanity hidden away in the background, but it rarely sees sunlight.

No one knows that better than Michael's mother, Diana Dill, who, like Diandra, took two paces back from the epicentre all those years ago but was never far away during the darker days of her son's life. It is from within the family that the Douglas clan draws its breath and seeks renewal. In the midst of what was a difficult time for her son, Diana, then seventy, was herself going back on stage in a play to be produced by her husband, Bill

Darrid. Sadly, Bill died suddenly in July 1992. Darrid had been the stabilising hand over the lives of Michael and Joel, especially in the early days when Michael was adventuresome.

As a tribute to Bill, Michael decided that the play should go ahead and staged it at an off-Broadway theatre. It was a Shaw play entitled *The Best of Friends* – an apt title, because that's what they all were. Diandra had tenuously forgiven her husband; he in turn had made promises and commitments about the future.

The circle had turned; time was the healer. Even the competitiveness with Kirk, which had endured for so long, had virtually gone, though not entirely; it probably never will, even when the father is dead. Speaking during those weeks on the promotion of *Falling Down*, Michael Douglas sounded uncannily like his father when he was much younger, not so much in tone or physical appearance but in the staunch forcefulness of his delivery, more than a pinch of arrogance, caring for no other opinion but his own, with a ring of confidence which tells everyone around that on this one Michael Douglas is not user-friendly and, be warned, can be tough when he wants to be.

Perhaps, next time, he will play the hero. 'People like heroes, don't they?'

A wrong question about his personal life brings an uneasy response. The jaw clenches square and shut, the cleft chin juts out, you can hear the molars grinding. The green eyes dart nervously. You can almost see the hair on the back of his neck bristling. Then, just when you think he is going to reach inside his jacket, pull out a shotgun and blow your head off, the lips unlock and reveal his perfect white teeth.

'Me?' he says, banging the palms of his hands on the arms of his chair. 'This time, I really am going to take a year off and show Diandra a good husband.'

The eyes moisten slightly, the face relaxes and cracks with a smile . . . it is the smile of the good guy again . . .

Which is where we came in.

266

Filmography

Hail, Hero! (1969) Producer Harold D. Cohen; Director David Miller.
Screenplay from the novel by John Weston. A Cinema Center Film/Halcyon Production. *Cast*: Arthur Kennedy, Michael Douglas, Teresa Wright, John Larch, Charles Drake, Peter Strauss

Adam at 6 a.m. (1970) Producer Cinema Center; Director Robert Scheerer.
Screenplay by Stephen and Elinor Karpf. A Cinema Center Film. *Cast*: Michael Douglas, Lee Purcell, Joe Don Baker, Grayson Hall, Charles Aidman, Meg Foster

Summertree (1971) Producer Kirk Douglas; Director Anthony Newley.
Screenplay based on a play by Ron Cowen. A Bryna Production, distributed by Columbia Pictures. *Cast*: Michael Douglas, Barbara Bel Geddes, Jack Warden, Brenda Vaccaro, Kirk Callaway, Bill Vint

When Michael Calls (1971) (For television) Producer Gil Shiva; Director Philip Leacock.
Screenplay by James Bridges from the novel by John Farris. Palomar Pictures/20th Century-Fox. *Cast*: Ben Gazzara, Michael Douglas, Elizabeth Ashley, Karen Pearson, Albert S. Waxman

Napoleon and Samantha (1972) Producer Walt Disney Productions; Director Bernard McEveety.
Screenplay by Stewart Raffill. Walt Disney Pictures. *Cast*: Michael Douglas, Jodie Foster, Henry Jones, Will Greer, Johnny Whittaker, Arch Johnson, Ellen Corby

The Streets of San Francisco (1972) (Pilot for television; 104 episodes were shown subsequently between 1972 and 1976) Producer Quinn Martin.
Cast: Karl Malden, Michael Douglas, Robert Wagner, Kim Darby, John Rubinstein, Tom Bosley, Andrew Duggan, Edward Andrews

Coma (1978) Producer Martin Erlichman; Director Michael Crichton.
Screenplay by Michael Crichton from the novel by Robin Cook. MGM. *Cast*: Geneviève Bujold, Michael Douglas, Tom Selleck, Elizabeth Ashley, Rip Torn, Richard Widmark, Lois Chiles, Lance LeGault

The China Syndrome (1979) Producer Michael Douglas; Director James Bridges.
Screenplay by Michael Gray, T.S. Cook and James Bridges. A Michael Douglas/IPC Films Presentation for Columbia Pictures. *Cast*: Jack Lemmon, Jane Fonda, Michael Douglas, Scott Brady, James Hampton, Peter Donat, Wilford Brimley, James Karen, Diandra Luker (Douglas)

Running (1979) Producers Robert Cooper and Ronald Cohen; Director/Writer Steven Hilliard Stern.
Universal Pictures. *Cast*: Michael Douglas, Susan Anspach, Lawrence Dane, Philip Akin, Eugene Levy, Charles Shamata

It's My Turn (1980) Producer Martini Elfand; Director Claudia Weill.
Screenplay by Eleanor Bergstein. Columbia Pictures. *Cast*: Jill Clayburgh, Michael Douglas, Beverly Garland, Charles Grodin, Steven Hill, Teresa Baxter, John Gabriel, Joan Copeland

The Star Chamber (1983) Producer Frank Yablans; Director Peter Hyams.
Screenplay by Roderick Taylor and Peter Hyams. 20th Century-Fox. *Cast*: Michael Douglas, Yaphet Kotto, Hal Holbrook, Joe Regalbuto, Sharon Gless, James B. Sikking, Diana Dill, DeWayne Jessie, Don Calfa, Jack Kehoe

Romancing the Stone (1984) Producer Michael Douglas; Director Robert Zemeckis.
Screenplay by Diane Thomas. 20th Century-Fox. *Cast*: Michael Douglas, Kathleen Turner, Danny DeVito, Alfonso Arau, Zack Norman, Holland Taylor, Manuel Ojeda

A Chorus Line (1985) Producers Cy Feuer and Ernest Martin; Director Richard Attenborough.
Screenplay by Arnold Schulman from the original stage play. Embassy/Polygram. *Cast*: Michael Douglas, Alyson Reed, Terence Mann, Greg Burge, Cameron English, Vicki Frederick, Nicole Fosse, Audrey Landers, Janet Jones

The Jewel of the Nile (1985) Producer Michael Douglas; Director Lewis Teague.
Screenplay by Mark Rosenthal and Lawrence Konner. 20th Century-Fox. *Cast*: Kathleen Turner, Michael Douglas, Danny DeVito, Avner Eisenberg, Spiros Focas, Holland Taylor, The Flying Karamazov Brothers

Fatal Attraction (1987) Producers Stanley Jaffe and Sherry Lansing; Director Adrian Lyne.
Screenplay by James Dearden. Paramount Pictures. *Cast*: Michael Douglas, Glenn Close, Anne Archer

Wall Street (1987) Producer Edward R. Pressman; Director Oliver Stone.
Screenplay by Stanley Weisner and Oliver Stone. 20th Century-Fox. *Cast*: Michael Douglas, Charlie Sheen, Darryl Hannah, Martin Sheen, Terence Stamp, Sean Young, Hal Holbrook, Sylvia Miles

Black Rain (1989) Producers Stanley Jaffe and Sherry Lansing; Director Ridley Scott.
Screenplay by Craig Bolotin and Warren Lewis. Paramount/UIP. *Cast*: Michael Douglas, Ken Takakura, Andy Garcia, Yusaka Matsuda, John Spencer, Shigeru Komaya, Stephen Root, Guto Ishimatsu, Tomisaburo Wakayama

War of the Roses (1989) Producers James L. Brooks and Arnon Milchan; Director Danny DeVito.
Screenplay by Michael Leeson from the novel by Warren Adler. 20th Century-Fox. *Cast*: Michael Douglas, Kathleen Turner, Danny DeVito, Marianne Sagebrecht, Sean Astin, G.D. Spradlin, Heather Fairchild, Peter Donat, Dan Castellaneta, Gloria Cromwell, Susan Isaacs, Jacqueline Cassell

Shining Through (1991) Producers Sandy Gallin, Howard Rosemann and Carol Baum; Director David Seltzer.
Screenplay by David Seltzer. 20th Century-Fox. *Cast*: Melanie Griffith, Michael Douglas, Liam Neeson, Sir John Gielgud, Joely Richardson

Basic Instinct (1991) Producer Allan Marshall; Director Paul Verhoeven.
Screenplay by Joe Eszterhas. Carolco/Tri-Star. *Cast*: Michael Douglas, Sharon Stone, George Dzundza, Jeanne Tripplehorn, Leilani Sarelli

Falling Down (1993) Producer Arnold Kopelson; Director Joel Schumacher.
Screenplay by Ebbe Roe Smith. Warner Bros. *Cast*: Michael Douglas, Robert Duvall, Barbara Hershey

Non-acting participation in Kirk Douglas movies: *Lonely are the Brave* (1962), as production assistant; *The Heroes of Telemark* (1965), credited as an assistant unit director; *Cast A Giant Shadow* (1966), production assistant

Producer only
One Flew over the Cuckoo's Nest (1976) Producers Michael Douglas and Saul Zaentz for United Artists/Fantasy Films; Director Milos Forman; Starring Jack Nicholson and Louise Fletcher

Starman (1984)
Co-producer Michael Douglas for Columbia Pictures; Director John Carpenter; Starring Jeff Bridges and Karen Allen

Flatliners (1990)
Co-producer Michael Douglas for Columbia Pictures; Director Joel Schumacher; Starring Julia Roberts and Kiefer Sutherland

Index

273